THE LANCASHIRE UNION RAILWAY

By

Dennis Sweeney

Triangle

Publishing

First published 2010 by Triangle Publishing.
British Library Cataloguing in Publication Data.
Sweeney D.J.
The Lancashire Union Railway
ISBN 978 0 9550030 42
Printed in Great Britain by The Amadeus Press Ltd, Cleckheaton.
Written, compiled and edited by D.J.Sweeney.
Cover design by Scene, Print & Design Ltd, Standish.
Designed and Published by
Triangle Publishing,
509, Wigan Road,
Leigh, Lancs.
WN7 5HN.
Tel. 01942/677919. www.trianglepublishing.co.uk

Cover. Stanier Class '5' No.44826 crosses bridge 13 at Garswood with a Leeds-Liverpool parcels train on 30th July 1965. *Brian Woodward.*

Rear Cover : Type '4' No.218 *Carmania* heads south on the Up Whelley line with a mixed freight on 25th August 1972. The route officially closed to goods trains as from 2nd October 1972, although it was used for WCML diversions during electrification, 12th - 15th January 1973. *Ian Isherwood.*

CONTENTS

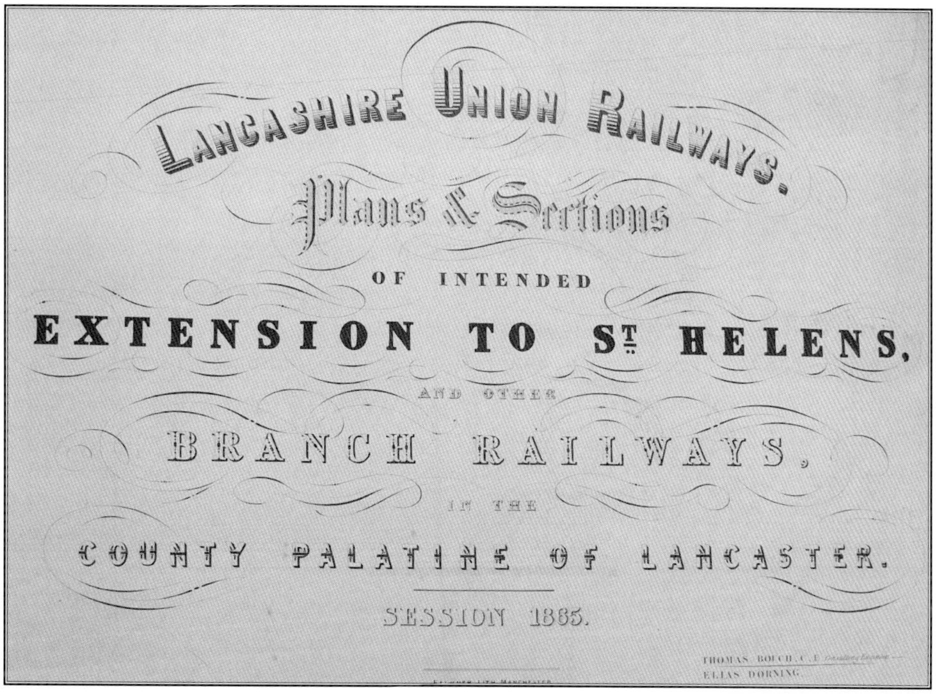

Fig 1. The Lancashire Union's 1865 line plan in its amended form from St. Helens to Hindley where it would meet the already sanctioned route to Haigh Junction, bears the names of Thomas Bouch and Elias Dorning.

INTRODUCTION AND ACKNOWLEDGEMENTS

As the nineteenth century moved on from the early embryonic period of the Bolton & Leigh, Liverpool & Manchester, and Wigan Branch Railway eras, the railway system of South Lancashire had become greatly enlarged by the 1880s and the proliferation of lines in the St. Helens and Wigan areas bear testament to this. The competition generated by such extension could only be good for the industrialists who would favour whichever company offered the best transit rates and it must not be forgotten that the canal companies provided intense competition against the railways, often undercutting their prices.

Amalgamations within the railway hierarchy in the North-West of England, had led to the formation of the 'Big Two', namely the London & North Western and Lancashire & Yorkshire Railways. Each had sought to build incursions into their competitor's back yard the London & North Western having the lion's share in South Central Lancashire and the Lancashire & Yorkshire more prominent in West and East Lancashire.

The latter in particular had proposed many schemes to infiltrate into the areas controlled by the former, most of which had come to nought and with the 'Quid-pro-Quo' operating between the two from the early 1860s the motivation was ripe for the industrialists to come up with their own plans as leverage against what was becoming something of a cartel. It is against this background that industry, principally Wigan coal owners, who were anxious to reduce transport costs to East Lancashire, formulated their plans for a railway from the London & North Western stranglehold at St. Helens, through Wigan, deep into Lancashire & Yorkshire territory at Blackburn. Thus the Lancashire Union Railway was conceived.

Only a part of the surveyed route now remains, that from Gerards Bridge to Ince Moss, where it joins the W.C.M.L. The 'Whelley' line which circumnavigated the eastern side of Wigan from Ince Moss to Haigh, and which was of immense value as a diversionary route, closed in the 1970s. The joint lines, Boar's Head - Adlington, and Chorley - Cherry Tree, succumbed to closure, like many lines in South Lancashire in the 1960s, the latter route standing in the way of the M61 Motorway.

Even the route to Ince Moss from St. Helens was a consideration for closure in the 1960s. Mercifully it survived the rationalisation of the 'Beeching Era'. Only now, with the increased congestion on the road network, can we contemplate the value of long lost lines.

I must express my sincere thanks to Gerry Bent, John Sloane, Alan Hart, Eddie Bellass, John Ryan, Ian Isherwood, Dr.J.G.Blears, Bob Maxwell, Brian Woodward and Peter Eckersley who have provided so much material for inclusion. Also to the staff at the Three Sisters Countryside Park who, apart from providing some excellent photographs have passed on their local topographical knowledge of the Bryn and Garswood areas most of which was swept away with the reclamation of the former colliery sites.

David Postle trawled endlessly through the late John Marshall Collection, bequeathed to the Kidderminster Railway Museum, to provide some unique views for inclusion.

Once again I acknowledge the experience of Bill Paxford, Peter Hampson and Tony Graham whose knowledge of signalling matters has, once again, been second to none.

To the staff at Leigh Archives, Preston Records Office and St. Helens Local History Archives, I gratefully acknowledge the assistance so readily given.

Again, for the industrial railway scene I have relied heavily on the works of C.H.A. Townley , J.Peden, & Co., supplemented by personal correspondences with C.H.A.Townley who provided so much information particularly with regard to the Wigan Coal & Iron Co. and their predecessors.

I have been greatly assisted with the unenviable task of proofreading by Gordon Rigby and Ian Pilkington and mere words are inadequate to express my relief at such assistance being so readily offered.

Lastly, to all of those too numerous to mention who have provided snippets of information and photographs I express my sincere thanks.

All scales and dimensions are given in Imperial Measure.

Dennis Sweeney,
Leigh,
2010.

I. ST. HELENS CONNECTIONS

St. Helens, like Wigan, had a complicated network of railway lines which began early in the chronology of Public Railways in Great Britain and, before the main subject of this book - *The Lancashire Union Railway* - is broached, it would be prudent to give a brief resume of the general arrangement of lines which percolated the centre of the town and have a relevance to the subject matter itself.

In 1829, at the request of local industry, the engineer C.B.Vignoles carried out a survey of the projected St. Helens & Runcorn Gap Railway. This would begin north of St. Helens, at Cowley Hill Colliery on a line roughly southwards, to a proposed dock on the bank of the River Mersey at Runcorn, a distance of approximately 9 miles. In addition to the main line, Vignoles' remit also provided for the inclusion of a number of branch lines to local collieries in the area most of which were located north of the Liverpool & Manchester Railway, then under construction. Plans for the St. Helens & Runcorn Gap Railway were therefore deposited before Parliament in November 1929.

In fact, Vignoles had surveyed two possible routes which may be conveniently termed 'Eastern' and 'Western'; Vignoles himself recommending the 'Eastern' route. On 16th February 1830 the Bill for construction of this route was presented to Parliament, duly receiving Royal Assent on 29th May that year.

As Chief Engineer, Vignoles was to receive a salary of £650 per annum which, when compared to the renumeration he would later receive in the same capacity on the Wigan Branch Railway of £500 seems generous. However, out of his salary, he was expected to contribute to that of his subordinate engineers!

The first section of railway from St. Helens to an east facing junction with the Liverpool & Manchester Railway (St. Helens Junction) was opened on 2nd January 1832. The first train from the Broad Oak Branch ran on 28th November 1832 to the as yet, unfinished dock at Runcorn. This dock would not be completed until 26th July 1833. In the interim period, the 'official' opening of the line had taken place on 21st February 1833.

The Ravenhead Branch, to a similarly named colliery, opened on 12th December 1834, but the full length of this branch, to Ravenhead Plate Glass Works, would not be completed until 1851/2. Construction northwards from Peasley Cross to Gerards Bridge was actually built by the Union Plate Glass Company on behalf of the St. Helens & Runcorn Gap Railway, opening in 1837. Like other embryonic railway companies they had found themselves perennially short of funds due to a combination of ambitious expansion plans, the need to repair and renew existing lines and intense competition from the previous transport monopolists in the area, namely the Sankey Brook Navigation, who continually cut rates of carriage, forcing the railway company to follow suit or lose the trade altogether. However, in 1845 the two protagonists were to amalgamate, becoming the St. Helens Canal & Railway Company, so for a few years at least, peace ensued in the vicinity. All the while though, envious eyes were being cast upon the mineral and industrial assets of St. Helens, particularly by the Grand Junction Railway.

In 1845, the Grand Junction Railway had absorbed the Liverpool & Manchester, and the Bolton & Leigh - Kenyon & Leigh Junction Railways, having already absorbed the Warrington & Newton Railway in 1835. In 1846 the Grand Junction became joint lessee, with the Manchester & Leeds Railway, of the North Union Railway. On 16th July 1846 the London & North Western Railway was formed by the amalgamation of the Grand Junction, Manchester & Birmingham and London & Birmingham Railways.

The first station at St. Helens had been at Peasley Cross on the Ravenhead Branch. On 19th December 1849 a new passenger station and goods yard opened on the south side of Raven Street which involved the construction of a new east to north curve off the Ravenhead Branch. This, in turn, connected with a colliery branch line from Sutton and, by extension, crossed the nearby canal by a swing bridge.

Plans for an extension to Rainford (by no means the first) by the St. Helens Canal & Railway Co. were deposited on 30th November 1852. This would run from a new junction with the Ravenhead Branch, again crossing the canal, passing to the east of the 1849 station and goods yard, going under Raven Street (now Parr Street) to a new station on the north side of Raven Street, south of the present station on Shaw Street. From the new station the line would make a junction with the Gerards Bridge Branch (Pocket Nook Jcts) from which, by continuance, would divert and pass over the Sankey Navigation at Gerards Bridge thence passing through open country to make a junction with the Liverpool -

Fig 2. The central area of St. Helens c1849 showing the St Helens & Runcorn Gap Railway lines to Ravenhead and Gerards Bridge and the first station at St. Helens, Peasley Cross on the Ravenhead Branch itself. Expansion of the railways in this area would continue unabated for the next forty-five years or so.

Wigan line at Rainford, a distance of approximately 6 miles 700 yards. The Bill received Royal assent on 4th August 1853.

In addition to the new station in St. Helens there would be stations at Gerards Bridge, Moss Bank and Rainford, which together with the route and its junction with the Liverpool - Wigan line opened to passengers on 1st February 1858, although the first coal train ran from Rainford to St. Helens on 5th December 1857. Stations at Rookery and Crank opened towards the year end. A connection with the East Lancashire Railway at Ormskirk was completed in March 1858.

Despite the continued expansion of the St. Helens Canal & Railway Co. by the construction of new docks, lines and doubling of single line sections, profits were often negligible after running costs, dividends and interest were taken into account. In truth, it was the canal operations which had kept the company solvent and, in 1860, the Company was leased to the London & North Western Railway. The St Helens Canal & Railway Company was finally swallowed whole by the former on 1st August 1864.

The London & North Western Railway's Act of 1865 included the provision of a branch line from the Liverpool & Manchester line at Huyton, to St. Helens, work on the route beginning in 1868. As the line approached the town it would cross over the Ravenhead Branch on a viaduct and cut across the 1849 station at Raven Street to reach the 1858 built station on the opposite side of Raven Street. The same Act also provided for a half-mile branch line from a junction on the original St Helens & Runcorn Gap line south of Peasley Junction (Broad Oak Junction) to north and south facing junctions on the Broad Oak Branch itself, enabling through running between the latter, the Blackbrook Branch and St Helens.

With the opening of the Lancashire Union's route from Gerards Bridge to Wigan in 1869, the increase in traffic into St. Helens that it produced prompted the London & North Western to build a new station slightly north of that built in 1858, opening on 17th July 1871. The 1858 station labelled as "a wretched little hole" was closed on the same day.

It appears that the new station was not what had been expected by the local populace and came in for some criticism. Over the years the London & North Western made some minor improvements to placate the detractors but the station remained substantially the same until rebuilt by British Railways in 1961. The station had become St. Helens Shaw Street on 1st March 1949 to distinguish it from the Great Central's St. Helens Central Station. It is ironic that it was renamed St. Helens Central in 1987.

Unfortunately, access to the goods yard was only available from the north and all traffic arriving from the south had to shunt back through Pocket Nook Junctions.

A section of line on the Gerards Bridge route, from Peasley Junction to Pocket Nook Junction, was rebuilt to a much higher standard to ease congestion through St. Helens Station, completed on 1st November 1869.

The route from Huyton Junction to St. Helens opened for freight traffic on 18th December 1871 and to passenger services on 1st January 1872. Stations enroute were at Prescot and Thatto Heath. A station at Eccleston Park opened in July 1891.

Plate 1. The view at St. Helens Shaw Street Station on 4th April 1964 looking south. By this period most of the London & North Western's buildings had been replaced by British Railways 'modern' designs, altogether more utilitarian in their construction and using a number of differing types of glass in its construction supplied locally by Pilkingtons.

Eddie Bellass.

Plate 2. Standard Class '4' No.76079 shunts St Helens Shaw Street Yard in March 1961. This view north from Corporation Street (formerly Sharp Street) bridge gives some idea of the amount of railway infrastructure to be found in the St. Helens area before 'rationalisation' really took hold. St. Helens No.2 box is extreme right. *Eddie Bellass.*

Plate 3. Ex-LMS 'Patriot' Class No.45516 *The Bedfordshire and Hertfordshire Regiment* is seen at St. Helens after arrival with a Rugby League Special from Warrington in March 1961. The line to Peasley Junction goes off to the left, or straight on for Huyton Junction. St. Helens No.3 box is seen on the far side of Parr Street bridge *Eddie Bellass.*

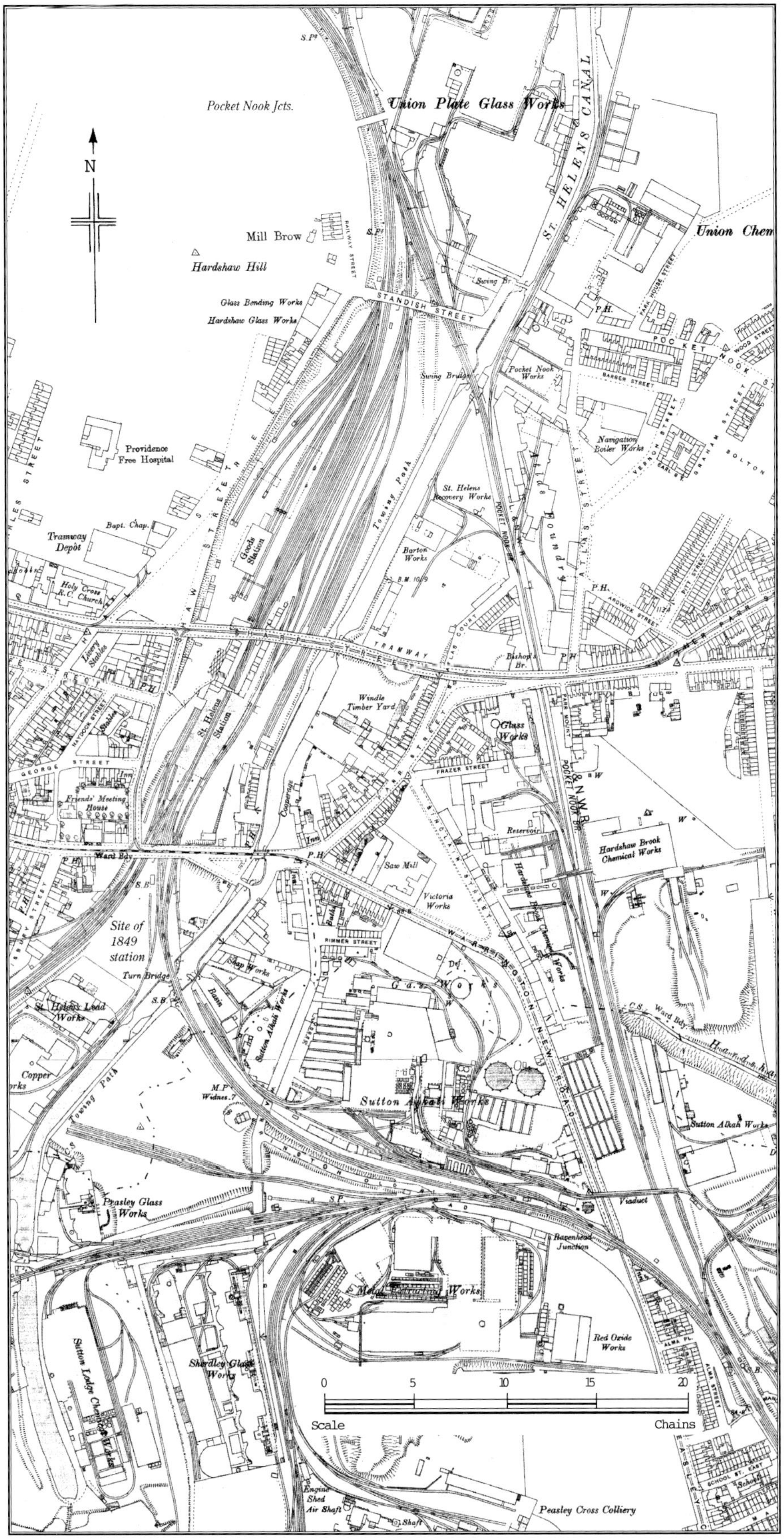

Fig 3. Ordnance Survey c1891/2. In some forty-odd years the central area of St. Helens had been transformed with the railways and industry taking up large tracts of land. The original St. Helens & Runcorn Gap Railway enters at bottom right, continuing out of frame, centre top. The 1849 built station, indicated south of Raven Street, now Parr Street, which was served by the new branch off the Ravenhead line, has been removed along with most of the sidings associated with it to make way for the line from Huyton Junction that had opened in 1871.

The Huyton lines and the 'new' station also took up much of the area previously occupied by the 1858 built station on the north side of Raven Street. It is this station which was renamed Shaw Street on 1st March 1949 and survives in its rationalised form today.

As can be seen, the goods shed and sidings could only be accessed from the northern end which often caused problems for freight arriving from the south and the need for reversal through the junctions at Pocket Nook.

Today, the railways of St. Helens are a mere fraction of what once existed. The Ravenhead Branch has almost succumbed in its entirety, that which served the Pilkington Oil Terminal, was lifted in 1992 when a new connection opened off the Huyton Branch, to a relocated terminal adjacent to the previous site.

From Gerards Bridge, the route to Rainford, except for sidings at Cowley Hill, is long gone and the last surviving stretches of the original St. Helens & Runcorn Gap Railway went on the demise of the mining industry in the town; except, that is, for a portion of the Gerards Bridge Branch from Peasley Cross to the now demolished Hayes Chemical factory, about a mile short of St. Helens Junction. This, together with the curve into St. Helens Shaw Street (as built for the 1849 station at Raven Street) survive and are a part of the Merseyrail Strategic Authority programme to reinstate passenger services over the route via a new St. Helens Junction connection. This would include a station at Peasley Cross, adjacent to the retail park and recently built hospital. In fact, just a few years ago, at the St. Helens end, pointwork for this branch was renewed and certain signalling works carried out, but at the time of writing, the tracks are rusting away and vegetation proliferating.

Plate 4. The scene at Ravenhead Junction on 7th March 1967 as BR Standard Class "4' No.76060 shunts an oil train, photographed from street level on Peasley Cross Lane.

John Sloane.

Plate 6, opposite. A four-car DMU departs the environs of St. Helens Shaw Street with the diverted 11.00 Liverpool Lime Street - Blackpool North on 23rd August 1981. The goods shed and associated sidings are long gone and a modern block of flats is now the prominent feature here. Over to the left, c2010, some sidings remain in situ, totally overgrown with trees.

Gerry Bent.

Plate 5. In 2007, Shaw Street Station was transformed once more, officially opening on 3rd December. Having been renamed St. Helens Central in 1987, glass once again, is a predominant feature of its ultra-modern construction and perhaps the name brings back memories of the former station of the same name closed to passengers in 1952, that of the Great Central Railway whose terminus did timber sheds an injustice!

Author.

Plate 8, left. One of the Rockware Glass 0-6-0 shunters stands at the foot of Standish Street bridge at Pocket Nook, also on 23rd August 1981. Two of these 200h.p. diesel-mechanical shunters had arrived at Rockware in 1973 from The Mersey Docks & Harbour Board having been built by Hudswell Clarke & Co. at Leeds in 1958, works Nos.D1038 & D1039.

The Union Glass Company had established its works here in 1836, the firm providing finance for the construction of the Gerards Bridge Branch. In 1864, the firm became a Limited Liability Company and, by that date, considerable expansion of the works had taken place. Further works extensions occurred before the second series Ordnance Survey was carried out in 1891/2. Cast plate production ceased by 1898 and in 1904 the Company began a process of liquidation which was not completed until 1920. Most of the works was eventually taken over by Forster & Sons, later Forster's Glass Company Ltd. from 15th July 1919. Forsters were taken over by the Rockware Glass Co. on 1st January 1948, but trading continued under the old name until 1966. In December 1981, Rockware announced its intention to cease production at Pocket Nook and the works closed in March 1982, rail traffic ceasing in February.

Gerry Bent.

Finally, before our survey of the Lancashire Union line proper begins, a series of photographs were taken by Eddie Bellass during a brake van special, organised by the Locomotive Club of Great Britain (L.C.G.B) North-West Branch, on 4th April 1964. The working was a return empties from Widnes, Tanhouse Lane, to Long Meg, on the Settle & Carlisle line. Although the party were not allowed to travel beyond Blackburn, an extra brake van had been added to the train at Widnes and it is from this van that most of the shots were taken en-route.

I feel it is entirely appropriate to show the views on this unusual trip, albeit that some are outside the parameters of the intended survey. I'm sure the railway enthusiasts will approve.

Plate 8. The train would be hauled, at least as far as Blackburn, by Stanier '8F' No.48750. The Fireman is seen attaching the required lamps to the engine at Tanhouse Lane.

Plate 9, (below). In 1961 a new chord opened between Tanhouse Lane on the Great Central & Midland Loop line, to Widnes No.1 Signal Box on the former St. Helens & Runcorn Gap Railway, enabling the anhydrite trains from Long Meg to access the United Sulphuric Acid Cos.(USAC) plant. 48750 and train, are seen on the chord passing the plant on approach to the junction near Widnes No.1.

Both, Eddie Bellass.

II. THE LANCASHIRE UNION RAILWAY

The Lancashire Union Railway was brought about by the requirements of Wigan coal owners to market their produce in East Lancashire, namely the towns of Burnley, Accrington, Blackburn and so on. Amongst the supporters of the Lancashire Union's proposals were the Earl of Crawford & Balcarres, John Lancaster, Lord Lindsay, Alfred Hewlett and James Diggle (Westleigh Collieries).

The proposers regarded the shipping of coal from Liverpool as too expensive, and the general idea of the proposed route was to gain access to Garston and Widnes on the Mersey Estuary where charges were more favourable. The Company was formed in 1863 with the nominal backing of the London & North Western Railway who saw a clear opportunity to make incursions into what was regarded as Lancashire & Yorkshire Railway territory.

Parliamentary powers first drawn up in 1863 envisaged a railway from a junction with the North Union at Boar's Head running to a new terminus in Blackburn by way of Adlington and Chorley, to the east of the existing Bolton - Preston route and, secondly, a main line from the St. Helens railway at Parr, meeting with the route from Boar's Head at Haigh, north-east of Wigan. This line would have passed through Haydock, making connections with the North Union at Bamfurlong, near Mains Colliery Sidings; with the Eccles - Springs Branch Junction route at Platt Bridge, still under construction at this period; a second connection with the North Union on the Springs Branch and, connections with the Lancashire & Yorkshire at Hindley, Adlington and Chorley. A short spur was included to serve Ellerbeck Colliery.

These proposals fired the Lancashire & Yorkshire into action and their counter proposals visualised a link from Chorley on the Bolton - Preston route to a junction at Cherry Tree on the Preston - Blackburn line, a short branch line to Horwich from a junction at Blackrod and a line from Hindley to the Bolton - Preston route at Red Moss (Hilton House Junction).

Due consideration was given by Parliament to all of the above. The Lancashire & Yorkshire plans were accepted in full, as were the Lancashire Union proposals for the line from St. Helens to Haigh, the Ellerbeck Branch, the links to the Lancashire & Yorkshire at Hindley, to the North Union's Springs Branch and the London & North Western's Tyldesley route at Platt Bridge. The proposed connection with the North Union at Bamfurlong was thrown out and only a section of the route to Blackburn, that between Boar's Head and Adlington, was allowed. The Acts of both companies received Royal Assent on 25th July 1864.

The initial survey of the Lancashire Union route was carried out by Elias Dorning and the Scottish Engineer Thomas Bouch. Elias Dorning had previously surveyed the Wigan-Tyldesley-Eccles and Leigh Branch routes for the London & North Western Railway in the early 1860s. He was also regarded as the foremost mining engineer on the Lancashire Coalfield. Thomas Bouch's name is synonymous with the first bridge over the River Tay which collapsed during a storm in 1879.

Having trained under Joseph Locke on the Lancaster & Carlisle Railway, Bouch had considerable experience and some notable constructions to his name. He had also

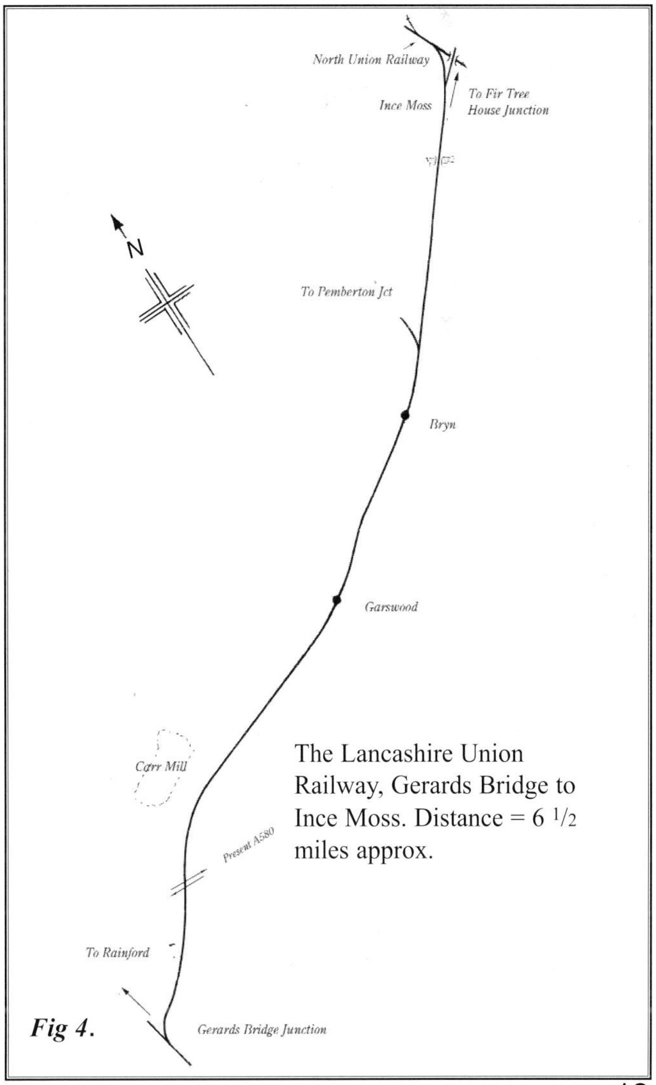

The Lancashire Union Railway, Gerards Bridge to Ince Moss. Distance = 6 1/2 miles approx.

Fig 4.

introduced a roll-on-roll-off system for ferries crossing the Forth and Tay which engineers came from all over the world to see and take note of.

Whilst accepting partial responsibility for the collapse of his bridge the overwhelming onus of guilt lay with others, notably poor maintenance of the structure and excessive speed of trains crossing the bridge which often exceeded 50m.p.h., against a recommended maximum of 25m.p.h. It has been suggested that the bridge was being shaken to death and in no state to stand the fury of an 80m.p.h. storm onslaught which ultimately brought down three centre spans on the morning of 28th December 1879 when 69 passengers and the locomotive crew lost their lives.

There is no doubt that this incident broke Thomas Bouch mentally, his health suffering as a result. He was to pass away in October the following year.

A competing scheme had been put forward by the South Lancashire Railway & Dock Company in 1864. The proposal was for a line from a new dock at Dingle, Liverpool, which would pass through St. Helens and make a connection with the North Union at Ince Moss, with the Springs Branch near Ince Forge, the Tyldesley route at Platt Bridge and, the Lancashire & Yorkshire at Hindley.

The Lancashire Union regarded the deletion of their Bamfurlong connection with the North Union in its original proposal as a serious setback and a revised plan was drawn up which, in fact, was not too dissimilar in its route from St. Helens to Wigan from that as proposed by the South Lancashire Railway & Dock Company.

As amended, the Lancashire Union proposal was for a route from a junction with the London & North Western's Rainford branch at Gerards Bridge, north of St. Helens station and, via Bryn (originally Brynn), Garswood and Ince Moss to Hindley, from where it followed the course already sanctioned by the 1864 Acts to Haigh. A new connection from Ince Moss to the North Union at Springs Branch was proposed, as was a spur from Fir Tree House to the Eccles - Tyldesley - Wigan line at Platt Bridge Junction; a branch from Bryn to Norley Hall Colliery ; a spur to the Lancashire & Yorkshire's Wigan - Liverpool route (Goose Green Junction - Pemberton Junction) and, a branch from Roundhouse to Kirkless Hall Ironworks. All these proposals were authorised in 1865. A proposed branch to Rose Bridge Colliery near Belle Green Lane was rejected.

Meanwhile, in 1864, negotiations had taken place between the Lancashire Union and the Lancashire & Yorkshire Railways and it was agreed that the Boar's Head - Adlington, Chorley - Blackburn routes, and the Ellerbeck branch, should be transferred to joint ownership, confirmed by the joint Act of 26th May 1865. Each Company was to pay half the construction cost and appoint five members to a joint committee.

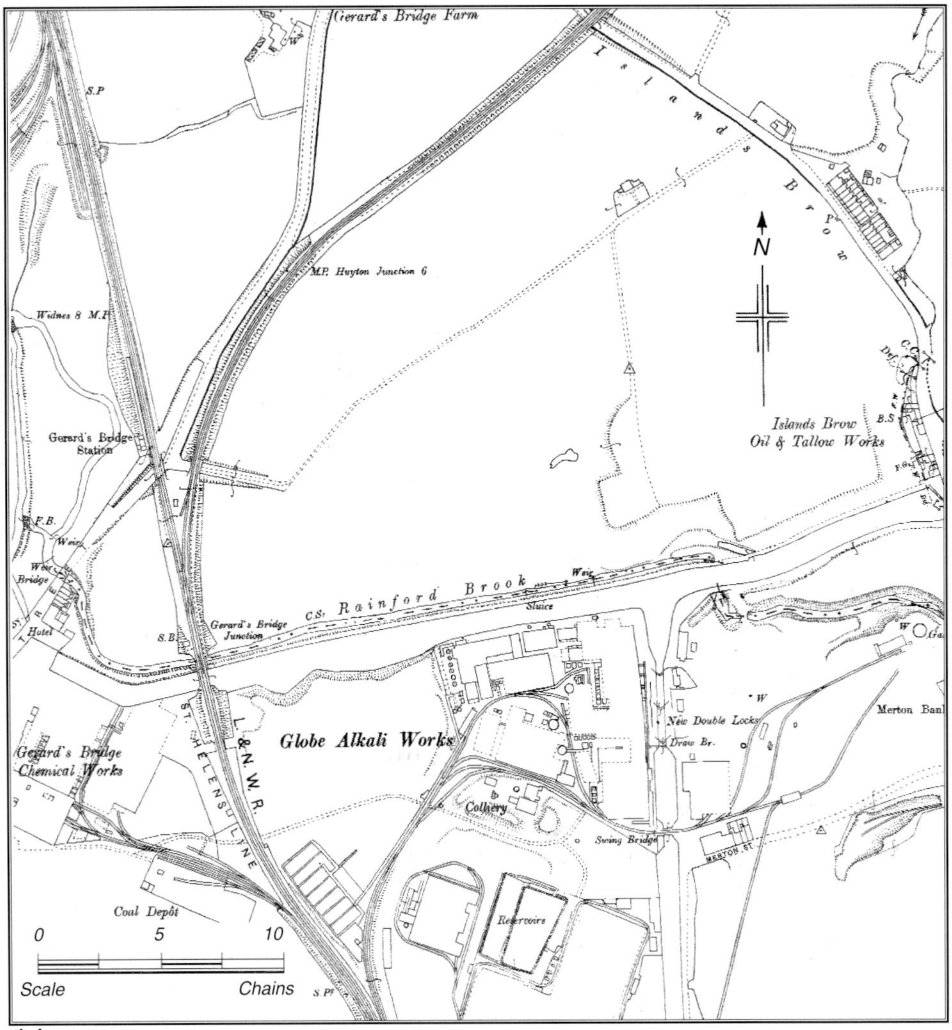

Fig 5. Gerards Bridge Junction from the second series Ordnance Survey. The station at Gerards Bridge was to close on 1st August 1904.

By a separate Act of 29th June 1865, powers were granted to the Lancashire Union to raise an additional £200,000 for the Gerards Bridge - Hindley section, having already been authorised by the 1864 Acts to raise £250,000.

Chief Civil Engineer for the London & North Western, William Baker, who had been engineer on the Wigan-Tyldesley-Eccles and Tyldesley-Leigh-Pennington lines completed in 1864, along with Sturgess Meek, Chief Civil Engineer for the Lancashire & Yorkshire, were appointed as Engineers for the joint lines.

In August 1866, the contract for the Gerards Bridge to Haigh route was awarded to Wm. McCormick for £170,00, later increased to £186,000. This was, however, cancelled on 24th November and transferred to Messrs Jameson & J.T.McCormick.

The Lancashire Union had decided to build passenger stations at Whelley, Hindley, Bryn and Garswood, built by Fairclough & Son whose tender of £7,350 was accepted on 2nd January 1869. However, the Inspecting Officer, Colonel Hutchinson, ordered, on 3rd May 1869, that Hindley was to be named Amberswood for Hindley to avoid confusion with the Lancashire & Yorkshire station of the same name. There was also Hindley Green on the Wigan - Tyldesley - Eccles route opened in 1864 and later, Strangeways & Hindley on the Wigan Junction Railway (renamed Hindley & Platt Bridge from January 1892).

Work on the Chorley - Cherry Tree route was delayed by negotiations between the Lancashire Union and the Lancashire & Yorkshire Companies, although work had actually commenced by December 1866, the contract for the 7 miles 60 chains route having been awarded to William Hanson on 2nd August that year. It was therefore necessary to apply for an extension of time to 25th January 1870. This was granted by the joint Act of 13th July 1868, which Act also vested the Ellerbeck branch between the two Companies. The construction of the latter branch was to begin immediately after 2nd August 1868, to be completed before 25th January 1870.

The Lancashire Union's Act of 16th July 1866 had authorised a 3 mile 275 yard branch from Garswood to Blackbrook, near Fleet Lane on the Broad Oak Branch, the latter built by the St. Helens Canal & Railway Company in 1851/2, plus a 1,320 yard branch to the Havannah Colliery. Neither of these branches were ever built in their original form. Additional powers of the Act had allowed the company to raise a further £80,000 in shares and borrowing of £26,000.

Length of line from Gerards Bridge Junction to Ince Moss Junction was some 6$^1/_2$ miles. Carr Mill, a local beauty spot known as Happy Valley, was crossed by an impressive viaduct consisting of six wrought iron, lattice girder spans of 40ft supported by brick piers 62ft 9in high. A junction (Carr Mill) would be made on the St. Helens side of this viaduct under the London & North Western's Acts of 22nd July 1878, which authorised a 1,320 yard extension of their Blackbrook branch from Parr, east of St. Helens, to a junction with the Lancashire Union, the contract let to G.Nowell for £4,300, opening on 23rd February 1880.

This was, in fact, a replacement for the abandoned Garswood - Blackbrook line proposed under the Act of 1866.

Plate 10. At the time of writing fuel oil is still delivered by rail to Pilkington's works at Ravenhead off a connection from the Huyton route which opened in 1992. Class '66' No.66 047 is seen north-east of Gerards Bridge Junction with return oil empties on 3rd April 2008.

From Gerards Bridge Junction itself, a half-mile section of the Rainford Branch is retained to serve Pilkingtons Cowley Hill Works, although it is some time since any traffic worked over the branch. *John Sloane.*

This branch was to provide a useful by-pass of St. Helens proper, particularly so for coal and heavy freight trains working to/from Widnes and Garston. The Long Meg anhydrite trains working off the Settle & Carlisle line via Hellifield, Blackburn and Chorley immediately spring to mind and would use this route to reach Widnes until closure of the branch on 6th April 1964.

In the 1930s a new bridge, between Carr Mill Junction and the viaduct, would be built to carry the railway over the new A580 East Lancashire Road.

Gradients of 1:86 and 1:84 predominated at a point west of Garswood station and with one slight rise before Bryn, it was downhill all the way to Ince Moss.

Just beyond Bryn Station, Bryn Junction served the branch to Pemberton and Norley Hall via Goose Green Junction. The Lancashire & Yorkshire Railway had running powers from Haigh Junction to St. Helens and worked over the branch to Norley Hall and Pemberton Collieries, some trains working from Aintree via Pemberton Junction. At its height, in the early 1900s, the branch was open 24 hours per day.

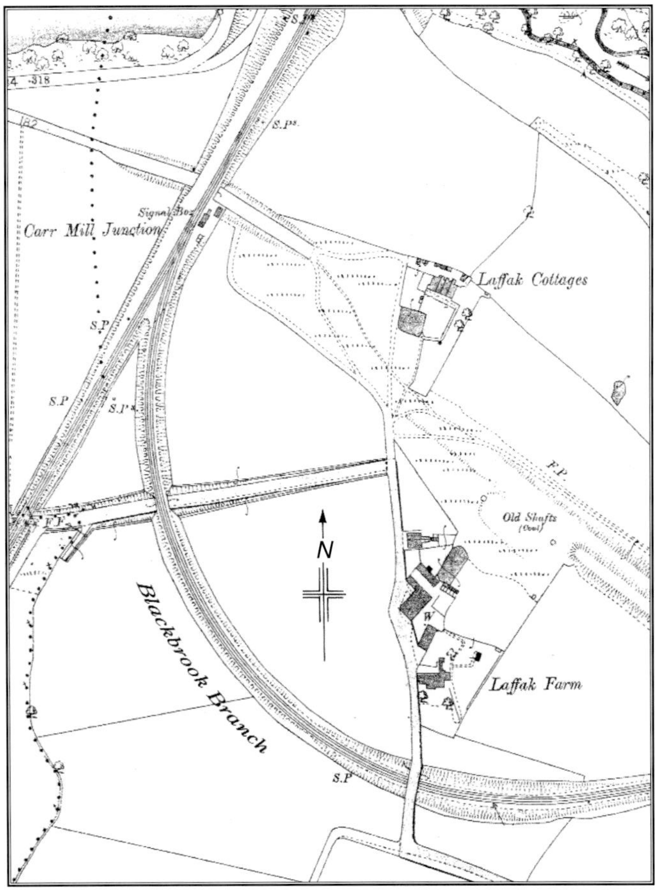

Fig 6. Car Mill Junction c1888 and the connections with the London & North Western's Blackbrook Branch.

At Ince Moss, connections were made with the North Union Railway by an east to north facing curve - Ince Moss Junction - St Helens Line Junction or, alternatively, on a rising gradient of 1:86 from Ince Moss, crossing the North Union lines for a connection with the Tyldesley route - Fir Tree House - Platt Bridge Junctions. Continuing eastward the railway passed over Warrington Road (A573) to Amberswood where, in 1886 connections were made with the Platt Bridge Junction Railway at Amberswood West Junction .

The railway then curved through 180 degrees with, from 1882, a connection with the Wigan Junction Railway which had opened in 1879 from Glazebrook to Strangeways Hall. By way of the London & North Western's Hindley Junctions Railway from Bickershaw Junction, connections were also made at Amberswood Junctions. The next point of contact was with the Lancashire & Yorkshire Railway by a spur from De Trafford Junction to Hindley No.2 Junction.

From De Trafford the railway takes a north-westerly course and after crossing the Springs Branch near Belle Green Lane, Rose Bridge and Round House Junctions are reached, the former connecting with the Springs Branch by a spur from Kirkless Junction, and the latter by a 1,078 yard long branch, with the Wigan Coal & Iron Co. at Kirkless. A cut and cover (Haigh) tunnel then carried the railway under the grounds of the Earl of Crawford & Balcarres for 374 yards towards Brock Mill Junction, the connection for Haigh Foundry, and Haigh Junction, the extent of the independent Lancashire Union's line. Here a junction was made with the joint Lancashire & Yorkshire/Lancashire Union lines from Boar's Head Junction on the North Union route some $3^{1}/_{2}$ miles from Wigan, to Adlington, thereby connecting with the Lancashire & Yorkshire's Bolton - Euxton route. It was then necessary to traverse Lancashire & Yorkshire metals to Chorley where, south of Chorley Station, was the colliery branch line to Ellerbeck and then the final section of joint line would be accessed at Blackburn Junction to take the railway up the steeply graded route through Heapey and Brinscall Bank, through Withnell and onward to a junction with the Lancashire & Yorkshire's Blackburn - Preston route at Cherry Tree. A total route distance from Gerard's Bridge to Haigh Junction of 11 miles 1,686 yards. Boar's Head to Adlington = 3 miles 911 yds. Chorley- Cherry Tree = 7 miles 1,068yds.

CARR MILL

Plate 11. Carr Mill Station as viewed c1900 looking in a north-easterly direction, that is towards Garswood. Only opened in January 1896, it was to close from 1st January 1917. The covered stairway egress/exit arrangements are of some interest being of corrugated sheet construction which seem peculiar compared to other L&NW stations, for the station buildings themselves are typical of the Company's wooden prefabricated constructions. The locomotive in the background appears to be crossing over the tracks as another waits by the signal box for permission to enter the station. Carr Mill Junction and signal box can be seen in the background at which point the four track section to Ince Moss begins.

Plate 12. A second view at Carr Mill from the same era which gives a view of the platform and its method of all timber construction which is typical of stations built on an embankment as was Carr Mill. One of the station staff poses for the camera alongside some period advertising.

Both, Courtesy of St. Helens Local History and Archives Library.

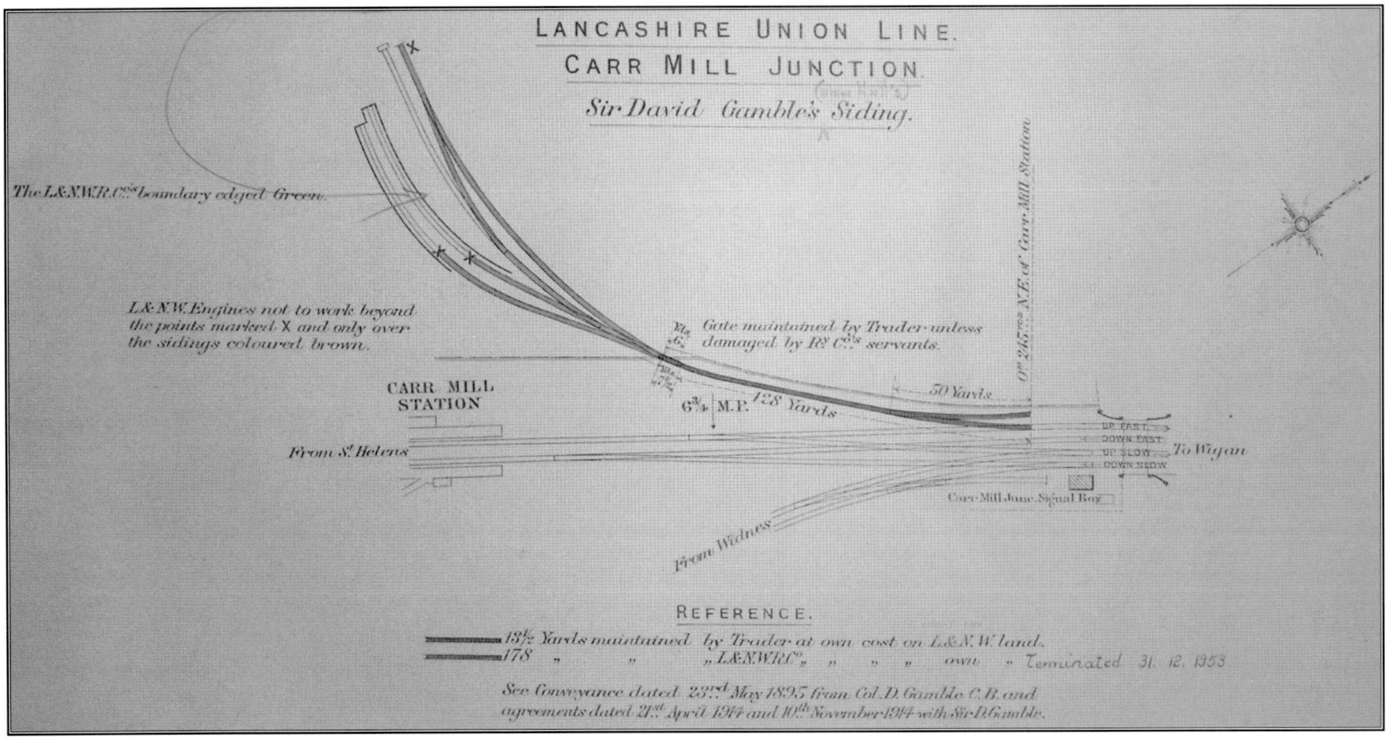

Fig 7. Sometime in 1894,work began on laying sidings on the western side of the main line north of Carr Mill Station. Known as Gamble's Siding, it served the estate of Sir David Gamble, the sidings agreement being completed in May 1895. Eventually there were four sidings and a small goods yard on the estate which was mainly used for agricultural traffic by the estates tenants, although a number of small colliery owners brought their coal by road to the sidings to be loaded into railway wagons. The agreement regarding Sir David Gamble's Sidings at Carr Mill is dated 23rd May 1895, with further agreements in April & November 1914 which covered extension of the sidings and the extent to which London & North Western engines could work.

The freehold of the sidings was later offered for sale to the L.M.S in 1936 by one Thomas Hull of Preston, apparently not taken up as the agreement with the owners was terminated by B.R. on 31st December 1953. The connection with the main line was removed in 1954.

Courtesy, John Ryan.

The London & North Western route from Huyton Junction to St. Helens had opened to goods on 18th December 1871 and to passengers on 1st January 1872. It was therefore possible for the introduction of a Whelley - St. Helens - Liverpool service comprising three trains per day each way and this commenced on the latter date. In the event, however, Whelley and Amberswood stations were closed on 1st March after just two months of operation which must rank as one of the shortest lived services on record!

Colonel Hutchinson inspected the route from Gerards Bridge to Ince Moss on 21st August 1869 but was not entirely satisfied. It was finally opened for goods on 1st November 1869 and for passengers on 1st December 1869. It is believed, the branch to Pemberton and the short connecting spur to the Lancashire & Yorkshire line opened on the same date.

The section from Ince Moss which passed over the North Union lines south of Springs Branch en route to Haigh also opened for goods on 1st November 1869, as did the connections to the Tyldesley route at Platt Bridge Junction, the Roundhouse spur to Kirkless Iron Works, Rose Bridge Junction to Kirkless Hall Junction on the Springs Branch itself and, the joint Boars Head to Adlington line. The latter opened to passengers a month later.

Some delay was encountered in the building of the Ellerbeck Branch resulting in an extension of time granted under the Lancashire Union and Lancashire & Yorkshire Act of 1868. It seems to have been opened on or before 19th June 1871, although the 'official' date as given by the Lancashire & Yorkshire is 6th January 1877.

The Bamfurlong Junctions Railway Act of July 1887 authorised powers for the widening of the Lancashire Union route between Carr Mill and Ince Moss, a distance of 5½ miles. A second Carr Mill viaduct was built in identical fashion to the original to take the new lines on the western side. However, the lines to Ince Moss from Carr Mill were built on the eastern side, becoming the

Plate 13, left. The brake van trip of 4th April 1964 had been scheduled to work via the Blackbrook Branch. However, the train was routed via St. Helens encountering some delay.The locomotive's crew were keen Blackburn Rovers supporters and, anxious to get a move on in order to make kick-off time as Rovers were playing at home, had a quick word with the Station Master and the Signalman, whereupon a locomotive was summoned to drag the train back to Peasley Junction to work as originally planned. Again, the train is photographed from the brake van, and seen on the Blackbrook Branch about 1/2 mile from Carr Mill Junction. *Eddie Bellass.*

slow lines, the original lines becoming the fast lines. This necessitated some slewing at Carr Mill, plus a further fifteen bridges had to be widened to take the additional pair of lines. The contractor for these works was Charles Braddock whose tender of £47,255 was accepted on 19th June 1889. The new lines were commissioned on 15th October 1892 and brought into use on the following day.

Plate 14, above. As viewed from the London & North Western's Blackbrook Branch extension, the return Widnes - Long Meg anhydrite empties train hauled by a Stanier 2-8-0 '8F' No.48750 approaches the junction with the Lancashire Union at Carr Mill. These and other freights were routed this way to avoid the centre of St. Helens. *Eddie Bellass.*

Plate 15. Another view of the same train now on the Lancashire Union route at Carr Mill Junction. A second brake van had been attached at Widnes on this trip for the use of L.C.G.B. club members who were allowed to ride as far as Blackburn. Other photographs of this working will feature in following pages. The date of this rather special 'special' was 4th April 1964. The first signal box at Carr Mill Junction is concomitant with the opening of the Blackbrook Branch extension in 1880. The second box, seen above, opened in 1892 and was a London & North Western type '4' having a 52 lever frame. This was to close on 24th September 1967. In B.R. days the box opened 5.30a.m. Monday to 2p.m. Sunday. *Eddie Bellass.*

Construction of the A580, East Lancashire Road in the early 1930s was carried out under the auspices of Lancashire County Council (L.C.C.) planning for which had begun in the 1920s. In total, thirteen bridges had to be built to cross railway lines plus one major canal bridge which are listed west to east below. Bridges over streams, culverts and roads etc are not listed.

Underbridge near Fazackerley South Jct.
Overbridge - St. Helens - Rainford line at Windle.
Underbridge - Lancashire Union line at Carr Mill.
Overbridge - Lowton -St. Helens line at Haydock.
Overbridge - Old Boston Colliery Rly at Haydock.
Overbridge - WCML at Golborne.
Overbridge - Wigan Junction Railway at Lowton.
Overbridge - Kenyon & Leigh Jct Rly at Lowton.
Overbridge - Bridgewater Canal at Astley.
Overbridge - Manchester Colls Rly at Mosley Common.
Overbridge - Eccles-Tyldesley line at Roe Green.
Overbridge - Roe Green - Bolton line at Roe Green.
Overbridge - Manchester Colls Rly at Roe Green.
Overbridge - Black Harry line at Swinton.

The construction of Carr Mill bridge was made more complicated by the existing topography of the area. To the north-east was Carr Mill Viaduct and the dam itself. To the south west was the junction for the Blackbrook Branch and the bridge over Laffack Lane. The location was, therefore, the only possible site to build the bridge, made more difficult as at the point of construction were four running lines plus a double junction between fast and slow lines. Work began in early 1931.

The former Lancashire Union lines were carried across the course of the A580 by a low embankment through which narrow trench slits were cut by hand and the spoil carried away by a narrow gauge tubway. In all, there were cuts for each end abutment and a further six, equally spaced over the bridge length of 102ft 2in.

As work progressed in cutting through the embankment the trench sides were close-shored and braced to prevent collapse. Prefabricated wooden trestles had to be assembled on site and slowly drawn into the trenches, each brace being removed in turn and replaced, allowing forward movement of the trestles. Once in position the trestles were wedged in position by timber chocks off the shoring sides.

Now, removal of the embankment between the trestles could begin. As this work progressed a series of overlapping RSJs were then positioned and packed to carry the railway sleepers above.

The bridge girders were fabricated at the Glasgow works of Sir Wm. Arrol & Co. Ltd., fourteen in all (seven per side), transported to site by rail which presented its own logistical problems because of their size. Each girder was 106ft 4in long x 8ft 3in deep x 2ft 2in wide at the flanges and weighed in at 36 tons 10 hundredweight.

It had been decided that the girders for the west side would arrive first, three on 30th August 1931 and two each on 13th & 27th September. Three east side girders would arrive on 18th October and two each on 1st & 5th November. Two heavy cranes from Bank Hall and Preston were used to unload the girders and place them alongside the railway as required, always arriving 'south' end first.

Plate 16. A view along an abutment trench giving some idea of the amount of strutting required and the close shoring to the trench sides. The narrow gauge tubway brought in materials, at this stage, bricks, some of which are half submerged in the waterlogged ground. The bricklayers have laid the first few courses of the abutment wall and the string line and pin can be seen near the brick on edge, right foreground. *B.R.*

Plate 17. Excavation of earth between the timber trestles has begun, the pick and shovel predominating in a physically demanding job. The narrow gauge tubway can be seen to good effect. Over on the left one of the bridge abutments rises from what would appear to most as being a jumble of men and materials, but was in fact a carefully planned operation. *B.R.*

Plate 18. Arrival of bridge girders at Carr Mill required the combined efforts of two cranes to offload these and deposit them in the assembly area adjacent to the site. B.R.

Before the two halves of the bridge could be assembled, timber baulks were laid between the trestles, extended beyond the assembly areas upon which rails and bogies were positioned.

On Saturday 23rd January 1932, lifting of the slow lines began followed by removal of all ballast, trestles and beams below track level. This work was completed by about 5.a.m. on Sunday morning. At 7.30a.m., rolling in of the east half commenced and when in position the bridge was jacked up off the bogies which were then removed and the bridge slowly lowered onto its abutments, completed by 11.a.m. Replacement of the permanent way was complete by 6.p.m. Two weeks later the whole operation was replicated for the rolling in of the west half. Once the centre joint between the two halves had been plated, excavation beneath the bridge for the A580 could begin in earnest.

Plate 19. A train approaches Carr Mill from Wigan hauled by a L&NW 19" goods engine as the slow lines are dismantled in readyness for removal of the supporting RSJs and trestles below. B.R.

Plate 20, below.. The operation to roll in the east half of the bridge is underway and the unfinished brick abutments at either end indicate that the bridge is probably being lowered into its final resting place. This view also gives some idea of the size of girders used in its construction. B.R.

Plate 21. A London & North Western locomotive, possibly Class 'C' or 'C1,' crosses Carr Mill Viaduct about 1910 with a freight heading for Wigan. Unusually, this photo is taken from the east side of the viaduct. *John Ryan.*

Fig 8, below The Billinge Collieries Sidings Agreement c1916, located at 1148 yards from Carr Mill Station in the 'Up' direction.

A colliery at Brown Heath, north of Carr Mill Dam, was sunk in 1914 by Billinge Collieries Limited. The firm constructed its own siding, again on the west side of the main lines, and this was linked by a narrow gauge tubway about 1/2 mile in length, probably rope worked by means of a stationary engine. It is presumed that a wagon tippler was used to transship the coals into standard gauge wagons at the siding for onward transportation by London & North Western locomotives.

Between 1914 and 1916 the siding had been worked on a temporary basis but a sidings agreement of 29th June 1916 states that the connections were to be made permanent . A new signal cabin - Billinge Colliery Sidings - had been commissioned at this location on 11th June 1916. The cabin was one of the new London & North Western Type '5s' having a 45 lever frame which seems extravagant as the plan does not show any crossovers here.

Brown Heath Colliery closed in August 1934, the sidings agreement being terminated on 29th September. The main line connections were removed in May 1935 and it is presumed that the signal box decommissioned at the same time as it is not shown in the 1937 appendix.

Courtesy, John Ryan.

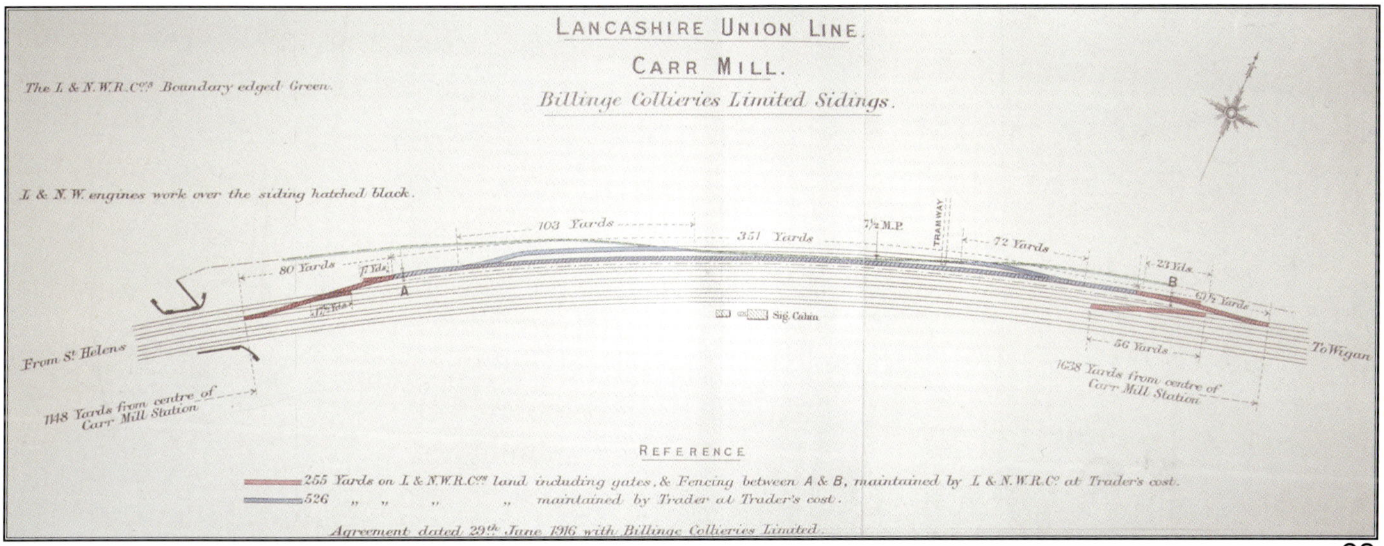

Plate 22. Carr Mill Viaduct, also photographed c1900. The area was known locally as Happy Valley, adjacent to the lake and obviously a popular recreation facility.

It is most likely that the photo was taken on a Sunday, the only day off work in those days for the vast majority of the working classes when every advantage would be taken to avail themselves, and their families, of some relaxation, knowing that the daily 'grind' would follow the day after.

Courtesy of St. Helens Local History and Archives Library.

Plate 23. A vintage London & North Western scene at Carr Mill about 1905 as an eight coach train hauled by an unidentified engine approaches the viaduct from St. Helens. *John Ryan.*

GARSWOOD

When the Lancashire Union Railway opened in 1869, the Garswood area was sparsely populated and it is surprising that the station here was of substantial construction, entirely brick and masonry with steeply pitched roofs complete with a stone parapet to each gable end.

The first signal or telegraph boxes on the route were inspected on 23rd August 1869. These were 'Type 1' Saxby & Farmer boxes, the locations being, as listed at Kew Records Office - Garswood, Bryn, Pemberton, Springs Branch Junction, Hall's Bridge Junction, Hindley, Whelley and Roundhouse Junction. The list may not be complete. Bryn certainly refers to Bryn Junction whilst Pemberton is thought to refer to Park Lane Sidings on the Pemberton Branch, this being the only box known to be open on the branch by this date. Hall's Bridge Junction is, in all probability, Fir Tree House Junction whilst Hindley would be De Trafford Junction. Whelley seems to refer to Rose Bridge Junction.

With the opening of J&R. Stone's Park Colliery in 1888, two cabins are operating at Garswood. The W.T.T. of 1899 lists these two boxes as Garswood Park Colliery & Station and Garswood Coal & Iron Company at a distance of 2 miles 350 yards from Carr Mill Junction, which in itself, one line distance for two boxes, is confusing. This is completely at odds with the logic of connections at this location which suggests that the first box of 1869 would have been named, simply, Garswood Station, and the additional box as Garswood Park Colliery Sidings, or similar. Is this a case of mistaken location as regards Garswood Coal & Iron Co.? The latter's nearest connections were at Ashton Pit Sidings, a further 1389 yards towards Bryn. However, by 1922 the W.T.T. gives only one signal box - Garswood, at a distance of 2 miles 431 yards from Carr Mill, which is more in keeping with the actual line distance to the Park Colliery connections. What is certain is that this cabin remained until closure in October 1972.

Plate 25. Ex-LMS 'Pacific' No 6201 *Princess Elizabeth* is seen between Garswood Road and Arch Lane bridges west of Garswood Station on 1st August 2009 with the returning 'Cumbrian Mountain Express to Liverpool Lime Street. A comparison with Gerry Bent's photographs, ***Plates 26 & 27,*** will show how the vegetation has proliferated over the intervening years eliminating all except the head-on shot. *Author.*

Plate 24, left. In the days after W.W.II., 'Patriot' Class No.5529 approaches Carr Mill with a train for Lime Street. *W.D.Cooper, Cooperrail.*

Plate 26. Class '47' No.47 282 approaches Garswood Road bridge with the diverted 12.40 Liverpool Lime Street - Newcastle on 23rd August 1981. Arch Lane bridge is in the background. *Gerry Bent.*

Plate 27. Photographed from Arch Lane bridge, Class '40' No. 40 152 climbs the bank westward from Garswood Station with empty ballast wagons from Ince Moss on 16th August 1981. *Gerry Bent.*

Plate 28. On 23rd August 1981 'Peak' class No.46 035 passes through Garswood Station with the diverted 07.50 Newcastle-Liverpool Lime Street. *Gerry Bent.*

Plate 29. On 16th August 1981 the diverted 11.00 Liverpool Lime Street - Blackpool North is worked by a four car DMU set with No.M50814 leading, seen passing through Garswood Station. *Gerry Bent.*

Plate 30. A pair of Manning Wardle 0-6-0 STs, *Wasp,* works No.1866/1915, and *Hornet,* works No. 1516/1901, are seen in tandem at J&R Stone's Park Colliery about 1935.

Author's Collection.

Plate 31. Local passenger services had gone over to diesel units before the end of the steam era on B.R. On 19th April 1969, a 2-car Class 110 BRCW unit calls at Garswood with the 11.07 Wigan North Western - Liverpool Lime Street service.

Courtesy, Kidderminster Railway Museum, John Marshall

Thomas Stone & Sons Downall Green Colliery appears in the mines lists from 1868. Here, a connection off the Lancashire Union, on the west side near Bryn Station, was provided under an agreement of 23rd February 1870. On the death of Thomas Stone in 1881 the firm became J&R Stone, but by 1891 the colliery was worked out and connections with the main line removed in October of that year.

However, in 1887, J&R Stone had sunk a new mine, Park Colliery, on the opposite (east) side of the Lancashire Union's lines, near to Garswood Station, where a sidings connection was provided on 29th February 1888. From Garswood Station, where the reception sidings were located, a half-mile long branch line ran towards the colliery which itself was sited at a much higher level than the Lancashire Union lines. Colliery engines had to push the incoming empties up a 1:90 gradient and beyond the screens to the colliery sidings from where the wagons then gravitated back beneath the screens, loaded and marshalled for dispatch.

The firm became J&R Stone Ltd in 1909, becoming part of the N.C.B. in 1947. Production ceased in 1960, although connections with the main lines remained in situ for a few years after closure.

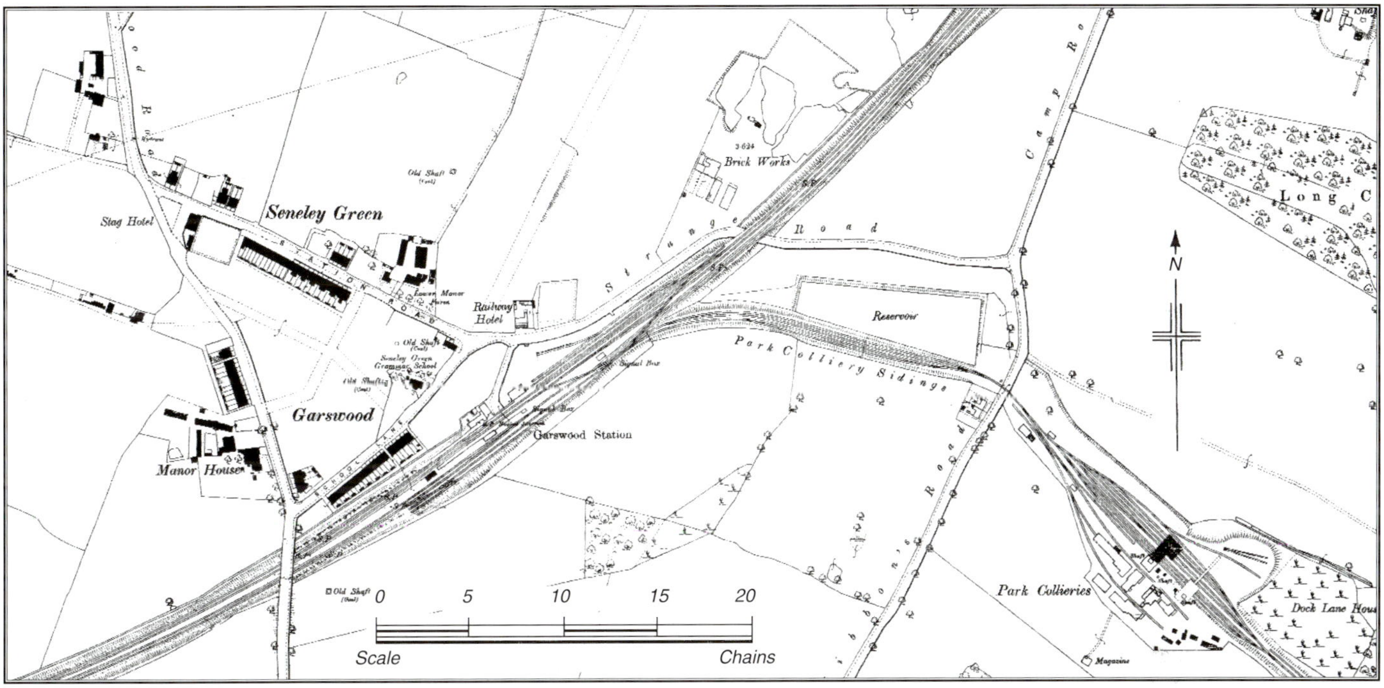

Fig 9. Garswood Station and Park Colliery Sidings c1892. As previously mentioned on ***Page 25***, two signal boxes are shown here within a few yards of each other -'Garswood (Park Colliery) & Station', between the slow and fast lines, the fast lines being those on the western side, and 'Garswood Hall Coal & Iron Co' near the colliery junctions. The new slow lines would only just have been laid at this period but nevertheless, the naming and location of two boxes here is quite odd.

Plate 32. In June 1965 '9F' No.92130 drifts through Garswood Station with a return Widnes - Long Meg empties. The dirt tips over on the extreme left are the legacy of Park Collieries operations.

Brian Woodward.

Plate 33. B.R.Class '9F' No.92091, receives banking assistance from '8F' No.48765 whilst working a Long Meg - Widnes anhydrite train on 30th July 1965. The banker is crossing bridge 13 approaching Garswood from Ince Moss. *Brian Woodward.*

Plate 34. After banking '9F' No.92091 from Ince Moss to Carr Mill, '8F' No.48675, runs light engine towards Ince Moss passing the 1892 cabin at Garswood which was situated between the fast slow lines, the latter having been lifted. *Brian Woodward.*

Plate 35. Another Stanier '8F' No.48511 approaches Garswood with a morning freight for St. Helens on 31st July 1965. The lifted slow lines were in the foreground and here were connections to Park Colliery. It is apparent that some re-modelling of lines took place to maintain links with the colliery which ceased production in 1960. These are seen still in situ. *Brian Woodward.*

Plate 36. Empties for Clock Face Colliery at St. Helens are hauled by '8F' No.48764 on 30th July 1965, seen approaching Garswood with a good head of steam as the fireman keeps his eye on the photographer. Again, bridge 13 is in the left background with the remains of pointwork into the goods yard which had closed in February 1963. *Brian Woodward.*

Plate 37. Stanier Class '5' No.45019 approaches Garswood with a St. Helens bound freight on 30th July 1965. *Brian Woodward.*

Plate 38. About 1935 a Stanier Class '5', which could not have been in service for more than a year or so, is seen on the approach to Bryn with a local train comprising some ancient London & North Western stock. It is presumably working a Liverpool - Wigan train. Ashton Pit Sidings had been sited on the left of picture. *Author's Collection.*

Plate 39. Over 70 years later, Class '60' No.60 091 *An Teallach* is seen between Garswood and Bryn on 6th March 2008 with empty fuel tanks from Pilkingtons. The location is almost identical to that of the L.M.S. Class '5' photo above, near Spindle Hillock, taken at a different angle from the nearby footbridge *Bob McClellan.*

BRYN

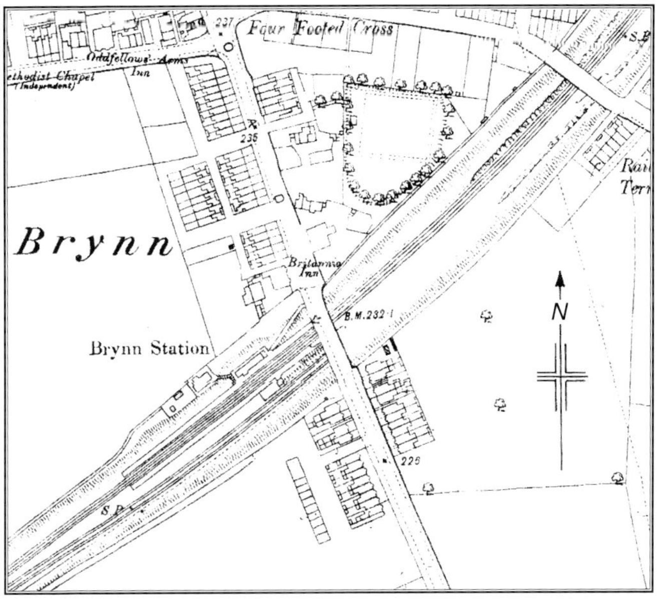

Fig 10. A section from the survey of 1892 shows the as yet uncompleted track quadrupling arrangements which stop at Wigan Road bridge adjacent to Bryn Station.

Like Garswood Station, Bryn also had buildings of substantial construction rather than the timber prefabricated type which lasted beyond the period of rationalisation and into the 1980s when the powers that be decided to remove these original structures and replace them with a bus shelter! Today they would have been candidates for a preservation order.

There had been a Saxby & Farmer box at Bryn Junction from 1869 which was replaced, clear of the new slow lines, by a L&NW Type '4', 64 lever box, in 1892. This, in turn, was replaced by a L&NW Type '5' having 70 levers, inspected on 1st September 1929 and sited in the triangle between the fast lines and the Pemberton Branch. It was to close in April 1959.

Ashton Colliery, south -west of Bryn Station, opened in 1888 and, according to the inspector's report of 21st May 1889, a new signal cabin was opened here between Garswood and Bryn which he lists as 'Coal & Iron Cos Wks.' at 1/2 mile south of Bryn Station. This can only be Ashton Pit Sidings at 1,389 yards from Garswood. As the owners of the mine were Garswood Coal & Iron Company, this adds to the illogical naming of the afore mentioned box at Garswood. It may be that some clerk at Euston got himself in a knot when compiling the W.T.T. of 1899, but we'll never really know!

The Ashton pits closed in 1910. The signal box is believed to have closed pre- 1922. However, it was still in situ c1931.

Plate 40. Bryn Station is seen here in Edwardian times as a tram passes by on Wigan Road above.The bridge on Bryn Road can just be seen to the rear, and beyond that the chimneys of Garswood Hall Colliery. The new slow lines instituted under the Bamfurlong Railways Act of July 1887, run on the right hand side, a new bridge being constructed to take these. *John Sloane Collection.*

Plate 41. On 12th July 2003, a Pathfinder Tours 'Anniversary Special' looking similar to a cattle train, passes through Bryn station with D345 in charge. *Alan Hart.*

Plate 42, below, right. 'Bryn for Ashton in Makerfield' says the station sign in white lettering on a blue background when photographed on 15th March 1971.
John Ryan.

Plate 43. In 1968, H.M. Queen Elizabeth II paid a visit to the 'Three Sisters' reclamation scheme which had then only just begun. She is seen in conversation with the Chief Planning Officer of Lancashire County Council under whose auspices the work started with the Department of the Environment providing grant aid. In 1974, Greater Manchester Council had authority for continuation of the scheme which passed into the hands of Wigan Metropolitan Borough for completion, opening to the public in November 1978.
Courtesy, Parks & Countryside, Wigan Leisure & Culture Trust.

Plate 44. Bryn Station is host to passing Class '47' No. 47 563 on 19th July 1981 working a Sunday diversion, the 10.40 Liverpool Lime Street to Newcastle. Note that the original station buildings are still in situ and although boarded up, look to be in good order. Unfortunately, they would not last much longer, being replaced by a bus shelter. *Gerry Bent.*

Plate 45. Bryn Station survives but reduced to the utilitarian 'bus shelter' accommodation typical of so many stations today.

On 12th July 2003 'Pacer' No. 142/043 calls with a Liverpool Lime Street - Wigan North Western service. *Author.*

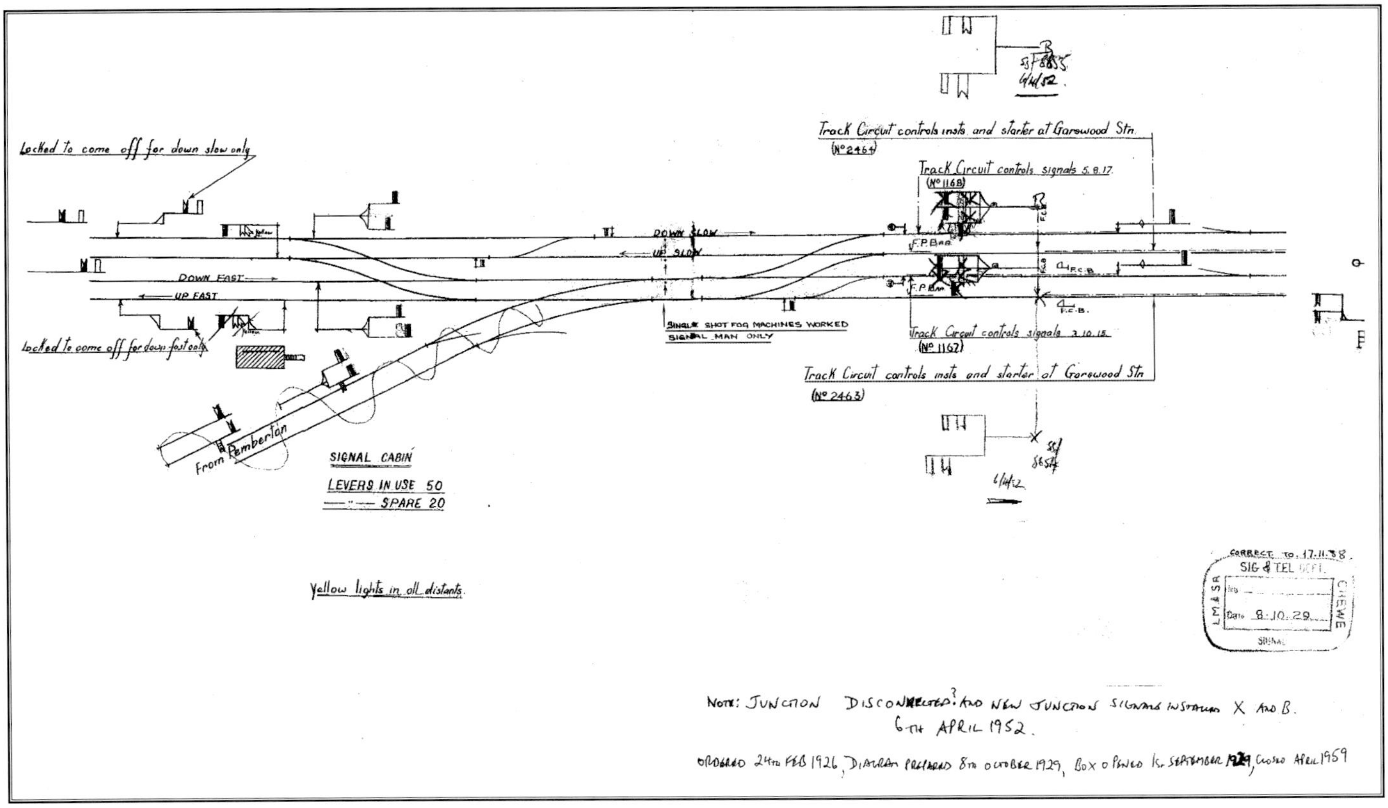

Fig 11. L.M.S. Crewe diagram for the new Bryn Junction signal box as prepared on 8th October 1929 and stamped correct to 17th November 1938. Notes for the removal of the junction and signal alterations, dated 6th April 1952, have been added. The new L&NW Type '5' box was ordered on 24th February 1926, opening on 1st September 1929. It is apparent from these notes that the diagram was prepared after the new box had opened. *Courtesy, Tony Graham.*

Plate 46. Class '40' No.40 087 approaches Bryn from Ince Moss with empty 'Mermaid' ballast wagons on 9th August 1981. Bryn Road bridge and part of the Three Sisters site, now landscaped, and new industrial buildings form the background. *Gerry Bent.*

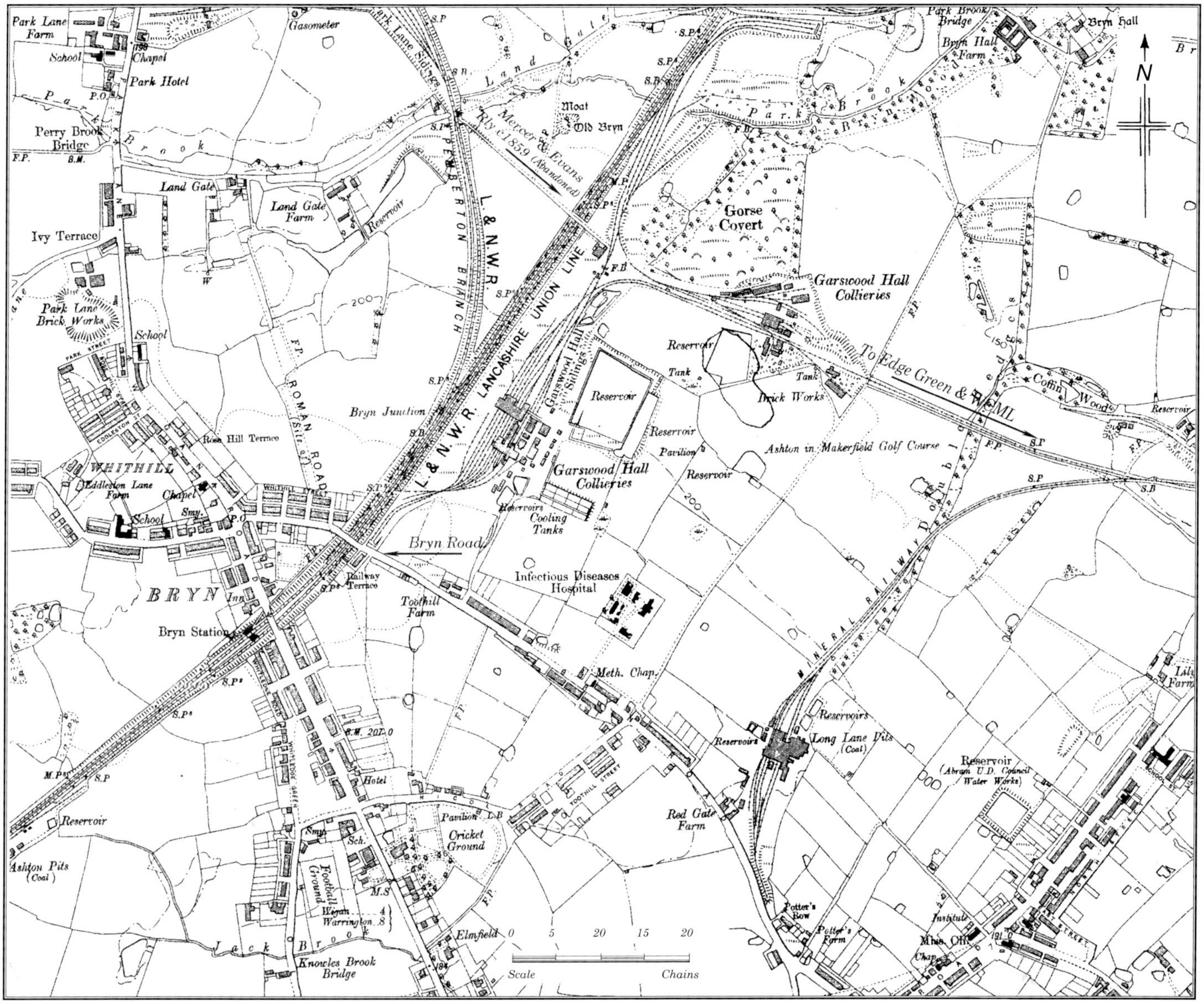

Fig 12. Bryn Junction left the main Lancashire Union lines north-west of Bryn Station This section is from an updated Ordnance Survey of the early twentieth century, after the sinking of Long Lane Colliery. The Park Lane pits are shown in more detail in ***Fig 24.*** (Pemberton Branch Chapter) but of interest is the abandoned portion of Mercer & Evans colliery railway from Park Lane. Also shown is Long Lane Colliery, sunk by the Garswood Coal & Iron Company in 1890 and from where a new line of colliery railway turned eastwards towards the North Union lines using the old Mercer & Evans alignment to Long Lane Sidings.* Ashton Colliery, bottom left, had been sunk by the Garswood Coal & Iron Company opening in 1888, the siding connections being completed in March 1890 under an agreement with the Railway Company of 13th December 1888.

Apparently the colliery was not a success, production ceasing in 1907/8, continuing as a pumping station until 1910.The Traffic Committee Minutes record that the sidings connections had been removed by November 1911.

The M6 Motorway now passes under the railway between the former Ashton Pits Sidings and Bryn Station.

Although it is not too clear on the above survey, the second signal box at Bryn Junction is sited alongside the new slow lines, but still at the same line distance as the original Saxby & Farmer Type '1' of 1869. The third box at this location would be sited in the triangle of lines at the junction some 125 yards nearer Ince Moss. Also shown is the second box at Garswood Hall Sidings, a L&NW Type '4', having 27 levers, sited alongside the fast lines and opened in July 1886. This had replaced a pre-1880s box and was to close on Sunday 8th September 1968.

See also* ***Pemberton Branch Page 98* *and* ***The Wigan Branch Railway Page 58.***

It is without doubt that the Telegraph, and the later Signal Box, owe their existence to the pioneering work of Michael Faraday, possibly the foremost scientist of the nineteenth century whose greatest discovery in 1831, after ten years of experiments, was that of the induction of electric currents. He proved the identity of electric currents from different sources in 1833; equivalents in electro-chemical composition, 1834; electro-static induction, 1838, and the relation between electric and magnetic forces.

The forerunner of the telephone was the electric telegraph invented by Cooke & Wheatstone in Britain c1837, the first 'Public Line' being laid between Paddington and Slough in 1843.

In the U.S.A., Morse invented a signalling code- Morse Code - and a recording telegraph was used commercially for the first time between England and France in 1851.

By the 1860s, the 'Railway Telegraph Box' was in widespread use on the railways of Great Britain and a number of these installations were open to public use for a fee.

Scotsman Alexander Graham Bell patented the apparatus which became the telephone in 1876. Born in Edinburgh and educated there and in London, he had gone to Canada in 1870, then on to the U.S.A. where he became Professor of Vocal Physiology at Boston University.

Hertz's discovery of electromagnetic waves showing that their behaviour resembled that of heat and light waves, led to Marconi's 'wireless telegraph', ancestor to the radio and modern communications.

From about 1875 onward and through to the late 1890s, the early telegraph boxes were being replaced by the Signal Box, the quintessential element of the working railway as we came to know it, and whilst many of the latter have been replaced by modern Power Boxes there are many signal boxes extant on Britain's railways today.

In the case of the Lancashire Union Railway the early Saxby & Farmer types were replaced by 'in house' designs of the London & North Western Railway although some of the former survived for many years, particularly on the joint lines, finding other uses as stores.

All of the above in some way or another, however, followed in the footsteps of Michael Faraday.

Plate 47. Bryn Station on 15th March 1971 as a Wigan Corporation bus passes on Wigan Road above, beyond which is Bryn Road bridge. Note that both platforms have long since lost their canopies but the station buildings seem to be in good repair. *John Ryan.*

Plate 48. A Post-Grouping scene at 'Bryn for Ashton in Makerfield'. After the opening of Ashton -in- Makerfield station on the Great Central's route the unwary passenger alighting here expecting to find himself in Ashton would, no doubt, be a little annoyed at having been misled by the station name. This was, however, common practice amongst the competing railway companies.
Lens of Sutton Association.

Plate 49. From Bryn Station the track curves left under Bryn Road bridge and begins to straighten out towards Ince Moss as it passes the former site of Bryn Junction seen left of centre on 15th March 1971. An abandoned mine tub adds to the scene. *John Ryan.*

Plate 50. Freightliner' liveried Class '66' No.66 506, is approaching Land Gate Lane bridge with a diverted Garston - Carlisle Merry-go-Round train on 13th January 2007.
Alan Hart

The Garswood Coal & Iron Company and Garswood Hall Collieries

The Garswood Coal & Iron Company was registered on 22nd November 1873 to take over the Mercer & Evans collieries.* In 1890 they sank Long Lane Colliery in the vicinity of Edge Green, Golborne, production beginning in 1894, and a new connection was made with what were now the London & North Western's lines through Golborne and Edge Green (WCML). As the colliery railway approached the main lines it would follow the course formerly used by Mercer & Evans between 1859 and 1869.

In 1929, Garswood Coal & Iron Co. were taken over by Garswood Hall Collieries, on the voluntary liquidation of the former. One of the first actions of the new owners was to close Park Lane pits on the Pemberton Branch as from 30th June, the connections with the former Lancashire Union lines being removed by October 1931. However, in the early 1930s, two of the pits were reopened by Landgate Colliery Co., eventually to pass into NCB ownership in 1947, finally closing in 1961. As production from these two pits was limited, rail connections were never reinstated.

The Garswood Hall Collieries themselves, date from the late 1860s, Nos. 1&2 pits situated north-east of Bryn Junction. Sidings connections had been made with the Lancashire Union under an agreement of 9th April 1870. Between 1874 and 1877, a further four shafts were sunk at the same location, others being sunk in the late 1880s. The company became a Limited concern on 24th March 1883.

In the Edge Green area of Golborne yet another mine, No.9 shaft, was sunk in 1901 at about 1/2 mile from Richard Evans' Edge Green Colliery .

A new colliery railway, circuitous in its route, was built from Garswood and, in part, ran parallel to the former Mercer & Evans' railway of 1859/69, passing through the new colliery site on its way to make a connection with the nearby Great Central route between Ashton and Edge Green.

Between 1931 & 1938, no less than five of Garswood Hall's mines were to close, including No.9 pit at Edge Green, with a further two shafts being used only for pumping and ventilation. Connections with the LNER in respect of connections at Edge Green were terminated on 31st October 1940, and with the LMS at Long Lane on 25th March 1943. The signalbox at the latter location had been removed by 14th October 1945. After this date any coal traffic from Garswood Hall's mines went out via the connections at Bryn.

At nationalisation in 1947, only Long Lane No.1 and Garswood Hall Nos. 3, 5, 6 & 7 pits were still in operation, becoming a part of the St. Helens, North West Division area and the five locomotives still working, all at Garswood Hall shed. Long Lane closed in 1955 and the pits at Garswood ceased production in August 1958. However, the washery at this location remained open until 1962 to process coal brought in from other collieries in the area.

* *see also* ***Pemberton Branch Page 97***

Plate 51. Long Lane Colliery is seen after closure in 1955. Demolition began in 1957 but was not fully completed until the 1960s.
Courtesy, Parks & Countryside, Wigan Leisure & Culture Trust.

Plate 52. With Bryn Road bridge in the background, Class '40' No.40 097 heads towards Ince Moss with a train of spoil wagons for Ince Moss Tip on 2nd August 1981. Next to the engine is an ex-Western Region brake van. The trackbed of the former Pemberton Branch can be determined by the line of bushes, top right. *Gerry Bent.*

Plate 53. Also on 2nd August 1981, Class '47' No.47 544 approaches Bryn with the diverted 09.55 Newcastle - Liverpool Lime Street. On the extreme left is the trackbed of the former Pemberton Branch as it turns northwards away from the Lancashire Union route north-east of Bryn Road bridge. It seems to have become a dumping ground for local farmers. In the right background are the abutments of the bridge which carried the Mercer & Evans colliery railway from their mines at Park Lane to reach the North Union lines near Mains Colliery. The next photograph is taken from this location. *Gerry Bent.*

Plate 54. The diverted 07.50 Newcastle - Liverpool Lime Street climbs the bank from Ince Moss on 2nd August 1981. On the right is the landscaped 'Three Sisters' area now put to recreational use. Ince Moss Tip and Land Gate Lane bridge are seen in the background. *Gerry Bent.*

Plate 55. A Lime Street - Wigan DMU approaches Land Gate Lane bridge on 15th March 1971. The descent to Ince Moss is seen to good effect beyond the bridge. *John Ryan.*

By the mid 1940s, the locomotive fleet of Garswood Hall Collieries was rather aged and an interesting set of circumstances surrounds the attempted purchase of a War Department 0-6-0 'Austerity' from the Hunslet Engine Company of Leeds.

The latter received an enquiry from Garswood Hall in March 1943 for an 0-6-0 17in, inside cylinder locomotive. Hunslet replied that an 0-6-0 'Austerity' with 18in x 20in cylinders would suit their needs at a price of £4,910. Apparently, nothing happened until May 1944 when Hunslet reiterated their previous offer but now with a price tag of £5,400, quoting an approximate delivery period of twelve months. Garswood Hall were advised that if a decision to proceed with the order ensued, then approaches must be made through official channels.

Approval by the Ministry of Fuel & Power was granted in July 1944 and the order placed with Hunslet on the 27th inst., asking for delivery by 31st March 1945. Hunslet replied that they may have problems supplying by that date due to their present commitments but advised " leave the matter in our hands", intimating that every effort would be made to supply by the requested order date.

It came as somewhat of a surprise therefore when, on 28th September 1944, Garswood Hall Collieries were informed by Hunslet that "we are today dispatching to you an 0-6-0 'Austerity'.

It appears that the Ministry of Supply (M.o.S.) Inspector was not on site at Hunslets when final hydraulic and steam tests were carried out on this particular locomotive, allegedly Works No.3302, the Inspector refusing to accept it. From Hunslets point of view, they now had a spare locomotive on their hands and quite logically took the opportunity to supply Garswood Hall, having already delivered to the M.o.S. their monthly quota.

On arrival at Garswood the 'Austerity' was immediately put to work but this was far from the end of the matter. It seems that the M.o.S. were displeased with the course of events and, on 23rd October 1944, Garswood Hall were requested by Hunslet to return the locomotive, which duly went back to them on 3rd November.

To confuse matters even further, it appears that the locomotive sent to Garswood was *not* No.3302 but No.3187, which should have been W.D. No.75137 but in fact had been numbered as W.D. 75147, Hunslet No.3188 becoming 75137.

To say that relations were now strained between Garswood Hall Collieries and the Hunslet Engine Company is perhaps somewhat of an understatement, so much so that Garswood now implied that they wished to cancel their order. At this period Manchester Collieries were seeking permission from the M.o.S. to purchase an 'Austerity' engine which was duly approved by the Ministry on 18th April 1945 and the Garswood Hall order subsequently cancelled by Hunslet.

Manchester Collieries had requested copper tubes instead of the steel ones normally fitted to these engines and also a blow-down-cock on the boiler. The copper tubes didn't present any problem but Hunslet claimed that insufficient time was available for any other modifications, instead offering to fit a mounting plate for the blow-down apparatus so Manchester Collieries could fit one themselves at a later date. However, on the day prior to the Austerity being dispatched, it appears that a blow-down-cock was stripped from one of the Manchester Collieries, ex-North Staffordshire 0-6-2 locomotives which were receiving new boilers at Hunslets. Therefore, Works No.3302 was sent to Walkden Yard on 1st August 1945 and there named *Stanley*.

At nationalisation in 1947, Garswood Hall Collieries Ltd. still had a number of pits at work on their original 1860s sites which continued in production until August 1958, the exception being Long Lane Colliery which closed in 1955. However, the washery at Garswood continued in use to process coal from other local collieries. By 1962 all operations had ceased and the sidings out of use.

Plate 56. *Stanley*, the 0-6-0 Austerity which strained relations between Garswood Hall Collieries, the Hunslet Engine Company and the M.o.S. in the 1940s, is seen on the Manchester Collieries system at Walkden Yard on 24th August 1958. *Peter Eckersley.*

Plate 57. The departure sidings at Garswood Hall No.4 pit are seen in the mid-1930s. The view is looking north-east and, just right of centre, having crossed over the Lancashire Union lines, a motor coach is making its way along Land Gate Lane, which must have been in a better state then than it is today. *Author's Collection.*

Plate 58 . Again, a shot from the mid-1930s at Garswood Hall Colliery with 0-6-0ST *King* taking water as the crew pose for the camera. This is thought to be near Garswood Hall's No.1 colliery. The locomotive is one of a number taken over by the National Coal Board in 1947. It would eventually be scrapped at Cronton Colliery, St Helens in 1968. *Author's Collection.*

Plate 59. A London & North Western G2/2A 0-8-0 passes Garswood Hall Sidings hauling a mixed freight bound for Liverpool in the 1950s, the photograph taken from the eastern side of Land Gate Lane bridge. In the sidings, a rake of ex-LMS bogie bolsters await collection having presumably been used for the delivery of mining equipment or perhaps, a P.W. working. Note Garswood Hall Sidings Signal Box on the right. In the far background, the overbridge still in situ at this period, is that believed to have been used by Mercer & Evans locomotives to transport coal from their Park Lane Colliery to the North Union lines near Mains Sidings. It would only have been in use as such for a short period, continuing in use thereafter as an occupation bridge.

Courtesy, Parks & Countryside, Wigan Leisure & Culture Trust.

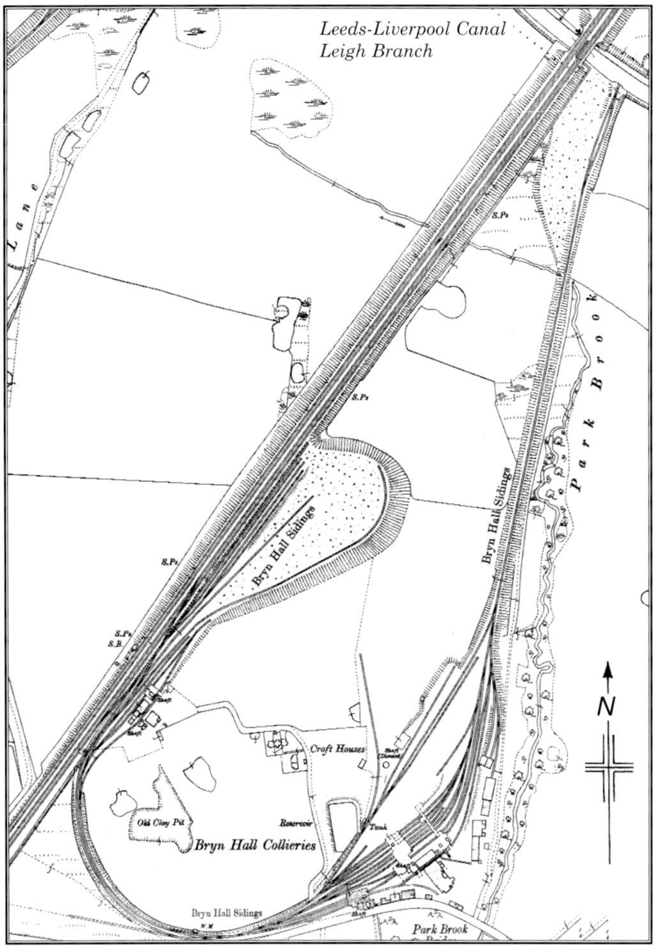

Fig 13. Brynn Hall Colliery and its railway system are shown about 1900 and any signs of the connection to the North Union before 1869 have disappeared without trace. Landgate Lane runs between Brynn Hall and the northern end of Garswood Hall Colliery Sidings. The length of line from colliery to canal was approximately 1/2 mile. Brynn Hall Sidings originally had a Saxby & Farmer Type '1' signal box from 1869. This was replaced by a 25 lever L&NW Type '4' in 1892, shown here alongside the fast lines. It was to close on 20th November 1956.

Plate 60, previous page. As a testament to the efforts of Lancashire Miners, the 'Three Sisters' rise like extinct volcanos above the surrounding area. At 150ft high these, together with other spoil heaps here, contained some 3 1/2 million tons of waste, reclamation of the former colliery sites beginning in the late 1960s. Some have said, and I wouldn't entirely disagree, they should have been left as a reminder of the industrial age; a fitting memorial to those who gave their lives to extract the 'black diamonds' from the bowels of the earth and the cost to mining communities generally and society as a whole.

As viewed from Bolton Road at Stubshaw Cross.

Courtesy, Parks & Countryside, Wigan Leisure & Culture Trust.

Brynn Hall Colliery

The original 'Brynn'* Hall Colliery was sunk in the 1850s and owned by John Smith & Sons who, by 1856, had constructed a colliery railway to the North Union south of Mains Colliery. Although much of Smith's route from his colliery is conjectural, at its eastern end it ran parallel to Mercer & Evans' line from their Park Lane pits on approaching the North Union. By 1869 the line and its connections with the latter had been lifted.

Brynn Hall Colliery's connection with the Lancashire Union was made under an agreement of 2nd December 1869 at which date it was under the ownership of Wm. Crippen. Sidings and main line connections were located north east of Garswood Hall Colliery's connections. New pits were sunk at Brynn Hall in 1873 and a railway built to a pierhead on the Leeds-Liverpool Canal. Over the years, little change occurred to the basic rail layout.

Brynn Hall Colliery Coal Company Ltd. was formed on 10th January 1893 under new ownership. However, in the early years of the twentieth century the firm was financially stretched and closure of two of the five pits here occurred in 1919. A proposal by shareholders to cease trading and close the company down was only narrowly avoided. Financial reconstruction took place in 1934, at which period the Chairman of Central Wagon Co Ltd., assumed charge until closure in 1945.

The first colliery engine on record at Brynn Hall was delivered in 1872 by the Hunslet Engine Co. It is presumed that prior to this date main line locomotives shunted the sidings. Another new locomotive, *Childwall*, also built by Hunslet arrived in 1891. In 1904 its boiler exploded killing the driver.

The Company seemed to acquire a mixture of mostly new locomotives in the early years and then, from the period of financial difficulty, only second hand ones from various sources. In 1933 an 0-6-0ST No.41, arrived from the Mersey Docks & Harbour Board. Built in 1918 by the Avonside Engine Co. of Bristol, on arrival at Brynn Hall it was named *James.* It worked at Brynn Hall until 1938 when it is believed to have been scrapped. A second *James* arrived in 1939/40, having been built by Hudswell Clark & Co. in 1920.

Phyllis was another 0-6-0 acquired from A.R.Adams & Co. Ltd, Newport machine dealers. This locomotive passed to S.Littler Ltd. scrap merchant, who set up on the former colliery site after it closed in 1945.

* *Spelling of colliery throughout its working life.*

***Plate 61*.** The doyen of its class, No.5552 *Silver Jubilee,* is seen climbing the bank from Ince Moss towards Bryn c1935 in the sparkling condition of an almost new locomotive complete with the chrome plated embelishments it carried on its emergence from Crewe Works in 1934. Note the Garswood Hall Colliery wagons in the nearby sidings, right.
Author's Collection.

Plate 62. Brynn Hall Colliery viewed in a North-Easterly direction about 1935. The 0-6-0 locomotive appears to be *Phyllis,* which would later pass into the hands of S Littler Ltd., who operated from the site after the closure of the mine. *Author's Collection.*

Plate 63. The present day view from Land Gate Bridge towards Ince Moss as Class 150/150 climbs the bank with a Wigan - Lime St. service on 4th March 2009. Over on the right the site of Brynn Hall Colliery and sidings are now totally overgrown. *Author.*

Plate 64. This is a view westward of the Leeds-Liverpool Canal that one would get from a passing train between Land Gate bridge and Ince Moss. Over 150 years of mining and industry have left their mark, the dirt tips in the foreground from nearby Ince Moss Collieries and those in the distance at Pemberton. Thankfully, ongoing reclamation schemes have seen much of this dereliction removed but it is a reminder of the scars inflicted upon the landscape.

At the top right hand can be seen the tops of three multi-storey blocks of flats at Worsley Mesnes, built between 1964/6, on which I finished my time as an apprentice joiner. I can recall coal trains on the ex L&Y Pemberton Loop which line passed by on the west side of the site. The trains were often signal-checked opposite one of the five storey blocks and the locomotive's crew would observe the activity going on around them. One particular day in 1965 I was moving some timber with the tower crane and, for a moment, took my eye off the job to look at the steam engine, a W.D. type, promptly receiving a thump on the shoulder as the timber swung around in the breeze which, luckily, left only a severe bruise; but oh for a camera in those days! *John Ryan.*

INCE MOSS & FIR TREE HOUSE JUNCTIONS

At Ince Moss, a connecting curve to the North Union at Springs Branch, St Helens Line Junction, was made. Extensive sidings would be laid here over the years particularly for the reception of coal trains from local collieries, re-marshalled for Garston and Widnes. Wigan-Liverpool passenger services, instituted on 1st January 1872, continue to use this route but most of the sidings, except for some on the inside of the curve have long since gone.

From Ince Moss, the gradient to Fir Tree House Junction was again 1:86. However, by the early BR period this had increased to 1:42. It was therefore necessary to have banking engines attached at Ince Moss and these would assist to Amberswood East or beyond if required. Some freights would reverse at De Trafford Junction to work towards Bolton via Hindley No.2 Junction. The banking engine would then become the train engine, dropping the leading engine off . The latter worked light back to Ince Moss or Springs Branch Shed.

Additional lines and sidings adjacent to Ince Moss Junction and between Ince Moss and the St. Helens Lines Junction at Springs Branch, - Springs Branch North Sidings - authorised in 1892, were completed in 1894. The Springs Branch - Wigan widening, authorised in 1890, was also completed in 1894.

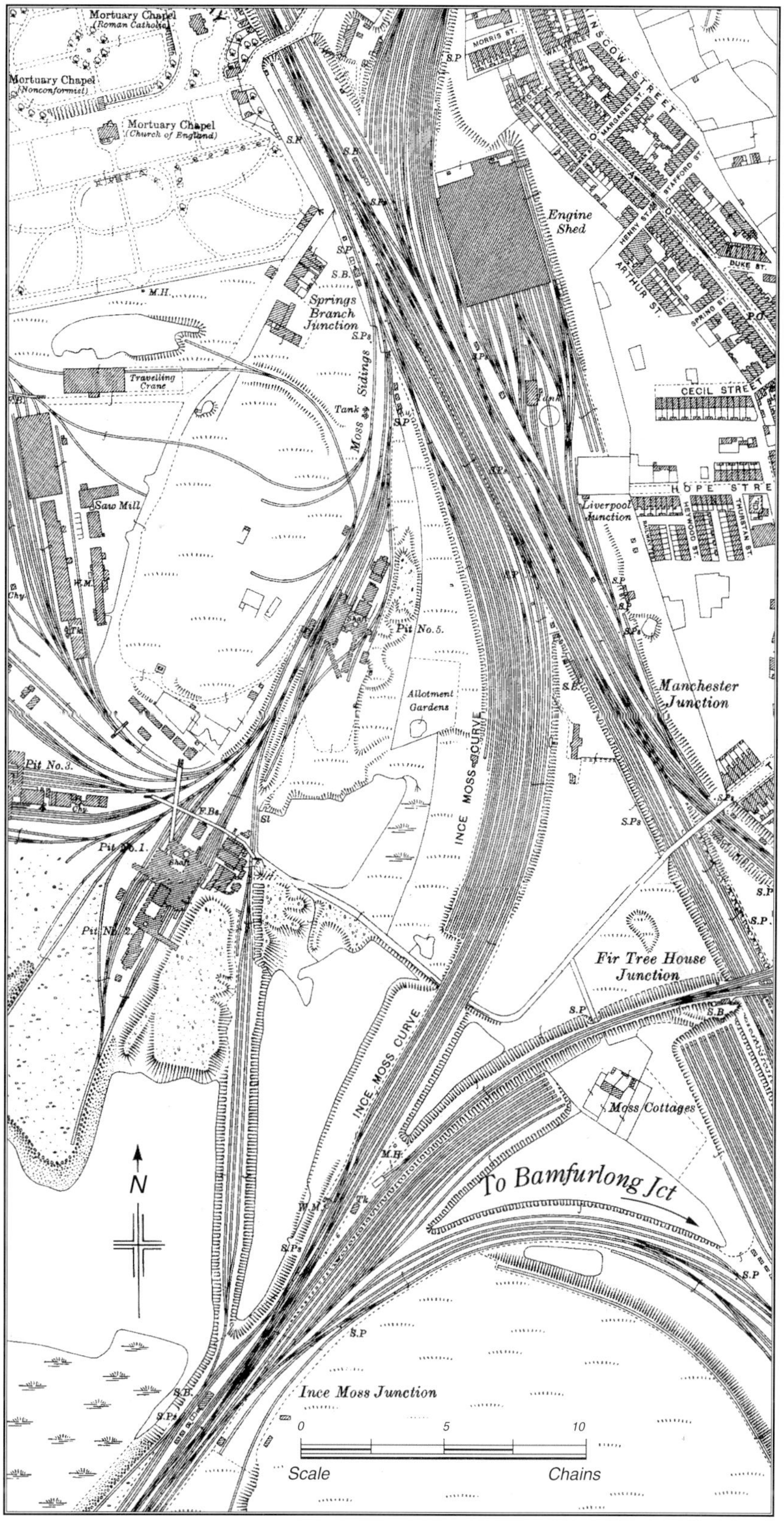

Fig 14. Beginning with a single line connection off the North Union lines to Pearson & Knowles collieries in 1863 and the opening of the Lancashire Union lines in 1869, the first additional sidings were installed at Ince Moss in 1873 to marshall freight trains "without touching the main lines", controlled by the 1869 Saxby & Farmer box. The next twenty-five years saw a continuing expansion of railway sidings and junctions at Ince Moss which, by the late 1890s, was virtually complete and are shown on this revision of the 1892 Ordnance Survey. Prominent at bottom centre are Ince Moss Sidings or Pemberton Corner, and the Bamfurlong Loop -Ince Moss Junction to Bamfurlong Junction curve. Adjacent is the connection to Ince Moss Collieries from the former Lancashire Union as authorised under the 1896 Act.

Under the Act of 4th August 1890, the Bamfurlong Sidings complex and loop lines were set out and brought into use in the summer of 1895 and a through sidings connection was opened at Ince Moss allowing connections with the former Lancashire Union line for traffic to/from St. Helens and Liverpool and the W.C.M.L. Up Slow at Bamfurlong Junction.

In the 1890s, some twenty coal trains per day departed from Ince Moss Sidings, or other sidings nearby, to work over the Lancashire Union route to Garston, via Blackbrook. Banana traffic worked in the opposite direction from Garston from 1912. In that year Elders - Fyffes relocated the discharge of bananas from Manchester Docks to Garston and in the first year of operations almost 49,000 tons of bananas were transferred from ship to rail, requiring three trains per day. In 1929, new discharge facilities were built enabling one shipload to be unloaded in one day, and by the 1930s almost 110,00 tons per year were unloaded from 72 ships. All went by way of the Blackbrook branch to by-pass St.Helens, working via Ince Moss and Whelley to Standish Junction. Most, if not all of Scotland's bananas travelled this way via Carlisle, other trains going to Blackburn and beyond. These steam heated trains ran throughout the 1960s but in similar fashion to the Long Meg workings were rerouted via St. Helens after closure of the Blackbrook Branch.

One of my former Signalman friends recalls a serious derailment to one of these trains at Ince Moss about 1950 and as this was a perishable cargo requiring special vans, the order came through to dispatch the whole lot to the tip. Needless to say, for a few days Wigan was awash with free bananas!

In the early years these long distance freights were worked by London & North Western 'Claughton' or 'Prince of Wales' class locomotives and subsequently by their 'G2/A' engines. In the LMS era, '8Fs' arrived on the scene and later, the much admired BR Standard '9F'.

'8Fs' and '9Fs' were the usual motive power on the Long Meg- Widnes anhydrite trains in the 1950s and 60s, which began their journey on the Settle & Carlisle route working via Hellifield, Blackburn, Chorley and Haigh Junction to access the Lancashire Union route until 3rd January 1966 when, upon closure of the Chorley - Cherry Tree line as a through route, they were re-routed via Bamber Bridge - Farrington Junction - Standish Junction - Whelley and, occasionally, by the W.C.M.L.

It is also worthy of note that in 1964 complete withdrawal of the Wigan - St. Helens -Lime St. passenger service and closure of all stations between Huyton Junction and Bryn were proposed by BR because, it was stated, of heavy freight workings, particularly coal, over the former Lancashire Union route. The fact that BR had closed the Blackbrook Branch and lifted lines on the Lancashire Union didn't seem to matter to the powers that were. Thankfully, due to local authority pressure, these closure proposals were withdrawn.

Carr Mill to Garswood Hall Sidings had been reduced to double track by 4th May 1958. Further rationalisation of the track between Garswood Hall and Ince Moss continued unabated for some years to come.

Signal box locations & line distances Gerards Bridge to Springs Branch No.1

1899		1922		1953	
Gerards Bridge Jct	Dist/To	Gerards Bridge Jct	Dist/to	Gerards Bridge Jct	Dist/to
Carr Mill Jct	1m 20yds	Carr Mill Jct	1m 20yds	Carr Mill Jct	1m 20yds
		Billinge Coll Sdg	1133yds		
Garswood Park Coll & Sta					
Garswood Coal & Iron Co.	2m 350yds	Garswood	1m 1058yds	Garswood	2m 431yds
	3m 370yds		3m 451yds		3m 451yds
Ashton Pit Sdg	1389yds				
Bryn Jct	1433yds				
	1m 1062yds	Bryn Jct	1m 1062yds	Bryn Jct *	1m 1187yds
Garswood Hall Sdg	911yds	Garswood Hall Sdg	911yds	Garswood Hall Sdg	786yds
Bryn Hall Sdg	517yds	Bryn Hall Sdg	517yds	Bryn Hall Sdg	517yds
Ince Moss Jct	1383yds	Ince Moss Jct	1383yds	Ince Moss Jct	1383yds
Springs Branch No.1	650yds	Springs Branch No.1	650yds	Springs Branch No.1	650yds
				**New Box 1.9.1929*	
	= 6m 1373yds		=6m 1454yds		=6m 1454yds

A Saxby & Farmer box had been inspected at Ince Moss on 23rd August 1869. In January 1880, this was replaced by a London & North Western type '4' Signal Box having 33 levers, which in turn was replaced in 1892 by another L&NW Type '4' cabin having an 84 lever frame. In 1949, a fourth box, an LMS Type '11' all timber cabin with a 85 lever R.E.C. frame opened here, surviving until closure on 1st October 1972 when Warrington Power Box was commissioned.

Opposite, the line distances between the signalling installations from Gerards Bridge and Springs Branch No.1 are given for 1899, 1922 and 1953 respectively. It will be noted that there is a discrepancy of 81 yards between the 1899 appendix and those of later years, and whilst every effort has been made to give accurate data, I again refer to my comments on ***page 25*** that someone at an undetermined date made an error as it is immediately obvious that the missing yardage seems to be accounted for between Carr Mill and Garswood.

It will also be noted that the distance between Garswood and Bryn Junction is constant, at least up to 1922. The 1953 appendix gives an additional 125 yards to Bryn Junction signal box, accountable to repositioning opposite the fast lines. This seems to be confirmed by the line distance to Garswood Hall Sidings: 786 + 125yards = 911yards.

Plate 65. On 22nd June 1985, Class '158' No.158/749 climbs the gradient from Ince Moss towards Bryn, approaching the bridge over the Leeds - Liverpool Canal, Leigh Branch, with a Blackpool North - Liverpool Lime Street service. The trackbed of the lifted slow lines occupies the right hand side of the picture. That the new lines were designated slow is not surprising as nearly all the colliery connections were on the eastern side, thus eliminating conflicting movements between Fast and Slow lines for slow moving coal traffic. In the far background is Winter Hill and its television mast. Since this photograph was taken, tree growth has claimed the vacant trackbed *Author.*

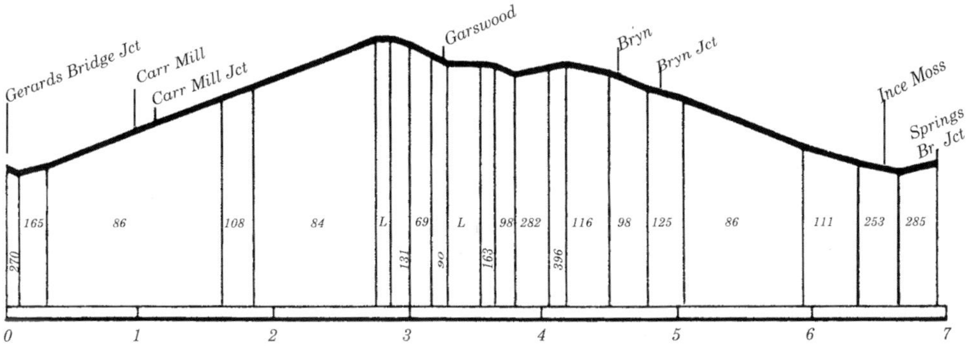

Gradient Profile, Gerards Bridge - Springs Branch.

Plate 66. Ince Moss Signal Box viewed towards Springs Branch on 20th April 1969. The lines to Fir Tree House Junction, pass between the two signal gantries and, on a rising embankment, cross the W.C.M.L. Just in view to the right of Ince Moss signal box is the Yardmaster's Office at Springs Branch. *Courtesy, Kidderminster Railway Museum, John Marshall.*

Plate 67. For the second view at Ince Moss, taken on the same day, the photographer has moved to his right and further north. The rising embankment which curves round towards Fir Tree House is seen to better advantage, as is the curvature of track towards the W.C.M.L. on the far left. *Courtesy, Kidderminster Railway Museum, John Marshall.*

Plate 68. Ince Moss Junction signal box is seen on 21st August 1971 and further rationalisation of the infrastructure here is well underway. This view is looking towards Bryn. *J.A.Sommerfield.*

Plate 69. On 3rd September 1965 '9F' 2-10-0 No.92161 is seen at Ince Moss about to start the climb toward Bryn whilst working one of the anyhdrite trains to Widnes from Long Meg Quarry on the Settle - Carlisle route, a roster particularly suited to these fine engines. The train would have stopped at Fir Tree House Junction to pin down the wagon brakes before descending to Ince Moss Junction. It was a gentle 1:253 incline here but increased to 1:86 within a half-mile, probably more with mining subsidence, the steepest section being just after Garswood Station at 1:69. These Long Meg trains ran via Blackburn, Chorley, Haigh Junction and Amberswood before closure of the Cherry Tree route in 1966. *Eddie Bellass.*

Plate 70. An ex-L&Y eight -wheeled tender from an 0-8-0 locomotive has found further use as a sludge tender when photographed at Ince Moss Sidings on 20th April 1969. The instruction for its return clearly seen on the side.

Courtesy, Kidderminster Railway Museum, John Marshall.

Plate 71. A Liverpool bound DMU with the early, small yellow warning panel, passes through Ince Moss on 3rd September 1965 as an unidentified '8F' idles away in the nearby sidings adjacent to the Bamfurlong Loop.

Eddie Bellass.

Plate 72. An ex-Liverpool & Southport Electric Railway carriage is being utilised as a mess van at Ince Moss Tip in September 1965, complete with new corrugated tin roof and stovepipe chimneys.

Eddie Bellass.

Plate 73. Bamfurlong Sidings 20th April 1969. The Down Main (Bank Road) and Up Main lines to Ince Moss Junction from Bamfurlong Junction are nearest the camera, on this side of the trap points. Bridge 28, left of signal box, has recently been rebuilt in preparation for the overhead electrification works and in a few years much rationalisation of the sidings here would take place.
Courtesy, Kidderminster Railway Museum, John Marshall.

Plate 74. Forty years later, on 13th March 2006, the Up and Down Main lines to Ince Moss Junction have been slewed right over in the rationalisation that followed, connecting with the Up and Down Loop lines from Bamfurlong Junction and all of the sidings have now been lifted. It is difficult for anyone not familiar with the railway history here to believe that Bamfurlong Sidings ever existed. Class '56' No.56 102 in Loadhaul livery, makes its way from Springs Branch on the Up Loop with the Kelbit Tanks. *John Sloane.*

Plate 75. On 1st August 1982, Class '25' No.25 195 approaches Ince Moss from Bamfurlong Junction with a spoil train for the Engineers tip. *Gerry Bent.*

Plate 76. A hive of activity on bridge 28 at Bamfurlong as reconstruction takes place on 20th August 1968. Some of the new concrete pillars and decking supports are already in place as work continues on lifting out one of the main beams. Note, no hard hats or high -vis jackets, the order of the day. *John Ryan.*

Plate 77. 'Transrail' liveried Class '60' No.60 066 *John Logie Baird* on Ince Moss curve with empty tanks from St. Helens on 30th January 2006. It will join the Up W.C.M.L. Slow line at Bamfurlong Junction.
Bob McClellan.

Plate 78(below). Some Ordnance Surveys show the Ince Moss curve to the W.C.M.L as lifted which is clearly not the case and it still sees some traffic. On 29th April 1989 Class '47' No.47 426 passes the remnants of Bamfurlong North Sidings on the approach to Ince Moss Junction with stock for a St. Helens - Wembley, Rugby League Cup Final Special. *Author.*

Plate 79, (below). In the 1980s, the remnants of Bamfurlong Sidings became nothing more than storage for redundant vehicles many of which were ex-departmental. On 15th November 1983, an ex-LNER coach, converted for overhead line use, is seen at the northern end of the sidings and has been the victim of repeated attacks of vandalism.
Author

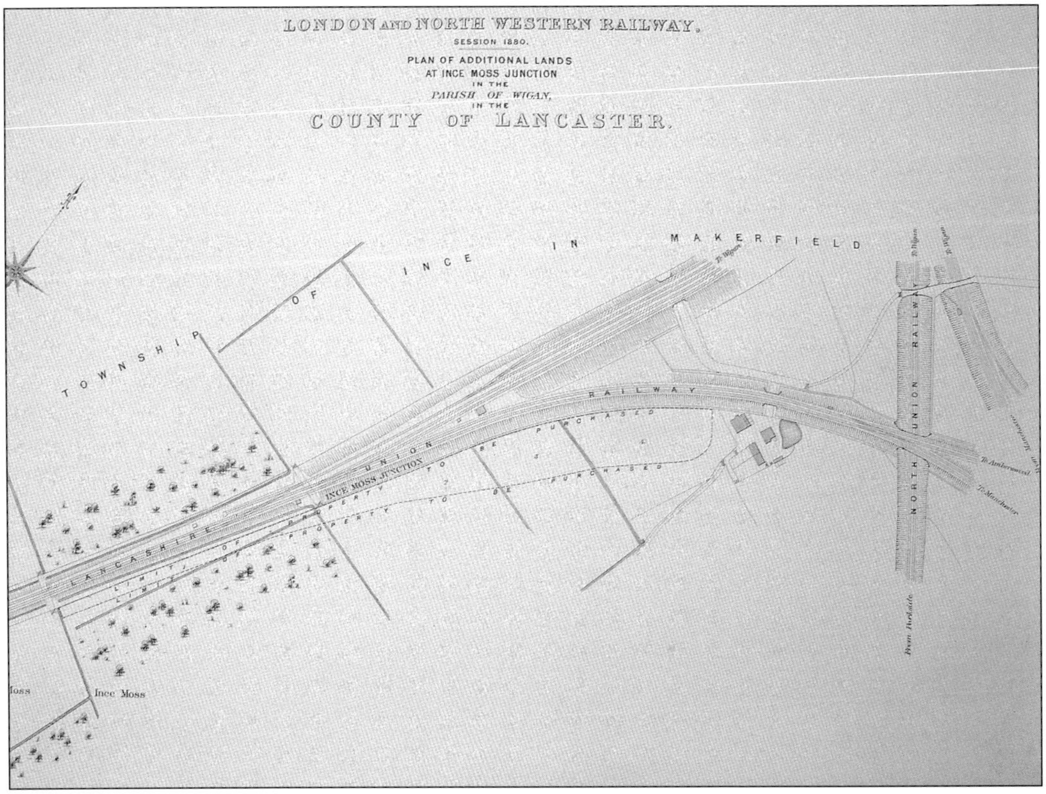

Fig 15. Ince Moss c1880. This plan shows the proposed land take for more sidings at Ince Moss at what later became known as Pemberton Corner.

Some additional sidings have already been laid here, on the inside of the curve to the North Union Junction at Springs Branch. These were built in 1873 to marshall freight trains without touching the main lines and controlled by the first signal box, a Saxby & Farmer 'Type 1'. This can be seen in the 'V' at the junction.

Wigan & Leigh Archives.

Plate 80. A panoramic view across the flash at Ince Moss as Class '47' No.47 381 works along the Bamfurlong Loop line towards Ince Moss Junction with a spoil train for the engineer's tip on 19th July 1981. The sidings at Bamfurlong North End were used for condemned vehicles at this period, and the glass works still received deliveries of sand by rail. The growth of vegetation and the erection of the ubiquitous steel fencing here, now prevents any photography on this curve. *Gerry Bent.*

Plate 81. The former Pearson & Knowles Ince Moss Collieries are viewed in the 1940s looking eastward. The WCML comes in at mid left going out of picture top right, with Taylors Lane bridge and Springs Branch No.1 S.B. partially obscured by smoke from No. 6 pit, centre. Adjacent to No.6 are pits Nos. 3 & 4, and behind these are pits Nos1&2 which had closed in the 1920s. Furthest left is pit No.5. The lines from Ince Moss Junction enter at upper right to cross over the W.C.M.L. and Tyldesley lines to exit at upper left. Across the centre the lines curve round behind No.5 pit towards the W.C.M.L., left. *John Sloane Collection.*

Thomas Pearson's involvement with the mining industry at Ince began in the 1840s with the sinking of Springs Pit alongside the Springs Branch and Crow Orchard near the North Union main line. ***(See The Wigan Branch Railway c2008).*** Thomas Knowles association with Pearson began in 1849, first as overlooker at the above pits, and later, from 1854 as a partner in the firm of Pearson & Knowles.

The first of the Ince Moss Collieries were sunk in 1863 on the western side of the North Union lines to which a connection was made under an agreement of 23rd April 1863, shown on the North Union line plans of 1865 and believed to have been constructed by the latter on land leased from W.G.Walmsley, the leasehold of which was later sold to Pearson & Knowles. The partners amalgamated with the Dallam Forge and Warrington Wire & Iron Company in 1873, the business being registered as Pearson & Knowles Coal & Iron Company Limited in 1874. An ironworks that opened on the site in 1872 by the Dallam Forge Company had closed by 1901. This may have been part of a reorganisation on the site to give more space for mining operations at Ince Moss and to concentrate their iron interests at Warrington.

Further expansion had taken place at Ince Moss in the 1870s to 1880s and in total six mines were sunk here. A second connection was made with the Lancashire Union Railway at Ince Moss Junction under an agreement of 31st March 1896.

Ince Moss Nos.1&2 pits were closed by 1928 and in 1930 amalgamations within the coal and iron industries led to the formation of the Wigan Coal Corporation of which Pearson & Knowles Coal & Iron Co. became a part.

The last of the Ince Moss Collieries closed in November 1962. Connections with the former N.U & L.U. lines were terminated on 31st October 1966.

Plate 82. The Lancashire Union lines curved to the north, where a junction was made with the North Union lines opposite Springs Branch sheds, south of the original connection to Pearson & Knowles Collieries of 1863. The Lancashire Union's Up and Down lines occupy the extremity of the curve, on the inside of which were laid out numerous sidings for coal and freight traffic - Springs Branch North Sidings.
John Sloane Collection.

Plate 83. On 6th June 1959 0-6-0 ST *No.1* is seen at Ince Moss Colliery shed. Built by Robert Stephenson & Co. for theWigan Coal Corporation in 1930, it arrived new at Ince Moss. The engine was at nearby Low Hall Colliery 1941/3 and again in 1947.
Peter Eckersley.

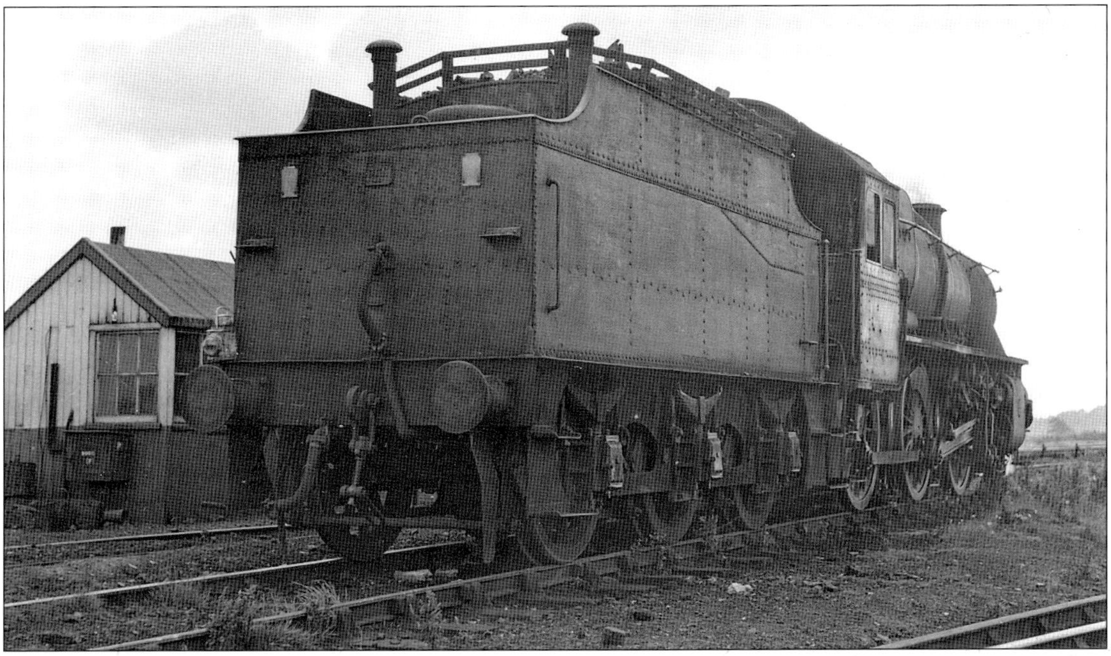

Plate 84. Stanier 'Mogul' No.42954 is seen between banking turns at Ince Moss parked up alongside the shunters cabin on 3rd September 1965.
Eddie Bellass.

Plate 85. An unidentified '9F' ascends the steep gradient from Ince Moss Junction towards Fir Tree House Junction in September 1965 with a return Widnes - Long Meg empties. In the background, the 'Three Sisters' are prominent. These were removed in the 1970s to form a recreation area and industrial complex. Ince Moss to Amberswood West Junction was to close on 19th May 1969, along with the Fir Tree House Junction - Platt Bridge Junction connection with the Tyldesley route. Originally, the gradient here was 1:86 but mining subsidence had made it much worse by B.R. days.
Eddie Bellass.

Plate 86. As viewed from its Southern side, Fir Tree House signal box is seen on 4th November 1967 as '9F" 2-10-0 No.92233 stops to take water before descending to Ince Moss Junction with a freight off the Whelley route. Two signalmen who were regulars in this cabin at the time were Horace Linacre and Tommy Ashcroft. *Dr. J.Gordon Blears.*

Plate 87. On 27th April 1991 a Class '47' takes the Bamfurlong Loop line from Ince Moss Junction with a Rugby League Cup Final special from St. Helens Shaw Street, departing at 09.15, to Wembley. Note that the landscape beyond is totally different when compared to ***Plate 85.*** *Author.*

Plate 88. Stanier Class '5' No.45156 *Ayrshire Yeomanry,* on Ince Moss Curve, approaching the W.C.M.L. with a R.T.C.S. special on 20th April 1968. Again the 'Three Sisters' at Bryn can be seen, left background. *Alex Mann.*

Plate 89. On the W.C.M.L an unidentified 'Britannia' heads north with a through freight in 1966 and is seen passing the connections with Springs Branch North Sidings and Ince Moss Colliery. The Yardmaster's Office is prominent extreme right, in the triangle between the former Lancashire Union and West Coast lines. *Tony Oldfield.*

Plate 90. Class '37' No.37 224 & Class '31' No.31 201 are seen in the remnants of Springs Branch North Sidings on 7th November 1997. It is thought that the connection to the WCML at this point had been lifted during electrification of the route, access now was only from the Ince Moss end, but a head-shunt remained here for a few years allowing a run-round facility. *Author.*

Plate 91. An example of the L.M.S. designed 2-6-0 taper boilered engines is seen from Taylor's Lane in September 1965 on the Down Goods Loop. This may be the Whelley stores working returning to Springs Branch. This train ran every week with various items, water, paraffin and the like, for the signal boxes on the Whelley line. *Eddie Bellass.*

Plate 92. A shot from Taylor's Lane overbridge on 3rd June 1965 with Class '5' No.45455 seen on the Down Fast working a Northwich-Corkickle soda ash train. On the right is Fir Tree House cabin and West Loop is visible under the bridge. Class '5' No.44907 has stopped to pin down the brakes before descending toward Ince Moss with a train of cattle vans. *Dr.J.G.Blears.*

Plate 93. The same '9F' as in ***Plate 85*** passes Fir Tree House Junction, the branch for the Tyldesley route which passed on the far side of the water tank where the Class '5' is standing. The Lancashire Union overbridges as seen here, would be demolished in 1971 as electrification of the W.C.M.L made its way northward. *Eddie Bellass.*

Plate 94. The route from Springs Branch, Manchester Lines Junction toward Tyldesley was on a steeply graded incline of 1:49, opening on 1st September 1864. In 1869 the Lancashire Union's St Helens-Ince Moss-Whelley route would cross this by the over-bridge seen in the background. The end of the return Garston cattle train empties hauled by Class '5' No.44907, as seen in ***Plate 92,*** is still out of shot. Crompton's Sidings signal box could not accept a Down Main Line train from Platt Bridge unless Springs Branch No.1 also accepted it because of the close proximity to the main lines. 'Jinty' No.47298 approaches Springs Branch Shed on the Up Goods Loop on 3rd June 1965. Over on the left the gate has been firmly closed across the trackbed of the former connections to Fir Tree House Sidings and the Crompton & Shawcross mineral line, which had originally been provided to allow Blundell's Amberswood Colliery an outlet after their mainline connection with the North Union was severed. 47298 is now preserved on the Seven Valley Railway *Dr.J.G.Blears.*

Plate 95. A Stanier '8F,' thought to be No.48494, ascends the bank light engine from Ince Moss towards Fir Tree House Junction in the mid 1960s. Ince Moss cabin can be seen left of the engine. *Alex Mann.*

Plate 96. Stanier Class '5' No.45390 works its way past Fir Tree House Junction, over the W.C.M.L. towards Ince Moss Junction with a Manchester - St Helens freight in September 1965. Under the bridge a freight can be seen coming from Bamfurlong Sidings, on the West Loop approach where it will join the WCML Down Slow. *Eddie Bellass.*

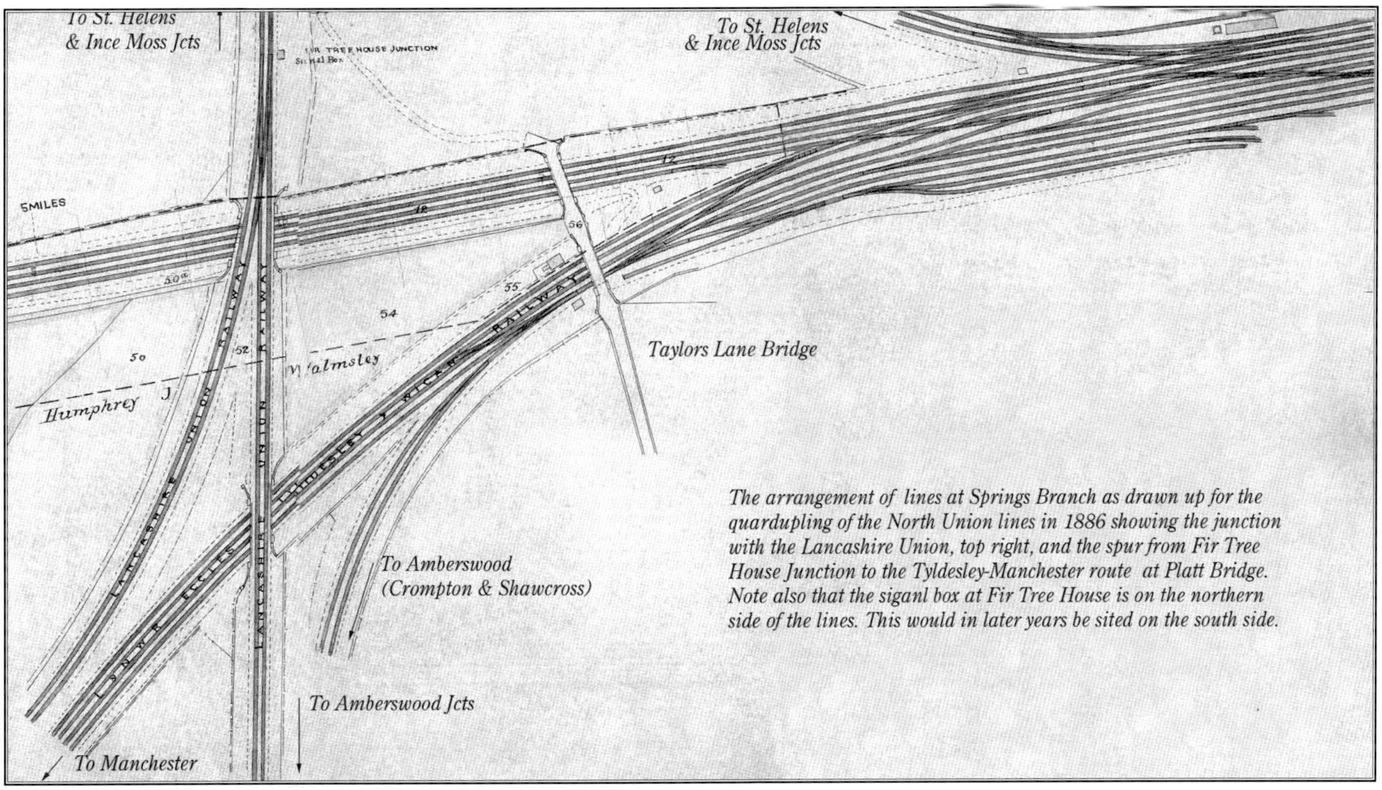
To St. Helens
& Ince Moss Jcts
To St. Helens
& Ince Moss Jcts
5MILES
Taylors Lane Bridge
Walmsley
Humphrey
To Amberswood
(Crompton & Shawcross)
To Amberswood Jcts
To Manchester
The arrangement of lines at Springs Branch as drawn up for the quardupling of the North Union lines in 1886 showing the junction with the Lancashire Union, top right, and the spur from Fir Tree House Junction to the Tyldesley-Manchester route at Platt Bridge. Note also that the siganl box at Fir Tree House is on the northern side of the lines. This would in later years be sited on the south side.

Fig 16. The Lancashire Union, North Union and London & North Western's Eccles - Wigan lines converge at Springs Branch prior to the great extensions which would occur at Bamfurlong and Ince Moss. This plan is extracted from the Golborne - Springs Branch widening plans of 1886, authorised under the 1883 Act. *Courtesy of John Hall.*

Plate 97. Fir Tree House Junction is seen looking up what was now reckoned to be a 1:42 incline with the points set for the Tyldesley route to Platt Bridge Junction. Note how the lines to Platt Bridge level out after passing the signal box whilst those straight on for Amberswood continue to rise. To the right of Fir Tree House signal box is Platt Bridge box on the Tyldesley route. This box also controlled traffic on the lower level Platt Bridge Junction Railway. *Courtesy Kidderminster Railway Museum. John Marshall.*

Plate 98. D428, later renumbered as 50 028, having worked south from Standish Junction with the diverted 09.30 Blackpool North - Euston on 25th June 1972, passes Spring View Cricket Ground on the approach to Platt Bridge. Note that over on the left the embankment of the former Lancashire Union route westward from Amberswood has been removed. *John Ryan.*

AMBERSWOOD JUNCTIONS

Plate 99. This is the going-away shot following on from ***Plate 240*** as seen in ***The Wigan Branch Railway*** by the same author. Stanier Class '5' No.45411 brings up the rear, as the train, now on Lancashire Union metals, heads towards Amberswood East Junction. Note in the foreground the line from Strangeways West Junction on the Wigan Junction Railway, to Amberswood West Junction. This short connection had been built by the Manchester, Sheffield & Lincolnshire Railway opening in 1882. The redundant timber signal post would have been the starter from the now lifted Amberswood Up Sidings. *Dr J.Gordon Blears.*

Plate 100. 'Britannia' Class No.70025 *Western Star* approaches Amberswood West Junction on 2nd September 1964 after working south from Standish Junction with a mixed freight. *Jim Peden Collection (B.Barlow).*

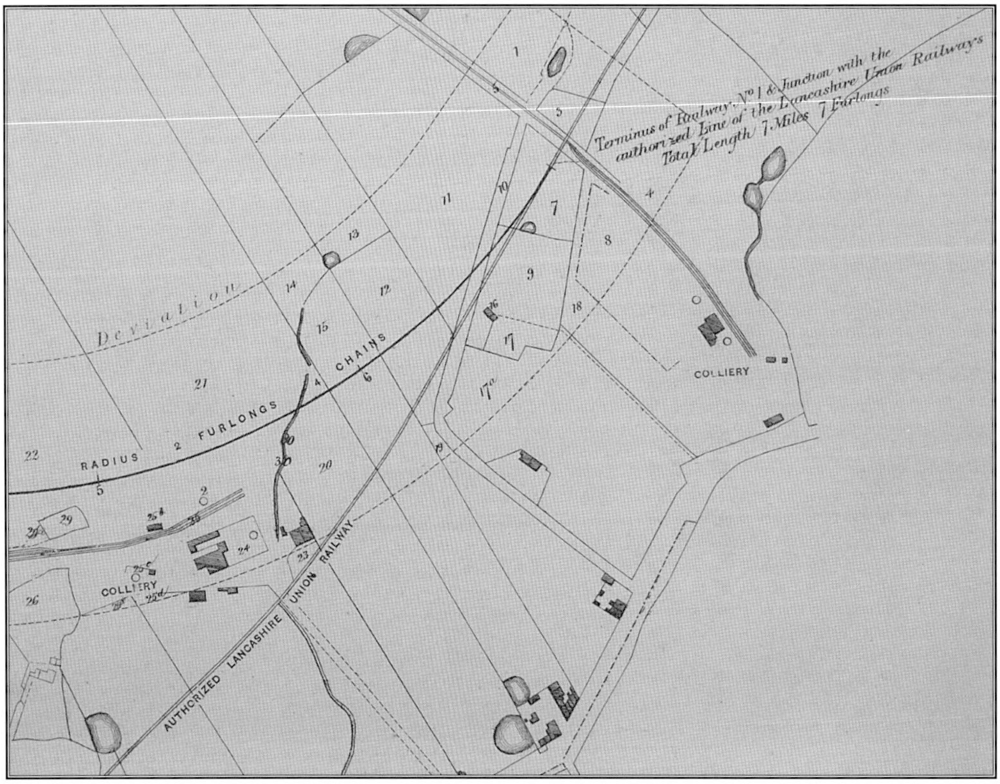

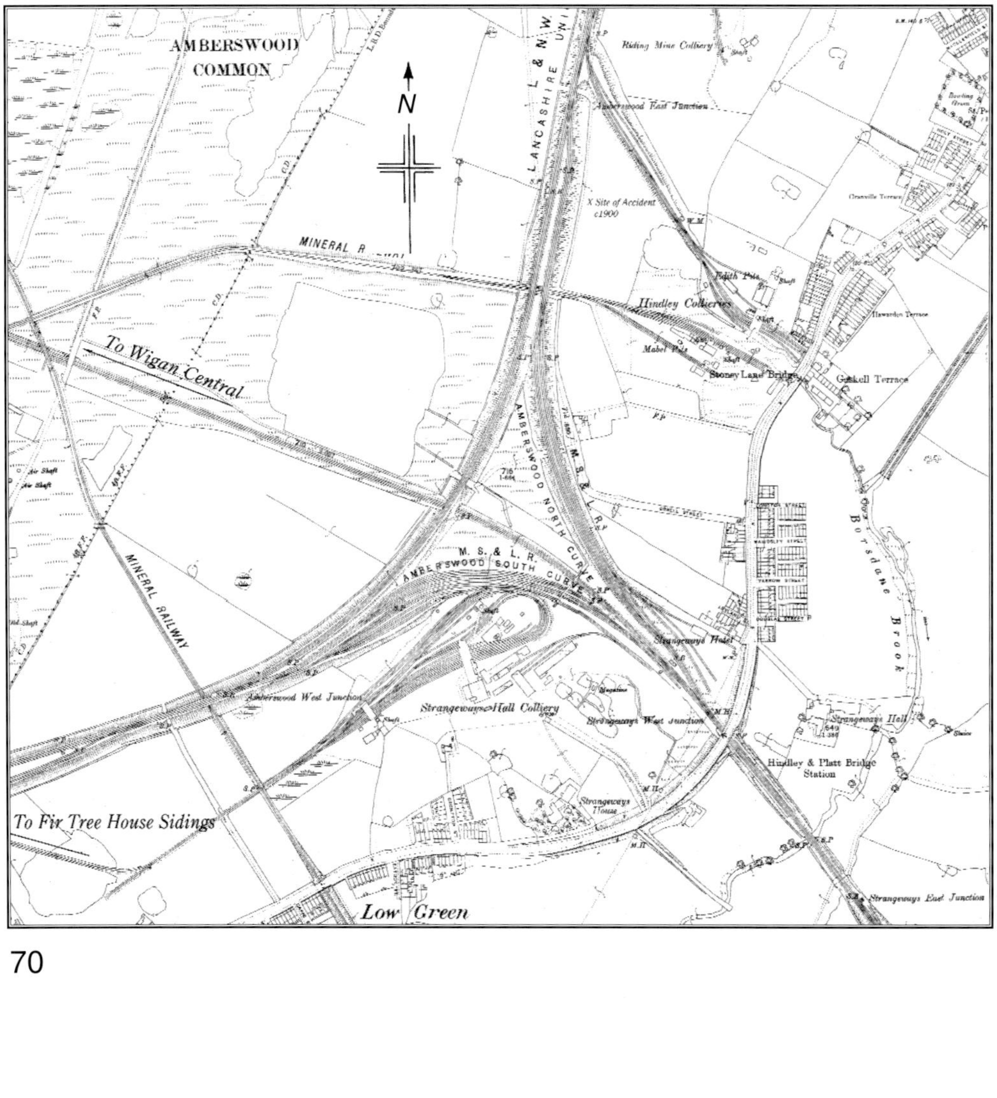

Fig 17. The Lancashire Union Line Plan c1865 at Amberswood left, also shows the previously authorised route from the 1864 Act. In the event, all of which, south of Amberswood East, was abandoned in favour of the former.

The railway companies did not always orientate their plans to Grid North, hence the apparent misalignment when compared to Ordnance Surveys.

Wigan & Leigh Archives.

Fig 18. Amberswood and Strangeways West Junctions c1892. The Manchester, Sheffield & Lincolnshire Railway arrived on the scene here in the shape of the Wigan Junction Railway in October 1879, then only as far as Strangeways to serve the nearby colliery. In 1884 the line had been extended to a temporary terminus at Darlington St, Wigan before being extended into the centre of Wigan proper, opening on 3rd October 1892. It seems that the London & North Western were working into Strangeways Hall Colliery Sidings off the Lancashire Union route from 1880 when the first Amberswood West signal box opened.

Connections were made with the Lancashire Union Railway, at Amberswood East & West Junctions, off the Wigan Junction Railway, paid for by the Manchester, Sheffield & Lincolnshire Railway. The north curve however, that is Strangeways West to Amberswood East Junctions, is not thought to have been completed until 1886 when the London & North Western, implementing their Hindley Junctions Railway as amended by Parliament, opened their connections from Strangeways East to Bickershaw Junctions on 25th October.

London & North Western notes give a signal box at Amberswood West Junction from 19th July 1880 which at this period probably controlled the Company's workings into Strangeways Hall Colliery which they were entitled to work into free of any toll charges, granted under the Manchester, Sheffield & Lincolnshire Railway Act of 1879. According to the Sidings Schedules, Railway No.4 of the Wigan Junction Railways Acts, that is Strangeways West to Amberswood West Junctions, (Amberswood South Curve) was completed in late 1882. It appears the trackbed of this curve, or at least a part of it, was laid to ballast level by Crompton & Shawcross under an agreement of 1st October 1878, but the track laid by the Wigan Junction Railway whose line from Glazebrook to Strangeways opened on 16th October 1879. A second signal box was opened at Amberswood West Junction on 11th October 1886 having 29 levers. This is entirely concommitant with the construction of the Platt Bridge Junction Railway which was to open on 25th October 1886.

Amberswood East Junction signal box also opened on 11th October 1886, having 27 levers. Strangeways West Junction to Amberswood East Junction (Amberswood North Curve) is believed to have opened later in the year, between 11th-25th October.

The plans for the London & North Western's Hindley Junctions Railway Act deposited in 1882, show a totally independent set of rails from Bickershaw Junction, running alongside the Wigan Junction Railway metals to the Lancashire Union. The same plan shows that the Strangeways West - Amberswood East Junctions curve has some tracks laid but unconnected to the Lancashire Union. However, the Act as passed by Parliament obliged the London & North Western to meet with the Wigan Junction Railway south of Hindley & Platt Bridge Station, running rights being granted to the London & North Western to work over the Wigan Junction route to Amberswood Junctions. It is apparent that the Wigan Company were acutely short of funds and in no hurry to make connections at Amberswood East. However, the Hindley Junctions Railway, in its amended form, opened on 25th October 1886, so connections at Amberswood East had, by then, been completed.

In 1892, another 4 levers were added to Amberswood East box frame as connections were about to be made with the Edith and Mabel pits sunk by Crompton & Shawcross. These mines appear in the Mines Lists for 1891 and were sited on the eastern side of the north curve with connections to the Lancashire Union a few yards north of East Junction under an agreement dated 11th May 1895.

One John Rayner had acquired a controlling interest in Crompton & Shawcross after William Crompton's death in 1892, he being the last surviving partner. By the early 20th century, Rayner had control of a number of collieries in the Amberswood and Hindley areas and had agreements with the main line railway companies, one of which was that he could run his engines between Amberswood East & West Junctions thereby working from the Edith and Mabel pits to Strangeways Hall Colliery and, in respect of his arrangements with the Great Central, to reach his Grange, Hindley Field and Victoria Collieries.

The Riding Mine, north of Edith and Mabel pits had, apparently, only been worked on a small scale by its owner. It is believed to have been sunk around 1890 but mining seems to have ceased between 1893 and 1898, when at the latter date it was taken over by one Henry Atherton. A sidings agreement between Atherton and the London & North Western dates from 18th September 1899.

A new connection had been laid from the Lancashire Union lines to the screening plant at Riding Mine in the early 1900s, authorised by the Goods Traffic Committee on 17th October 1900, under a separate Sidings Agreement of 1st February 1901 with Henry Atherton. On the same site there was an opencast clay pit and brickworks. The Sidings Agreement was transferred to Crompton & Shawcross Ltd.,- alias John Rayner in 1907, who had taken over operations at Riding Mine. The mine was to close in 1910, although the sidings remained in use to serve the brickworks until 1914. After the latter date the sidings remained unused although permission had been granted to the partnership of Messrs Kershaw & Topping for its use to access a planned wagon shop which never materialised. In 1917 the sidings and its connection with the Lancashire Union lines were removed.

Following the opening of the Hindley Junctions and Platt Bridge Junction Railways the London & North Western had at last a useful avoiding line to by-pass the congested through - Wigan main lines and whilst initially intended for freight, some passenger trains were routed via Whelley*. The first of these were through trains from Manchester to Blackpool which, from the summer of 1887, were directed via Bickershaw and Amberswood East Junctions. **The Lancashire Union became fully absorbed by the London & North Western in 1883.*

Come the amalgamation of the London & North Western and the Lancashire & Yorkshire railways in 1922, some services were, from July 1924, routed via Hindley No.2 and De Trafford Junctions. Manchester - Blackpool holiday specials regularly worked over the Whelley route and not only those originating in the L.M.S. areas; specials from further afield, for example, Nottingham, Sheffield and Leicester, working by way of Glazebrook Junction on the former Cheshire Lines route would work Whelley to Standish Junction, a process that would continue for many years.

Regular passenger services continued working 'Whelley' over the years, including the 5pm Windermere train from Manchester Exchange which went this way from 1911 via Tyldesley and Bickershaw Junction. For a short period it was routed via Dobbs Brow and Hilton House Junctions -1934 to 1937*, when, to avoid interference with the 'Coronation Scot,' it was routed by the Walkden High Level lines to Hindley No.2 and De Trafford Junctions. The service was interrupted in W.W.II but resumed over the Walkden route in 1946, ceasing as a regular working in 1964.

Hindley South Junction (originally Strangeways West, later Hindley & Platt Bridge Junction) to Amberswood East Junction closed to seasonal passenger services as from 5th September 1964 and to goods trains on 22nd February 1965. Manchester Central - Wigan Central via Glazebrook passenger services were withdrawn on 2nd November 1964. Hindley South to Amberswood West closed to goods on 15th March 1965. The route between Lowton St. Marys and Hindley South closed on 4th January 1965, therefore preventing any workings via former CLC lines. However, goods trains continued to work to Wigan G.C. by way of Bickershaw Junction until 6th November 1967.

Regular passenger services ceased to work via Hindley No.2 and De Trafford Junctions as from 15th June 1969 but excursion specials ran this way until 2nd October 1972. On the latter date, Amberswood West to Standish Junction ceased to be used for goods trains. However, between 12th and 15th January 1973, W.C.M.L. diversions used the route and occasional engineers trains until 1976.

Part of the route to Tyldesley**, (just over 4 miles) from Springs Branch to Howe Bridge West, remained open for coal traffic from Parsonage and Bickershaw Collieries. On 11th February 1975, Howe Bridge West to Bickershaw Junction closed as these mines, along with Golborne Colliery, were now connected underground and all coal for rail transport was wound at Bickershaw. All the remaining pits in the area, Bickershaw, Parsonage and Parkside, closed in 1992 (Golborne had closed in 1989) but the track remained in situ between Bickershaw and Springs Branch until the Autumn of 2003 when it was lifted by private contractors and taken away by road transport. Except, that is, for a short headshunt of about 200 yards left in situ from Springs Branch to a point near the A573 railway over-bridge on Warrington Road at Platt Bridge. The deck of this bridge has since been removed and fitted with the compulsory spiked metal fencing which now adorns many a mile of our railway network.

* *Departure times varied.*

***Eccles - Tyldesley - Howe Bridge West and Tyldesley - Leigh - Kenyon Junction closure given as 5th May 1969, but in effect closed from midnight on 3rd May on return of BICC Blackpool - Leigh - Tyldesley specials.*

Plate 101. Stanier Class '8F' 2-8-0 No.48633, approaches Amberswood West Junction with a through freight having worked south over Whelley from Standish Junction on 2nd September 1964.
Jim Peden Collection (B.Barlow).

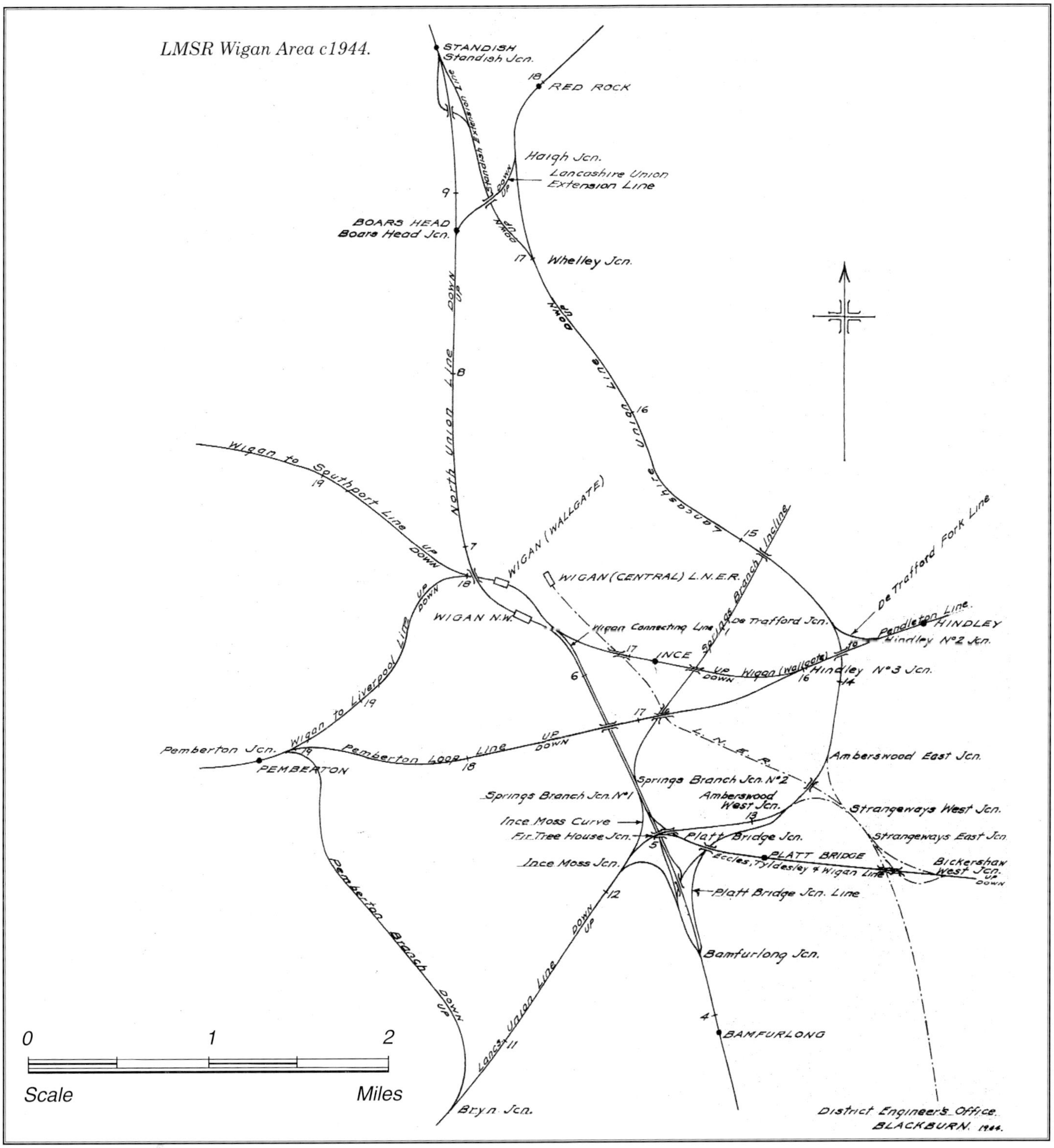

Fig 19. The general arrangement of lines in the Wigan area c1944 showing the circuitous route taken by the Lancashire Union Railway around the Eastern side of Wigan to Haigh Junction where it made connections with the joint line from Boar's Head. It will be noted that the designated Up & Down lines for the Lancashire Union route changed at Bryn Junction, thus being in sync with the W.C.M.L. and other connecting lines at Springs Branch. However, in the Working Appendices the change-over point is given as Fir Tree House Junction. Perhaps this was a proposal with the closure of the Pemberton Branch in mind!

The milepost distances given here for the Lancashire Union route are from Huyton Junction. Those on the W.C.M.L. are from Parkside. *Courtesy, John Hall.*

At Amberswood East Junction on 24th July 1900, a return holiday special from Blackpool to Manchester derailed just after the junction, killing the driver, one passenger and injuring twenty five others, some seriously. The engine was an 0-6-0 (Cauliflower) No.555 and tender No.495. The train had left Blackpool (Talbot Road) at 3.55p.m. with ten vehicles on and at approximately 5.10p.m. the engine left the rails at Amberswood, dragging with it the first four coaches down the embankment, the fifth derailing and tilting towards the 6ft way.

It is apparent, from the Inspecting Officers Accident Report, that the evidence given at the resulting inquiry is, to say the least, contradictory, the exact point at which the engine left the rails called into question.

At this particular location, the lines of what was now the London & North Western's railway, met those of the Great Central, the boundary being the set of points which gave egress from the Up line at Amberswood East Junction, onto the former Wigan Junction Railway's line to Strangeways West Junction, which route the train would have taken, via Strangeways East Junction to access Bickershaw West Junction and onward to Manchester via Tyldesley and Eccles Junction.

The London & North Western were anxious to prove that the derailment occurred on Great Central metals, whilst the latter determined to secure the opposite.

Evidence given by the fireman of the stricken engine who had joined at Preston stated that the driver shut off steam before the Amberswood East distant signal but could not say if the engine left the rails before, at, or after the junction. It was the first time he had worked the route.

The guard in the brake van next to the engine also came on at Preston. Having worked the line many times he estimated the train's speed at 45-50mph at 200 yards before the junction, slackening to 25-30mph at the junction. He maintained that his van had passed over the crossing before anything untoward happened. A similar account is given by the brakesman in the rear van who had joined the train at Blackpool.

The signalman at Amberswood East box is more positive. At 5.09p.m. he had received 'train entering section' from De Trafford and saw the train approaching his home signal at 200 yards distance. He saw the engine pass the facing point and crossing, then turned away to give 'train entering section' to Strangeways West cabin. Looking again towards the train he noted that the leading section "was off the line." "Up trains" he added, "usually run through this junction at the same speed as this train did". Apparently, there was a rule that Up trains be 'nearly' brought to a standstill at this junction. It would seem though it was a rule generally ignored and regarded as an unnecessary one.

Plate 102. This view of the accident is looking south and a multitude has gathered to gaze at the devastation. The chimney, centre of picture projecting above the coach roof right of the telegraph pole, is that of Strangeways Hall Collieries. *Author's Collection.*

Plate 103. This is a view of the Amberswood accident looking north towards East Junction. The colliery sidings, right, are those of Crompton & Shawcross' Edith Pits from where two of their employees gave what might be described as an unbiased account of the accident. Edith Pits had a sidings and connection to the Lancashire Union just north of Amberswood East Junction.

Author's Collection.

A London & North Western ganger standing opposite the crossing judged the trains speed at 30 mph and, he said, "watched the engine run over the facing point quite smoothly". He seemed confident that the engine had reached 50 yards from the head of the crossing when it lurched and derailed.

A Great Central ganger who gave evidence says that about 4.45p.m., he inspected the rails right up to to the point of the junction and noticed nothing wrong. "We take close up to the crossing, but not the crossing itself" he said. "The spaces between the joints were all right, about 1/4 inch apart" he added. It had, apparently been a hot day, but the ganger insisted the joints were "not too close together" and he did "not suppose that any of the joints were touching". Then he states that he "cannot say for certain whether any of the rail ends were touching". He returned to the site at about 5.30p.m. after the accident. On examining a broken rail he commented that "the two ends of the rail were not as far apart as they are now" and reiterated his previous judgement that "the line appeared to me in first rate order".

Two Great Central platelayers had been employed on mowing the embankments at Amberswood East Junction that day. Both state that they were a yard down the bank, about 14 yards beyond the nose of the crossing, saying that the estimated speed of the train "when approaching the junction was 40 mph" and that the "engine gave a jump" at the crossing and, "the front wheel of the engine caught the nose of the crossing".

Henry Ince, engine driver, and Samuel Allen, brakesman, were both employed by Crompton & Shawcross and at the time of the accident were standing on the footplate of their engine on the colliery railway which served Edith Pits. Being on an embankment opposite Amberswood East Junction, these men would have had a good view of the proceedings. Both give a similar account, maintaining that the engine and its first two coaches negotiated the junction at 26-28 mph and some 40 yards on, derailed. Their last comments concern the two platelayers 'mowing'. Driver Ince states:- "I saw two platelayers mowing on the side of the embankment, they were at the bottom of the bank. At the time the accident happened they were lying down at the bottom of the embankment, they were not standing up at the top" and, "I had shouted to them just before the engine came. There was a little boy with these men". The brakesman reported in similar fashion "I saw them lying at the bottom of the bank".

Plate 104. Amberswood East Junction signal box about 1964. This particular box opened on 11th October 1906 and had 27 levers and appears to have been photographed from a passing train approaching from Hindley & Platt Bridge. This cabin replaced that of 1886. C1940s until closure this was a one turn cabin working 8am - 4pm. Between Amberswood East and De Trafford Junction was a stop block of massive proportions with a set of traps off the Down line in the event of any runaways on the rising gradient to De Trafford. The distance between Amberswood East and West signal boxes was 788 yards. *Author's Collection.*

The railway at this location is on a 20ft high embankment. For an Up train approaching East Junction from Standish, the line is almost straight for the last 1/2 mile on a falling gradient varying from 1:60 to 1:362 for the last 3/4 mile: after passing through the junction the gradient continues to fall at 1:100 towards Strangeways West Junction.

The junction was relaid by the London & North Western in 1899 with rails at 90lbs per yard, chairs at 45lbs each and fishplates at 16lbs each. On the former Wigan Junction lines the Permanent Way consisted of rails that originally weighed 81lbs per yard, chairs at 40 3/4lbs each and fishplates at 29lbs per pair. Rails and chairs had been in situ since 1886, (which means since the Strangeways East - Amberswood East connection opened) but new sleepers and fishplates were provided in 1897.

All vehicles of the train seem to have safely negotiated the facing points but at the crossing there were distinct marks of some vehicle/s having mounted the 'V' rail on the right hand side and a corresponding mark on the wing rail opposite the crossing on the left hand side of the line. From these marks it would appear that some vehicle had been derailed on the right hand side, towards the six-foot way. This is consistent with a number of witness statements that the engine slewed into the six-foot before tumbling down the embankment.

However, next to the London & North Western's crossing, where the Great Central's line commenced, the first two rails on the right hand side were broken, about 2ft on each side of the fishplate between them. These were found on the London & North Western's main lines some 100 yards from their original position. The broken end nearest the facing point showed evidence of having received a severe end-on blow after the break occurred. From the pointwork onward, the Permanent Way was wrecked, sleepers almost cut through and the rails twisted and bent.

Acknowledging that much of the evidence was contradictory, and particularly commenting on that given by the platelayers and the Crompton & Shawcross employees, the inspector judged that the derailment was not due to points or crossings. He pays particular attention to the speed of the train which he considered to be at least 30mph, noting that the curve of 8 1/2 chains was not provided with a check rail and had practically no superelevation. The Great Central's rails were found to weigh only 64 1/2lbs per yard, having lost 20% since being laid in 1886. Therefore, the inspector concluded that the speed of the train and the weakness of the rails adjoining the junction were the determining factors of the accident.

Plate 105. Ex-London & North Western Class G2/2As Nos.49436 and No.49311 banking, are seen on a heavy coal train working north on 4th September 1956. Amberswood East signalbox can just be seen in the background .

In February 1899 an expansion of sidings capacity had taken place at the Crompton & Shawcross sidings from connections at Amberswood East. Listed under 'Miscellaneous Instructions':- 'These sidings are now in use. Nos 1&2, nearest the main line are for Colliery purposes. No.3 for L&Y trains to attach. No.4 for North Traffic for L&N.W trains to pick up. Nos 5&6 for empties, but engines must not go beyond the points leading into these sidings'.

Peter Eckersley.

Plate 106. In 1915, Hindley Urban District Council had agreed, in committee meetings with South Lancashire Tramways and Wigan Tramways, to lower the roadway on Wigan Road between Hindley and Ince, under the Lancashire Union's railway bridge, in order to allow double deck trams to run from Hindley to Wigan. However, there is no physical evidence that this was carried out. It seems that a reinforced concrete bridge deck, as in the photo above taken on 8th January 1986, was built to give the additional clearance required, and as such, may have been the first bridge in the area to use this type of construction giving, in this instance, a clearance of 14ft 8in.

With the advent of increased axle loads giving rise to larger HGVs in the later 20th century, the bridge clearance had again become inadequate to allow the passage of such vehicles and in the early 1990s the bridge was demolished. Oxidisation of the reinforcing had 'blown' patches of the concrete cover away in parts exposing the bars leading to further corrosion and as such was a potential safety hazard.

Author.

DE TRAFFORD & HINDLEY No. 2 JUNCTIONS

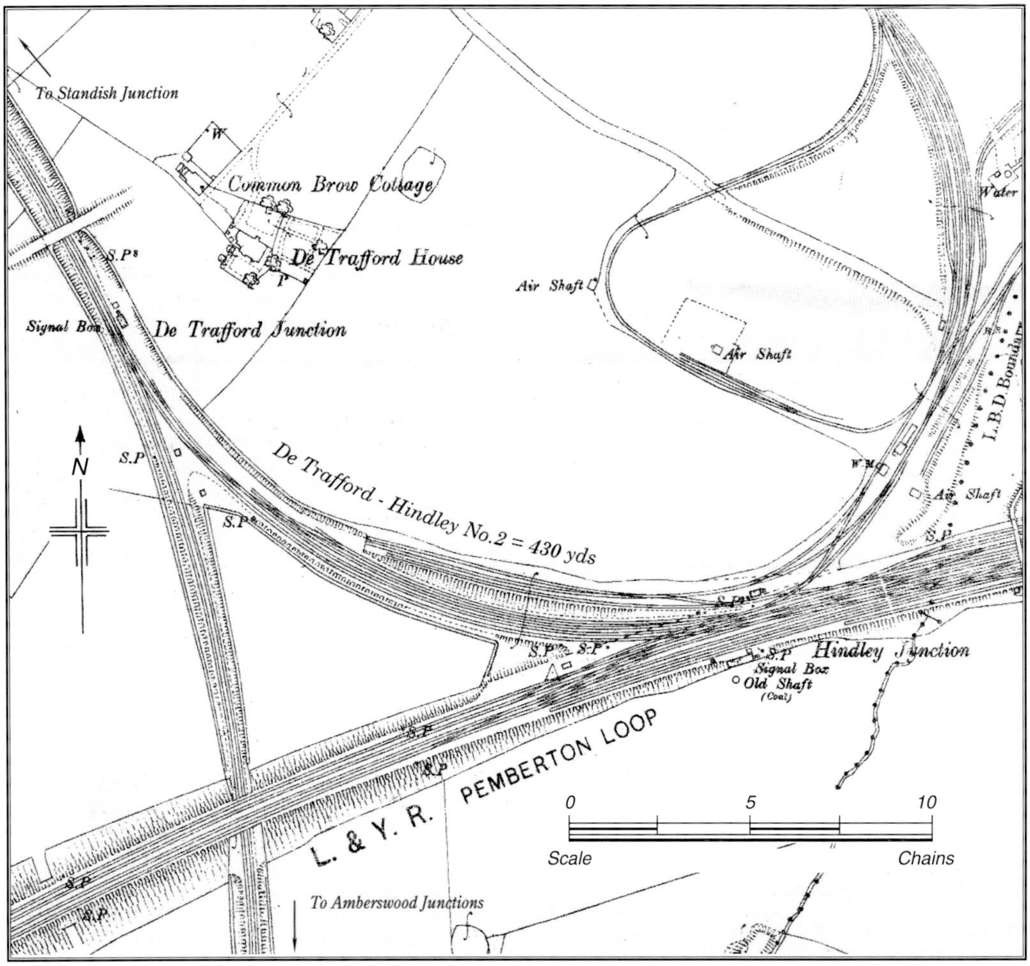

Fig 20. De Trafford Junction from the second series Ordnance Survey.

This appears to be the second signal box that is shown here, positioned just beyond the junction itself, the first was a telegraph box. The third cabin as seen in the following photographs dates from the early twentieth century and was sited within the triangle on the curve from Hindley No.2 Junction, possibly where the original box had been.

At top right are the Wigan Coal & Iron Co's. lines to Kirkless and the Springs Branch.

Hindley No.2 to De Trafford Junction closed to regular passenger trains as from 15th June 1969 and to excursion traffic on 2nd October 1972. Amberswood East to De Trafford had closed to seasonal passenger traffic on 5th September 1964. However, a few excursions used the route between 6th July - 7th September 1968.

Plate 107. The lines of the Lancashire Union Railway passed below those of the Lancashire & Yorkshire west of Hindley No.2 Junction. On 14th September 1986, a two-car DMU unit working a Wigan Wallgate - Manchester Victoria service, passes over the abandoned Lancashire Union trackbed. It is now possible to walk a fair proportion of this towards Whelley from Amberswood. *Author.*

Plate 108. At Hindley No.2 Junction in the early 1960s, all the lines are still intact as Stanier '8F' No.48504 negotiates the pointwork with a Class '3' freight . *Alex Mann.*

Plate 109. A Class '25' passes Hindley No.2 Junction with an eastbound train of coal empties in 1971 and soon there will only be two tracks at this location. Here, traffic from the ex-Lancashire & Yorkshire lines worked onto the former Lancashire Union lines which can be seen going off to the right towards De Trafford Junction. This route was closed to regular passenger services on 15th June 1969 but excursion trains continued to go this way until October 1972.

The photograph is taken from the iron bridge which is still extant, but the signal box, gantry and junction have long gone. Only two tracks remain and, like many other former 'open' railway locations prolific vegetation has taken over. *John Eckersley.*

Plate 110. A DMU takes the route to De Trafford Junction and the Whelley route in 1971 with a holiday special to Blackpool. Much track lifting is in evidence as the ex Lancashire & Yorkshire's Pemberton Loop has now been abandoned. *John Ryan.*

Plate 111. A Class '110' DMU on the former Lancashire Union lines at De Trafford Junction having worked via Atherton Central and Hindley No.2 Junction on 7th August 1971 with a Summer Saturdays only Pendleton to Blackpool Train. A couple of landmarks in the background are St. Peter's church at Hindley, and far left, Scowcroft's tip at Hindley Green. The previous signal box at De Trafford had been sited on the extreme left, just beyond the junction itself. It is probable that the box as shown here gave a better sighting of traffic from Hindley No.2 Junction, out of view at top left. The bridge, far right is that seen in ***Plate 107.***

Jim Peden (B.Barlow).

Plate 112. De Trafford Junction signal box is seen on 16th August 1972. A telegraph box opened here on 1st December 1869, replaced by a second cabin in 1887. The distance from Amberswood East to De Trafford was 1,229 yards.

Jim Peden (J.A.Sommerfield).

ROSE BRIDGE & ROUNDHOUSE JUNCTIONS

After passing over the Springs Branch route at Belle Green Lane, Rose Bridge Junction, for a connection with Kirkless Hall Junction and the Springs Branch is made.

The Lancashire Union Act of 1865 contained provisions allowing the Earl of Crawford and Balcarres, and the Kirkless Hall Coal & Iron Co., to work their own trains over the Lancashire Union to Widnes, Runcorn and Garston. However it is not certain if this was ever implemented.

The remainder of the Wigan Coal & Iron Co's. operations over the main line were covered by an agreement between the Earl and the Lancashire Union dated 13th May 1865, which permitted the Earl, and his tenants, to make use of the line between the junction with the Springs Branch (Rose Bridge - Kirkless Hall) and Adlington. As the Earl was one of the promoters of the railway this would not have been too difficult to achieve.

The Adlington workings seem to have finished before W.W.I., but trains continued to run as far as Brinks Colliery Sidings until about 1930, the connection at Brinks out of use in 1931. Brinks washery could also be reached over the Wigan Coal & Iron Co's. private lines and this would account for the lack of balanced workings over the Lancashire Union lines in later years.

It appears that the Kirkless and Lindsay pits of the Wigan Coal & Iron Co, although connected by the internal railway system, albiet a rather tortuous route, preferred to use the main line for at least part of their traffic and it may be that these trains started much earlier than the Working Time Tables suggest, perhaps from the opening of the Lancashire Union line.

Plate 113. Ex-LNW 'G2A' No.48895 approaches Rose Bridge Junction on the single line from Kirkless Hall Junction c1962 with a couple of vans. This link with the Springs Branch at Kirkless was re-instated in 1958 and was the only way to reach the engine shed and works at that period. *Harold Hunt.*

Plate 114. Now doesn't every boy's grandfather take him trainspotting! but footplating - now that's something else. A young Derreck Killin on the footplate of 48895 as the engine waits for the road at Rose Bridge. The driver is believed to be Albert Whittaker. *Harold Hunt.*

Plate 115. After a short stop at the junction waiting for the road, 48895 and its ensemble, moves off north-bound. The engine was based at Springs Branch from the 1940s and is believed to have been withdrawn from there in 1962.
Harold Hunt.

Plate 116. Stanier Class '5' No.45321 stops at Rose Bridge Junction about 1950. The junction here to Kirkless Hall Junction had closed in July 1938 but because of the cutback of the Springs Branch line was re-opened on 13th May 1958, finally closing on 15th May 1965.
Courtesy, Bill Paxford.

Plate 117. This North-Westerly view at Rose Bridge is from 1962. The pile of slag from Kirkless Iron & Steel Works, dumped alongside the Up line behind the water tower over decades was known to locals as 'rab-bit rocks'. Pit waste from Rose Bridge Colliery is seen on the far left. The tall signal is the Roundhouse distant.
Harold Hunt.

Plate 118. On 17th July 1965 Class '9F' No.92115, heads north at Rose Bridge Junction with a Ford block train from Halewood on which 'Anglias' seem to predominate. The Roundhouse Junction distant signal is 'off' giving the driver a clear road.

Jim Peden Collection (B.Barlow).

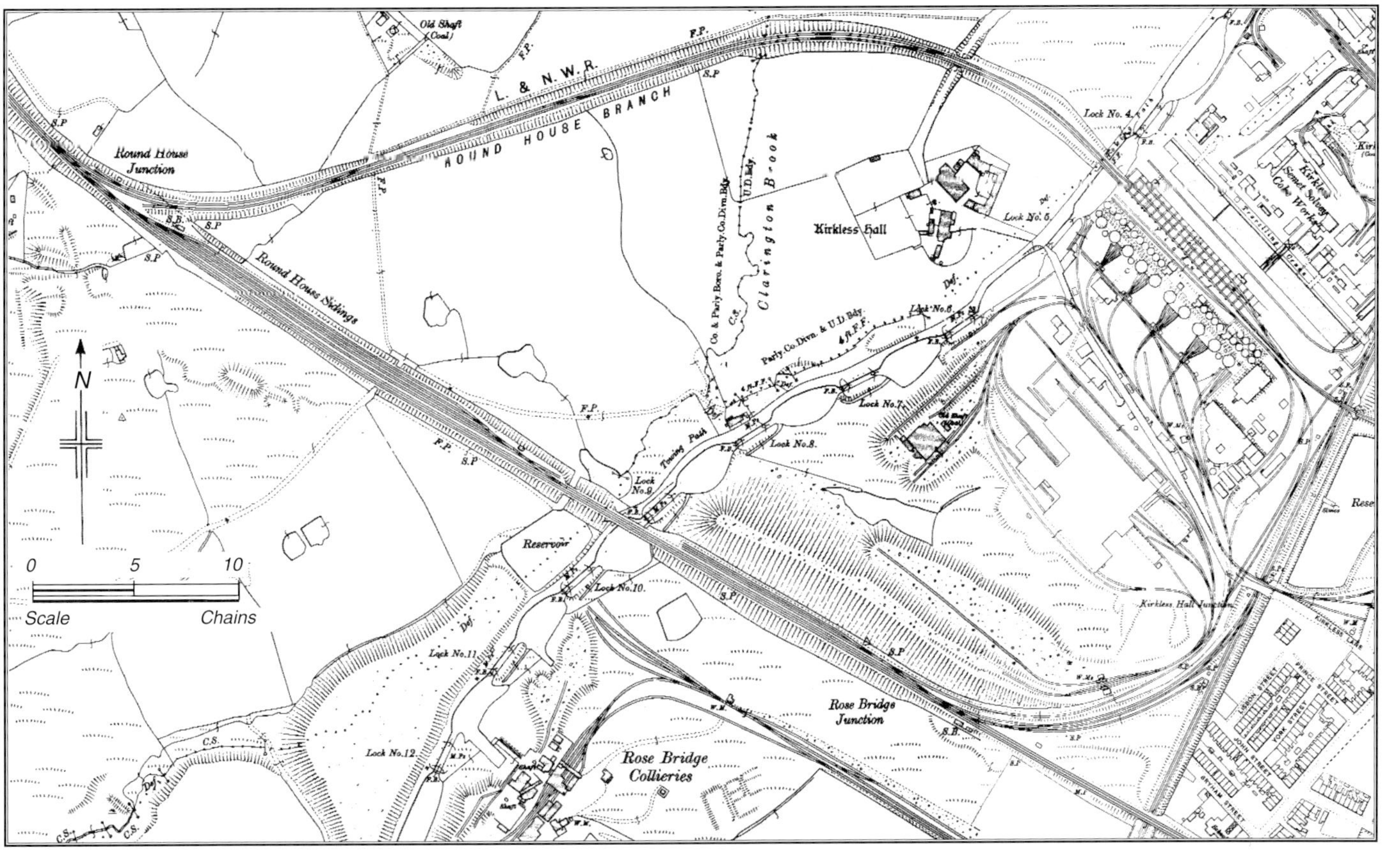

Fig 21. The high level railway of the Wigan Coal & Iron Co. made an end on connection with the branch from Roundhouse Junction in 1869. Coke, iron ore and limestone traffic for the iron works was handled via this junction to sidings from where they discharged directly to the furnaces below until closure of the works in the 1930s. It had been reduced to a single line in 1922 and closed completely in 1938. Between 1870 and 1900 there were sidings on the South-West side of the main lines here, serving Fidlers Platt Lane Colliery. *See **Fig 22.*** In 1883 a proposal to eliminate a level crossing here also shows the area for the future Roundhouse Sidings on the North-West side. Rose Bridge signal box closed c1938. The sidings are shown here in the early years of the twentieth century, before the construction c1913, of a new bank of sidings built to the west of lock 4 on the Leeds - Liverpool Canal.

Plate 119. Stanier Class '5' No.45397, passes Rose Bridge Junction with a good head of steam working a northbound van train about 1962. *Harold Hunt.*

Plate 120. Kirkless Hall Junction Signal Box, probably photographed in the early years of the twentieth century. It is a Type '4' London & North Western design and has replaced an earlier signal cabin which had been sited on the opposite, Up side of the lines. *John Sloane Collection.*

Plate 121, below. Stanier Class '5' No.45023 is seen southbound passing Roundhouse Junction Sidings about 1959/60. As the locomotive does not carry a reporting number and has only one lamp at the top of its smokebox door which indicates 'Ordinary Passenger Train', it is somewhat of a mystery, a Preston - Manchester Victoria perhaps, due to some blockage via Euxton Junction, or a Saturdays only, booked holiday train. Note Roundhouse Sidings in the background referred to in ***Fig 21.*** *B.Nichols.*

Fig 22, opposite. Roundhouse Junction is portrayed here from the Lancashire Union plan of 1883 showing Fidlers Platt Lane Colliery, its connections with the railway and the first signal cabin at this location. The purpose of the plan was to show planned alterations to a level crossing which was to be abolished and substituted by an underpass. It also gives details of the proposed land take for Roundhouse Sidings. *Wigan & Leigh Archives.*

Plate 122. The Lancashire Union Railway crossed the Leeds - Liverpool Canal between locks 9 & 10 at Higher Ince. This view westward probably dates from about 1962. Rose Bridge Colliery was sited on the extreme left, as evidenced by the waste tips. The tips on the far side of the canal are from Platt Lane Colliery.
Wigan & Leigh Archives.

Plate 123, right. Unrebuilt 'Patriot' Class No.45524 *Blackpool* crosses the Leeds - Liverpool Canal southbound with a van train in August 1951. *H.Hurst.*

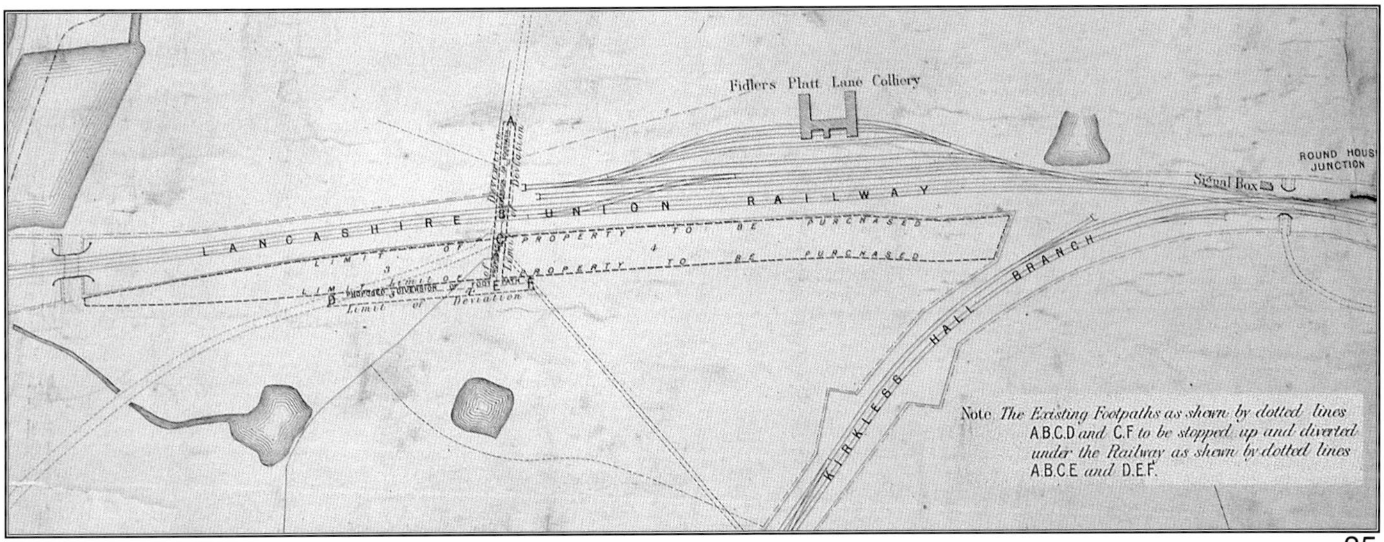

Plate 124. This is the scene at Rose Bridge Junction on 13th August 1966. The occasion is a 'Wigan Area Railfans Society' (WARS) railtour which had Stanier 'Mogul' 2-6-0 No.42968 in charge throughout. Included in the tour were a number of scheduled photo stops. The starting point of the tour was Springs Branch MPD at 09.25hrs. Enroute, the lines to Adlington, Horwich, Standish, Hindley, Ince Moss and Bolton were covered, terminating at Wigan North Western at 15.06hrs.

Brian Taylor, courtesy the Stanier Mogul Fund.

Plate 125. An unidentified B.R Class '9F' heads south over the Leeds-Liverpool Canal between Roundhouse and Rose Bridge Junction with empty hoppers on 18th November 1967.

Plate 126. The canal was still in use at this time for commercial traffic and barge *Taurus* is seen between locks 9 & 10 at Higher Ince on the same day.

Both, John Ryan.

Plate 127. Roundhouse Sidings signal cabin on 16th August 1972. This cabin worked three turns and had about 25 levers controlling the junction here. Banking engines often left north-bound trains here unless that is, the engine driver had asked to be banked to Coppull Hall or, up Brinscall Bank if working to Blackburn. A crossover road here allowed banking engines to work back light engine to Bamfurlong or Ince Moss.
J.A.Sommerfield.

In the 1830s, on the South-West side of the later Roundhouse branch, a number of small collieries were in operation. Cheshire Hole Colliery had a narrow gauge tramway which ran towards the Leeds-Liverpool Canal at Ince, passing under the Wigan-Hindley road by a tightly gauged tunnel, to a basin below lock 17. Another pit, Roundhouse Colliery, had a tramway to a wharf below lock 8.

By the 1850s, these two collieries became collectively known as Platt Lane Colliery, becoming Platt Lane Coal Co. on 18th October 1865. They were subsequently taken over by the Wigan & Whiston Coal Co., with a Mr. Fidler, a partner in the Platt Lane Coal Co., appointed as Managing Director, also in late 1865.

In the late 1860s, a new shaft was sunk near the old Roundhouse Colliery, which, along with Cheshire Hole Colliery was abandoned. The new Platt Lane Colliery was served by connections with the Lancashire Union, provided under an agreement of 4th November 1869, opening for traffic in January 1870.

The colliery was leased to W. &J. Latham in 1888 who worked it until the mid 1890s. However, in 1896, the owning company were in liquidation and the colliery abandoned the same year. By 1900, according to the Sidings Schedule, all connections had been removed.

Even before these were removed the Lancashire Union proposed to construct sidings on the North-East side of the main lines in 1883*. A number of sidings were constructed in the 1880s by the Wigan Coal & Iron Co. for the storage of incoming traffic for the iron and steel works at Kirkless; coke, iron ore and limestone. From these sidings a high level line had been built for the transfer of these materials to the furnaces which crossed over the Springs Branch adjacent to Kirkless Lane. Slag from the furnaces was worked out by the same route for tipping south of said sidings. A second high level line, also crossing the Springs Branch, was built in 1868, just a few yards south of where Kirkless Hall Sidings Telegraph Box would be sited. This would give a much easier discharge of materials to the furnaces.

In 1869, the connection from Roundhouse Junction to the Wigan Coal & Iron Co's. high level lines opened and raw materials went into Kirkless by this route. A crossover at the Kirkless end allowed mainline locomotives to uncouple and run round. It seems likely that the empties from the Kirkless plant were shunted into Roundhouse Sidings by Wigan Coal & Iron Co. locomotives. Just before W.W.I., a bank of sidings were constructed on the north-west side of the Leeds-Liverpool Canal for the reception of iron ore and limestone traffic worked in via Roundhouse Junction by the London & North Western. Now though, from the sidings the wagons were released by Wigan Coal & Iron staff and, by gravity, to the various unloading points serving the furnaces.

These new arrangements required alterations to the levels of the Roundhouse Branch over Kirkless Hall Lane and the canal, the cost of which, some £16,420, was charged to the Wigan Coal & Iron Co. As the account was settled in November 1913 it seems likely that the new procedures were in use before that date.

As a consequence of this new procedure, only incoming traffic was dealt with over the Roundhouse Branch the empties going out via Rose Bridge Junction and eventually in 1922, Roundhouse was singled but continued in use until the closure of the Kirkless Iron & Steel Works in the 1930s. The Sidings Schedule records that instructions were given to remove the junction in 1935 but it may have remained in situ for a couple of years thereafter. The sidings at Roundhouse remained in situ until the mid 1960s. **See Fig 21.*

LINDSAY PIT TO HAIGH JUNCTION

Plate 128. Type '2' diesel No.D5257 is seen with a north-bound coal train passing Lindsay Pit Sidings on 22nd September 1971. The working is probably from Golborne Colliery.

Lindsay Pit signal box was a single turn cabin in B.R. days opening Monday-Friday 10a.m. - 6p.m. It became customary to close the box after the passage of the afternoon Manchester - Windermere train, usually about 5.40p.m. Saturday hours were 10a.m.-2p.m. *Ian Isherwood.*

Plate 129. Although Whelley Station lost its passenger service after only two months of operation the station buildings survived until demolition in the early 1970s. The station was sited about half-way between Roundhouse Junction and Lindsay Pit Sidings. This view of a southbound Type '2' is from 1st April 1969. *Courtesy, Kidderminster Railway Museum, John Marshall.*

Plate 130. In the early years of British Railways ownership, one of the ex-Lancashire & Yorkshire Aspinall 0-6-0 '3Fs' passes Lindsay Pit Sidings with a north-bound mixed freight train composed mostly of wooden bodied wagons of various types. The two exceptions, that second next to engine and the third last, are of the all steel variety.

John Sloane Collection.

After Roundhouse Junction, Lindsay Pit Sidings are passed, just beyond which are the grounds of Haigh Hall where, originally, a cut and cover tunnel was constructed at the behest of the Earl of Crawford & Balcarres, landowner. The Haigh Tunnel was 374 yards long with cover varying between 6in and 2ft. Almost immediately after opening of the route, water was found to be seeping from an ornamental pond above, into the tunnel. Although this was rectified, it seems that mining subsidence was the real problem.

Something obviously had to be done to finally rectify this problem and in 1882 it was decided to open out the tunnel. The subsequent cutting was to be fenced off and a bridge constructed to carry the Earl's 16ft wide, shrubbery lined driveway, over the cutting. The contractor who carried out this work was Charles Braddock for a price of £4,284, the original tunnel being dynamited and the spoil dumped alongside the North Union Railway in preparation for the Golborne - Springs Branch widening. The Earl was paid £6,800 in compensation by the railway company, not bad considering it was probably his own mining operations which had caused the subsidence in the first place!

The nearby Lindsay & Alexandra Pit Sidings had an outlet here to the Lancashire Union and were also connected to the colliery railway system which, from the pits ran northeast, crossing the Lancaster Canal by Shedfield Bridge, to connect with the Springs Branch at New Springs.

Plate 131. Another ex-Lancashire & Yorkshire 0-6-0 heads north through the grounds of Haigh Hall between Lindsay Pit and Whelley Junction. It was here that a cut and cover tunnel was originally built only to be removed by dynamite in 1882 because of subsidence. The work was completed in 1884. *H.Cheetham.*

Plate 132. Type '4' No.D1834 is seen in Haigh cutting on 22nd September 1971 working the 14.18 Carlisle - Willesden parcels. Unbelievably, at Privatisation in 1996, Railtrack, the body then in charge of the infrastructure on the railways, published a report on its future aspirations, one of which was to re-open this route for freight traffic. One can only wonder at the lack of foresight of the powers that were for ever allowing it to close in the first place. Even in the 1970s it was obvious that road traffic was increasing at an alarming rate and the railways, given a fair chance, could have eased the steadily increasing burden of road transport; -and, as they say, the rest is history. *Ian Isherwood.*

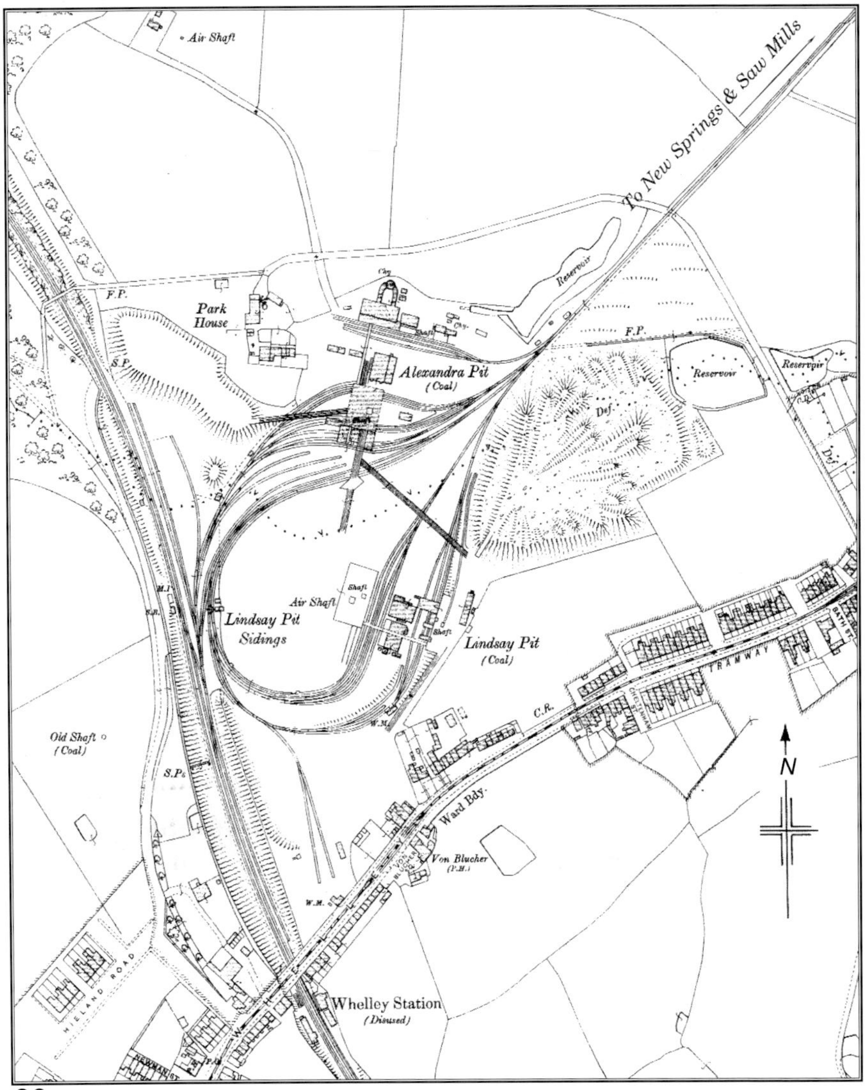

Fig 23. Sinking of Lindsay Pit began in the 1850s. An extension of the Earl of Crawford & Balcarres' private railway from a point north of the Lancaster Canal near Haigh Saw Mills was built to Lindsay Pit by 1857, being later extended to Brock Mill Forge and Haigh Foundry. This line of private railway would, with the arrival of the Lancashire Union's route, need to be rebuilt from Brock Mill Junction at Haigh. *(See **Page 93**).*

Sinking of the Alexandra Pits began in 1874 and by 1890, both Lindsay and Alexandra Pits had been deepened to reach lower seams.

The private line to Haigh Saw Mills, from 1865 a part of the Wigan Coal & Iron Co's. railway, was removed after the closure of Kirkless Works in the 1930s, Lindsay Pit being abandoned in 1932. Alexandra Pit continued working until June 1955, having been taken over by the National Coal Board in 1947. The sidings and connections with the former Lancashire Union lines were, however, to remain in use until 1962 as coal was sent by road from the Dairy Pit for screening at the Alexandra Pit plant. Dairy Pit had been reopened in 1955 having been closed for some time. It was sited just north of the Lancaster Canal, north-west of Haigh Saw Mills.

Plate 133. This is a view northwards of the 374 yard long Haigh Tunnel site from its southern end, opened out in 1882/4. In the background is the ornamental bridge constructed to carry the Earl of Crawford & Balcarres' driveway. This area through which the railway passed is generally referred to as 'The Plantations'. *Courtesy, Kidderminster Railway Museum, John Marshall.*

Plate 134. Wigan Coal & Iron Co. locomotive *Manton,* is seen at Alexandra Pit in 1908. This locomotive, only recently built when this photo was taken, would spend much of its life at Manton Colliery in the Midlands where the Wigan Coal & Iron Co. had other mining interests. Lindsay Pit is on the right. *Wigan & Leigh Archives.*

Plate 135. D388 heads north through the plantations and under the ornamental bridge with a sand train on 26th June 1972.
John Ryan.

Plate 136. A four-car DMU heads south on 25th June 1972 approximately 10 minutes ahead of the 12.30 Blackpool North - Euston which apparently, did not run. Was this a substitution? The photo is taken from the ornamental bridge. *John Ryan.*

BROCK MILL JUNCTION

Between Whelley and Haigh Junction was Brock Mill Junction from where a branch line descended steeply down the Douglas Valley to where Brock Mill Forge and Haigh Foundry were located.

A number of iron forges and mills had been established here from the mid 17th century, the power being provided by the River Douglas. In 1788, the 6th Earl of Crawford & Balcarres, together with his brother, Robert Lindsay, in association with one James Corbett, built the Haigh Ironworks and, at about the same period, took control of Brock Mill Forge. Apparently, the Haigh Ironworks was not successful and the blast furnaces blown out pre- 1815. However, some of the buildings on the site were used to manufacture machinery and steam engines.

In 1804, Robert Daglish was appointed Chief Engineer and built the first steam locomotives in Lancashire here in 1812. These were based on the Blenkinsop cog pattern, with some detailed differences, as demonstrated on the Middleton Colliery Railway near Leeds in 1810/11. The engines as built by Daglish were for use on the Orrell Colliery Railway, north-west of Wigan where Daglish was Colliery Manager. At Orrell these engines were referred to as the 'Yorkshire' or 'walking' horse*.

After the accession of the 7th Earl in 1828, Brock Mill Forge and Haigh Foundry were leased, in 1835, to a partnership of Evans, Ryley & Burrows. Between 1835 and 1856 over 100 locomotives were built here, mostly for main line use and the client list is a veritable 'who's who' of notable names and companies involved in the construction and running of Britain's embryonic railway system vis:- The Liverpool & Manchester, North Union, London & Birmingham, Great Western, Manchester & Bolton and South Devon Railways to name but a few. Haigh Foundry also built a number of locomotives for Bury & Co. of Liverpool under sub-contract and supplied others to Gooch & Evans and also to Rennie & Co. At least 3 were built for the War Department for use in Crimea.

The Haigh Foundry Company was formed in 1856 with the Earl of Crawford & Balcarres at its head, as Evans and his partners had not renewed their lease. The new company now concentrated on mining machinery and by 1860 Haigh Foundry and Brock Mill Forge had been connected by an extension of the Earl's colliery railway system from the north bank of the Lancaster Canal where connections had been made with the Springs Branch in 1838.

It is also worthy of note that prior to the arrival of this rail connection all the locomotives built at Haigh had to be drawn by teams of horses hauling stout carts up Leyland Mill Lane which then wound and rattled their way through the streets of Wigan en route to their purchasers. This must have been an endurance task as presumably the locomotives had to be stripped down into manageable loads for reassembly at their final destinations.

* *See Norley Hall Collieries* ***Page 104***.

Plate 137. On 25th June1972, D7527&5183 are at the head of 1LO2, a Chester/Northampton - Blackpool North special heading towards Whelley Junction having passed through the Plantations. Whichever way you look at it, it's an odd way to get to Blackpool!

John Ryan

The Lancashire Union route, when built, would cut across the Earl's railway at Haigh. In 1865 an agreement was signed to the effect that the Lancashire Union would construct a new branch from Haigh, Brock Mill Junction, to Brock Mill as a replacement, the Earl providing all the track materials with the Lancashire Union paying the cost to trackbed level. Opening of the branch to Brock Mill was probably concomitant with the opening of the main lines and Wigan Coal & Iron Co. trains worked over it from the outset, having running powers from Lindsay Pit Sidings to Haigh, and from Boar's Head to Brinks Sidings on the route to Adlington.

After a period of uncertainty when both Haigh Foundry and Brock Mill Forge were advertised for sale, the Haigh Foundry was taken over by J.Petford Ltd. in 1899, makers of iron bedsteads. It is thought that the Wigan Coal & Iron Co. worked their traffic as Petfords still had a coal yard at Leyland Mill. Petford Ltd. was liquidated in 1908 and various concerns have since leased premises on the site. Brock Mill Forge was converted to a textile works in the 1880s, later the Haigh Dyeing Co.

It is believed that the branch closed in 1919 as by February 1920, all the track, and the connection near Haigh Junction had been lifted. One of the Earl's sidings at Haigh Junction was taken over by the London & North Western on 7th April 1919, a chute being installed whereby the Haigh Dyeing Co. were allowed to unload coal for the works to be carried by road transport. In the 1930s the works was taken over by the Post & Chronicle Group and up to recent times a number of light industrial firms rented the premises. *See **Fig 30, Page 109** for O/S.*

Plate 138. A View from the abandoned trackbed towards Haigh Junction on 7th April 1968, affords a good view of the juxtaposition of Whelley Viaduct, left, and Boar's Head Viaduct, Centre. Victoria Colliery, alongside the W.C.M.L. between Boar's Head and Standish is the prominent building, left, just below the telephone wires. *Courtesy, Kidderminster Railway Museum, John Marshall.*

Signal Box locations & line distances Ince Moss to Haigh Junction

Ince Moss	Dist to c1933	Box closed
Fir Tree House Junction	547 yds	18.5.1969
Amberswood West Junction	1356 yds	11.5.1969
Amberswood East Junction	788 yds	18.5.1969
De Trafford Junction	1229 yds	10.1972
Rosebridge Junction	1177 yds	7.1938
Roundhouse Junction	810 yds	1.10.1972
Lindsay & Alexandra Pit Sidings	776 yds	3.1957
Whelley Junction	1m 127 yds	19.6.1967
Haigh Junction	1112 yds	18.6.1967
	5m 882yds	
Standish Junction	1m 829 yds	15.1.1973

Plate 139. Stanier '8F' No.48249, with a good head of steam, arrives at Haigh Junction about 1960 on a northbound freight with four cattle vans next to the engine.

Plate 140, below. 'W.D.' 2-8-0 No. 90257 passes Haigh Junction cabin with another northbound freight, also about 1960.

Courtesy, Kidderminster Railway Museum, John Marshall.

Plate 141, below. The view from the rear brake van at Haigh Junction on 4th April 1964 as the train of return empties makes its way along the route to Adlington Junction. Whelley Junction - Haigh Junction was originally double track, singled in November 1952, closing completely on 23rd January 1967, having had no booked traffic since 25th April 1965.The Boar's Head line is on the right which, like the route to Cherry Tree had been constructed jointly with the Lancashire & Yorkshire Railway. It was here at Haigh that the ceremonial cutting of the 'first sod' was carried out by the Chairman of the London & North Western Railway, Richard Moon, on 31st July 1866, work commencing immediately.

Eddie Bellass.

Gradient Profile,
Ince Moss -
Haigh Junction.

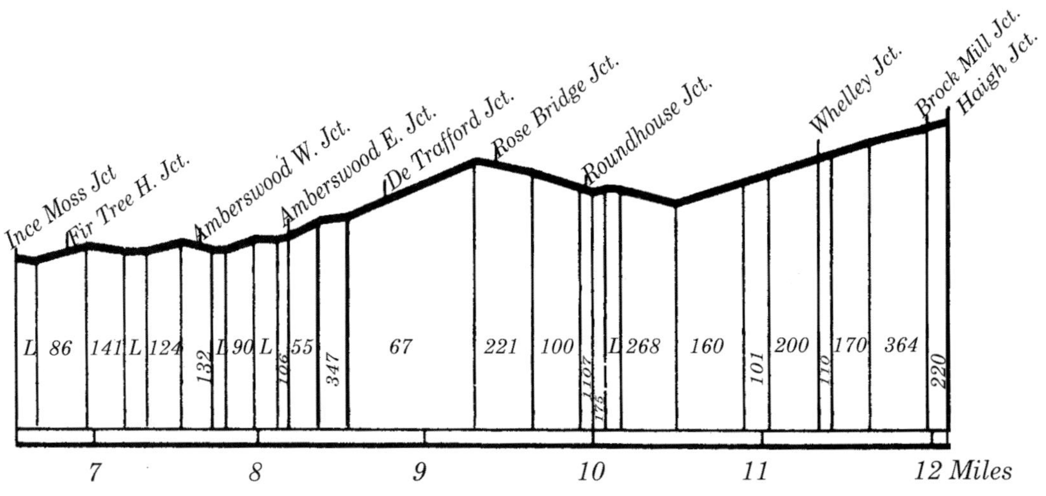

Plate 142. These two wagons, c1920s, may be of some interest to modellers. The location is believed to be Park Lane Colliery on the Pemberton Branch, but definitive proof is lacking. Nevertheless, it makes an interesting pairing, the L&Y 20 tonner and the smaller 8 ton Park Lane wagon with the company logo. *Wigan & Leigh Archives.*

THE PEMBERTON BRANCH

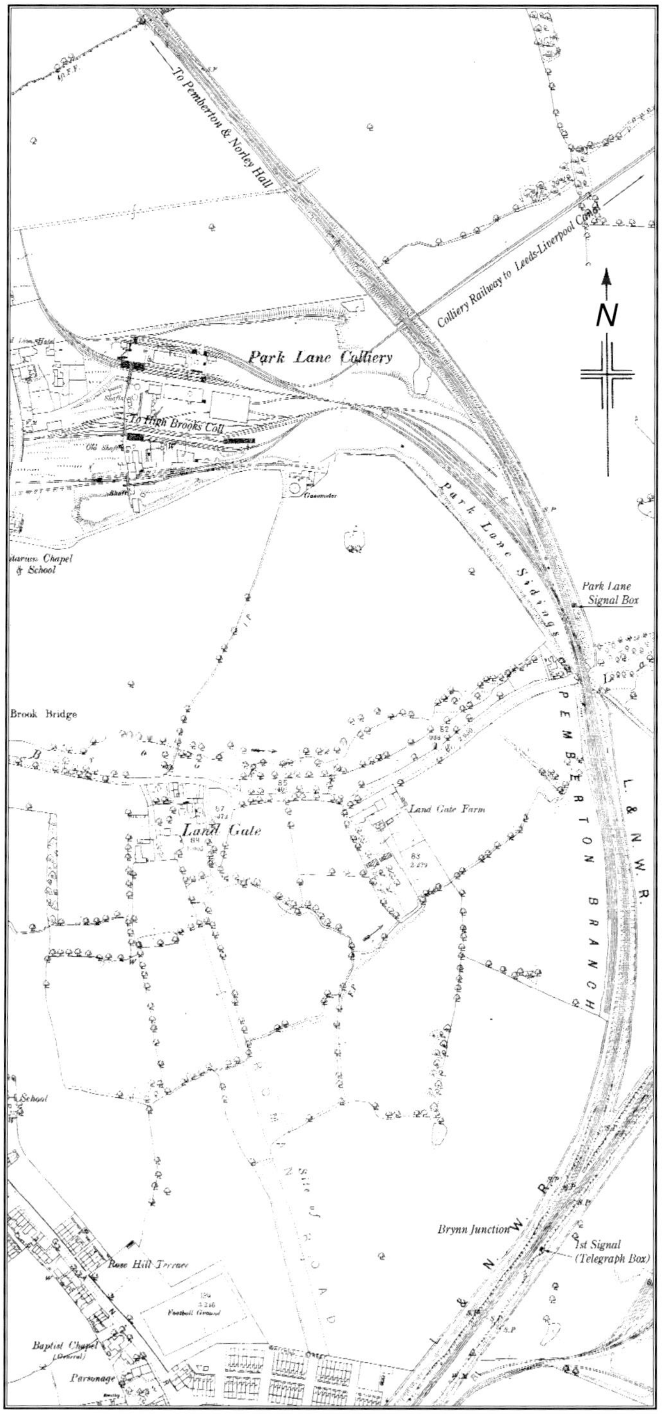

Fig 24. From the second series Ordnance Survey. The Park Lane Collieries sunk by Mercer & Evans were taken over by Garswood Coal & Iron Co Ltd in 1873 and by the time this survey was carried out further expansion at the collieries had taken place. These pits were to close in 1929 when the firm became Garswood Hall Collieries. The first signal box at this location is shown where, later, the new slow lines would be.

The Pemberton Branch, authorised under the Lancashire Union's1865 Act, ran from Bryn Junction in a northerly direction towards Norley Hall with a spur to the Lancashire & Yorkshire's Wigan - Liverpool line at Pemberton Junction. En route, connections would be made with Park Lane Collieries, Winstanley Collieries, Blundell's Pemberton Collieries and finally, Norley Hall Collieries. It is believed that the branch opened in its entirety on 1st November 1869, concomitant with the opening of the Gerards Bridge - Ince Moss - Haigh Junction route, except, that is, for the Goose Green - Norley Hall branch which in all probability didn't open until 1871. No regular passenger services ever worked the branch. Length of line from Bryn Junction to Pemberton Junction was 2 miles 493 yards. From Goose Green Junction, London & North Western locomotives were allowed to work as far as Norley Hall No.4 pit, provided that the colliery company maintained their way adequately.

As is the case with all lineside communications along the route at this period, Saxby & Farmer boxes would have been in place. At Bryn Junction, the first box appears to have been sited on the south-east side of the then two track main line. At the time of quadrupling this was replaced by a new L&NW Type '4' box on the same side of the tracks having 64 levers. In 1929, this, in turn, was replaced by a new cabin, a L&NW Type '5' with 70 levers, sited in the triangle of lines some 125 yards nearer to Ince Moss. The branch was worked as permissive block from Bryn Junction to Goose Green Junction, train staff being used on the single line section to Norley Hall.

PARK LANE COLLIERY

Working northwards along the branch the first connection was at Park Lane Junction. Two collieries, High Brooks and Park Lane, were sunk in the 1850s and collectively became known as Park Lane from 1869, owned by Mercer & Evans. A line of railway, some two miles in length had been built in the 1850s, running to a pier head on the Leeds-Liverpool Canal from High Brooks, connecting with Park Lane on the way. A second line of railway opened in 1859, ran eastwards for about 2¼ miles to the North Union Railway where a connection was made near Mains Colliery.

Upon completion of the Lancashire Union Railway in 1869, the line to the North Union was abandoned and a new connection made with the Lancashire Union's Pemberton Branch, shown in ***Fig 24*** opposite. The line

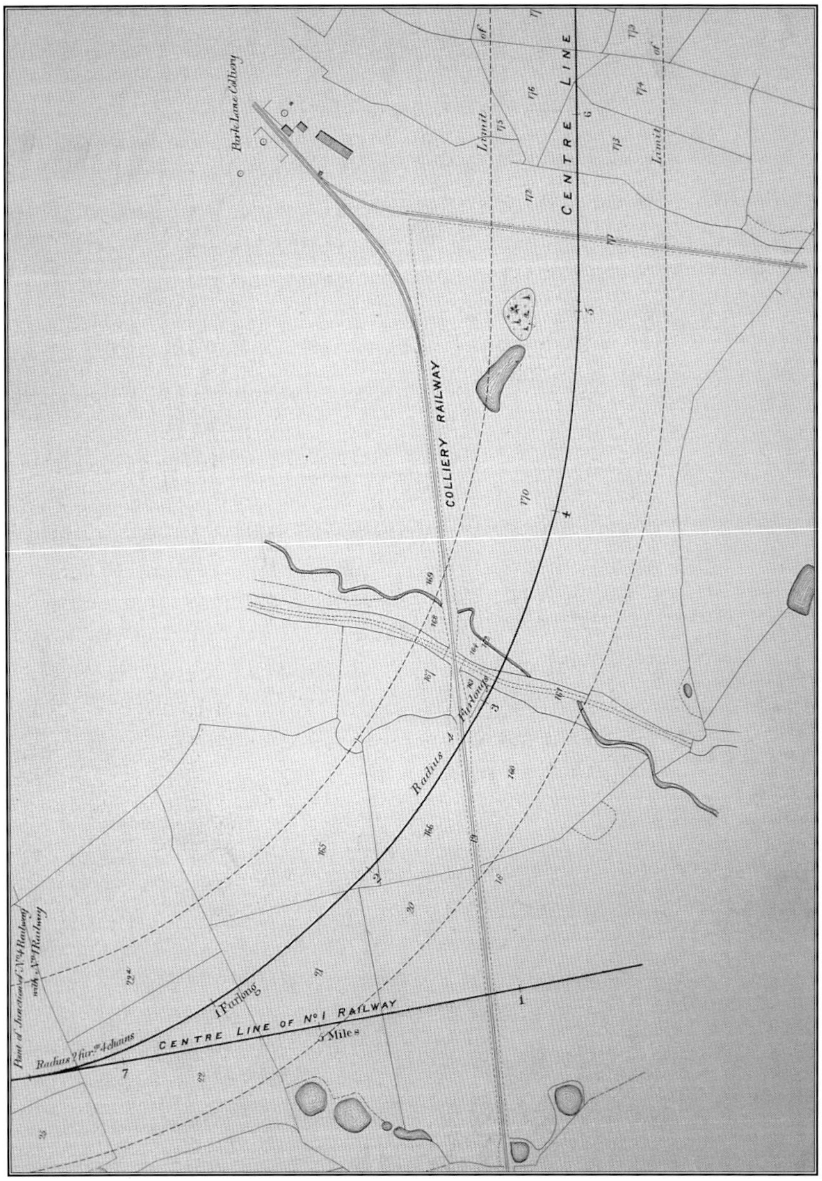

Fig 25. Extracted from the 1865 Lancashire Union Line Plan, this section shows the proposed Bryn Junction, far left, and the arrangement of colliery railways in the vicinity. The Park Lane Colliery of Mercer & Evans has a line of railway which ran to the Leeds - Liverpool Canal, upper right. A second branch line, built in 1859 and shown running eastwards from the colliery, ran for a little over 2 miles to the North Union Railway near Mains Colliery and would be intersected by the Lancashire Union's Pemberton Branch, and its main lines to Ince Moss. This colliery railway is thought not to have survived for long in its original form after Mercer & Evans Collieries were connected to the Pemberton Branch. Certainly, by the time Park Lane was taken over by the Garswood Coal & Iron Co. Ltd in 1873 the section from Park Lane Colliery to Garswood Hall Colliery was lifted, although the line to the Edge Green area of Golborne is shown on the second series Ordnance Survey and saw further use.

to the canal was retained and passed beneath this branch.

Park Lane Collieries purchased their first locomotive in 1869, *Caliban*, which had been built for the Grand Junction Railway in 1837 by Sharp Roberts & Co., Manchester. A second locomotive, *Helica,* which had been built locally by the Haigh Foundry as a 2-2-2 for passenger service, also for the Grand Junction Railway, arrived in 1861, having been rebuilt as an 0-4-0 goods engine in 1844.

Mercer & Evans Park Lane Collieries were taken over by the Garswood Coal & Iron Co. Ltd. on 22nd November 1873. A proposal to become involved in the manufacture of iron products was not pursued and it was decided to redevelop Park Lane Colliery by sinking further shafts in the same locality. By the early 1880s the company employed over 2,000, had three locomotives, 1,500 wagons and a total of nine shafts. Not all were successful, as Ashton Colliery sunk in 1888 about $^1/_2$ mile from Bryn Station, had closed by 1908. Main line connections with the colliery were instituted from March 1890. After closure the colliery was used for a few years as a pumping station. By 1911 the sidings connection here had been removed.

A Saxby & Farmer signal box having 16 levers is known to have been in operation at the junction for Park Lane Collieries in 1869. It was to close on 4th November 1931, after closure of Park Lane Colliery.

WINSTANLEY COLLIERIES

One Thomas Claughton had obtained leases to mine coal to the north-east of the Pemberton collieries in 1822 and consequently constructed a 4ft narrow gauge tramway to the Leeds - Liverpool Canal at Parson's Meadow which, from the early years of the twentieth century became more commonly known as Wigan Pier. In total, there were four separate pits which had a connection to the tramway route but by 1864 operations at these early mines had ceased. However, in the interim the tramway had been extended south-west of Pemberton towards Winstanley where, between 1830 and 1845, a number of pits had been sunk. These and the colliery tramway, are shown on the first series Ordnance Survey of 1845/6.

From No.4 pit at Windy Arbour, the distance to the canal was approximately 3½ miles, consisting of 'T' section rails at 15ft in length, laid on stone blocks. Horses in use here travelled down to the canal in dandy carts in order to haul the wagons back up the inclines. By 1867, a third rail had been laid on much of the system allowing standard gauge wagons to work through to a connection with the Lancashire & Yorkshire west of Pemberton Station. A link with the Pemberton Colliery railway was to provide an additional outlet with the Lancashire Union Railway in 1869 at Blundell's Sidings. It is believed that the locomotives were in use from the late 1870s on this system.

The Bankes family had been owners of these mines at Winstanley until 27th October 1885 when Winstanley Collieries Company Limited was formed by Tomlinson, Rogers and Simpson who had leased the mines since July the same year. In 1886/7, all remaining narrow gauge lines were relaid to standard gauge, including that to the canal at Wigan Pier, and a new connection with the Pemberton Branch authorised by the London & North Western in July 1886, just in time to appear on the second series Ordnance Survey.

Plate 143. En route to Goose Green Junction the Pemberton Branch crossed the A49, Warrington Road by an overbridge, seen left. The view is believed to date from the winter of 1948/49.

The second vehicle approaching is a Series I Land Rover and although a few prototypes were running in 1947, the production model was not introduced to the general public until the Amsterdam Motor Show in April 1948. It is extremely unlikely that the first of these rolled off the production lines before 1949. That being the case, it calls into question the various closure dates of the branch which have been banded about previously - between 1946 and October 1948. However, Bill Paxford's account of a scrap train working the branch c1949/50 *(see **Page 102)*** calls all of the above dates into question. It is however, quite possible that access from Pemberton Junction had ceased by late 1947, the date favoured by most sources for closure. That the branch was still accessible from Bryn Junction, at least to Blundell's Sidings, is not only confirmed by Bill Paxford's recollections, but also by ***Fig 11, Page 36,*** which states that the junction was not removed until 1952. *Courtesy, Cliff Reeves.*

Plate 144. Unbelievably, this is the same location in April 2009. The A49 of earlier years, barely wide enough for the passage of vehicles, has undergone a complete transformation into a dual-carriageway, instituted concomitantly with the construction of the M6 motorway and link road from junction 25 to Land Gate. Part of the Pemberton Branch embankment is still visible here, out of shot on the extreme right. *Bob McClellan.*

By the 1890s, the earlier Winstanley pits were becoming exhausted and a new mine was sunk in 1888 at Billinge Lane. This was not entirely a success, closing in 1900. In 1899, Leyland Green pit came on stream and the colliery railway was extended to serve it.

The first locomotive on the standard gauge system *Eleanor*, was an 0-4-0 supplied by Walker Brothers of Wigan in 1879, followed by *Louisa,* another 0-4-0 to work the 4ft gauge lines supplied by Hunslet of Leeds in 1882. The latter was sold on when conversion to standard gauge of the remaining lines on the system took place. In due course other locomotives followed, *Winstanley* in 1905 from Andrew Barclay and from the same maker, *Billinge* in 1916, both 0-4-0s.

Tomlinson, Rogers & Simpson had, from the 1890s, owned the Worsley Mesnes Colliery and its associated ironworks and connection from here to the Winstanley Colliery's railway permitted traffic to be worked out via the Lancashire Union.

Leyland Green Colliery closed in 1927 and the railway to it taken out of use, the company going into liquidation on 29th July 1927. Sidings with the former Lancashire & Yorkshire route at Pemberton, Bankes' Sidings, were removed in 1928. Those with the former Lancashire Union line continued in use until 1930. Instructions to remove the Winstanley connections were issued on 20th December 1933.

The remaining colliery railway to Wigan Pier, and the discharge apparatus, were removed in the 1930s by E.Calderbank & Sons Ltd. It is ironic that some fifty years later Wigan Pier would be reopened as a tourist attraction.

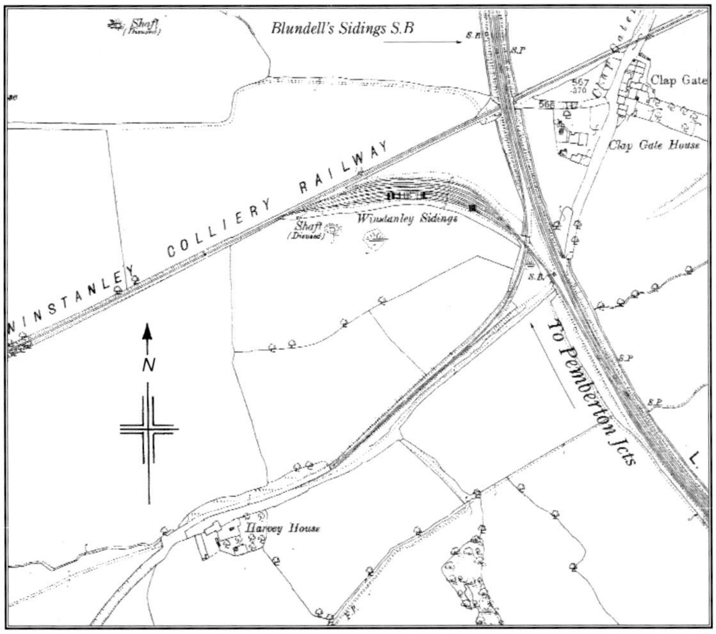

Fig 26. Winstanley Collieries and their connections with the Lancashire union c1890. The colliery line from Winstanley en route to Wigan Pier passes beneath the Pemberton lines. A south facing connection was made with the Lancashire Union in 1886 by a single lead junction which accessed two reception sidings sited alongside the main line. Presumably Winstanley Colliery engines shunted traffic to/from these to the colliery itself. Previously, Winstanley Collieries had used Blundell's Pemberton Colliery connection from 1869. The signal box at Winstanley Sidings dates from 1887. Having only 6 levers, it was to close c1929/30.

By a circuitous route, connections from the Winstanley Colliery Railway would be made with Worsley Mesnes Colliery which was sited in the area between the Lancashire & Yorkshire's Pemberton Loop and Wigan lines.

PEMBERTON COLLIERIES

From the 1820s, a number of collieries in the Pemberton area had been linked to the Leeds-Liverpool Canal at Seven Stars Bridge by 4ft gauge tramways. One was operated by the German family; these were never to have mainline connections. The second tramway in this area was owned by Henry Hollinshead Blundell, whose pits date from 1815. His tramway, built c1827, ran for much of its length parallel to that of German's as it approached the canal. In 1842 Richard Blundell, who had inherited his father's estate in 1832, sank Amberswood Colliery which had a connection with the North Union south of Springs Branch. In 1848, connections with the Lancashire & Yorkshire Railway were made at Pemberton where five pits were now in operation.

In turn, Richard was succeeded by his son Henry on the former's death in 1853 and there followed a period of expansion at Pemberton, notably King and Queen pits, sinking of which began in 1867. By 1870, Blundell's tramroad to the Leeds - Liverpool Canal had been abandoned, part of which course would become Victoria Street, an extension of Billinge Road from Pemberton to its junctions with Ormskirk and Warrington Roads.

With the arrival of the Lancashire Union Railway on the scene, a connection was made at Blundell's Sidings under an agreement of 14th December 1869. Located at 1 mile 1,262 yards from Bryn Junction, a 10 lever Saxby & Farmer box was here in the early days. This was either replaced by a new signal box, or extended to 21 levers in 1899. Closure is given as c1944/48.

North of Blundell's Sidings was Goose Green Junction which gave a connection to the Lancashire & Yorkshire's Wigan - Liverpool route at Pemberton Junction, east of which would see a further connection on 1st May 1889 when the Pemberton Loop lines from Hindley opened for goods, and to passengers a month later. This Wigan by-pass route, which had seen only passenger traffic in its last year or two, was to close on 14th July 1969.

The Pemberton Colliery Company Limited was registered on 7th December 1900, but the association with the Blundell family was not relinquished until 1929 when Pemberton Colliery (1929) Limited was formed, by which period production had dropped to 300,000 tons per year, from a peak of 600,000 tons in the early years of the twentieth century. A further name change to Pemberton Colliery Limited, occurred in August 1938.

The colliery closed on 3rd November 1946 but since 1943, all traffic had been dispatched by the former Lancashire & Yorkshire connections. Although a drift mine opened here in 1945, the coal from this was taken by road to Pemberton Station and loaded into railway wagons. Eventually, on 1st January 1949, the drift mine came under National Coal Board ownership, continuing in operation until 1966.

Opencast coal had also been delivered by road to Pemberton screens from other opencast sites in the Wigan area and dispatched by rail as from 16th July 1943. These operations ceased about 1964 but the plant remained until the private sidings agreement was terminated in August 1967.

Plate 145 . This view of the Pemberton - Goose Green area dates from 1971. The most familiar benchmark from which other locations may be determined is the former Lancashire & Yorkshire's Wigan - Liverpool route which enters upper right to exit at top left. Mid right the same company's Pemberton Loop enters, passing the multi-storey flats at Worsley Mesnes (mentioned in the caption to ***Plate 64)*** and joins the Liverpool line at Pemberton Junction, centre, where Little Lane overbridge crosses. The trackbed of the former Lancashire Union lines enter lower left and would have passed over the A49 Warrington Road as in ***Plate 143.*** The trackbed is then intersected, first by industrial building, and second by housing around Highfield Grange Avenue which connects with the A49 and Poolstock Lane left of centre. Mid left the Lancashire Union trackbed is again discernable, as is the wasteland of the former Pemberton Colliery and Goose Green Junction sites. Thence continuing under Little Lane and the Lancashire & Yorkshire routes the Lancashire Union would have crossed Ormskirk Road, ***Plate 148***, towards Norley Hall Collieries where, at top right, sits the housing estate. The curvature of Heather Grove, off Ormskirk Road, closely follows the former railway alignment.

Wigan & Leigh Archives.

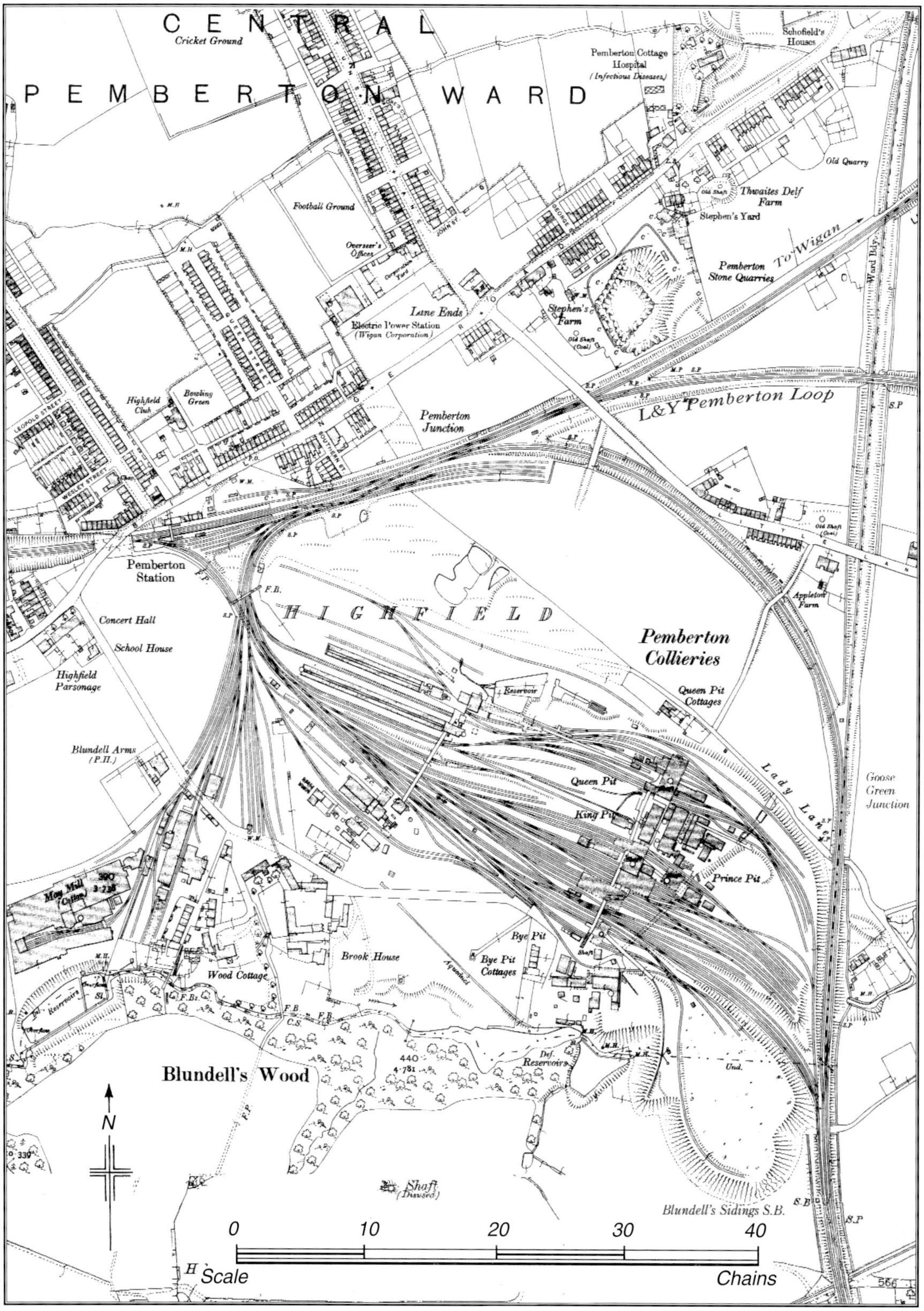

Fig 27. The arrangement of lines and junctions at the northernmost point on the Pemberton Branch from the updated survey of 1907.

Blundell's Sidings connection was north of the Winstanley line, the signal box here sited on the western side of the Lancashire Union's lines at 1mile 1,262 yards from Bryn Junction and 991 yards from Pemberton Junction. Immediately north of Blundell's Sidings was Goose Green Junction and signal box, shown here sited in the triangle between the single line to Norley Hall and the curve to Pemberton Junction. It is believed to have opened in 1899, but the survey of 1888-92 shows an earlier box on the eastern side of the main lines at 2 miles from Bryn Junction. Blundell's Sidings box took over the function of Goose Green box in 1901.

At Goose Green, the Pemberton Branch turned westward to make a connection with the Lancashire & Yorkshire's Wigan - Liverpool line at Pemberton Junction or, continuing northwards, to Norley Hall Colliery. Goose Green to Norley Hall was always single track, worked by train staff.

Former Signalman Bill Paxford recalls being sent to Blundell's Sidings box c1949/50 to receive a scrap train. This was to be propelled in from Bryn Junction to collect scrap metal from the colliery sidings which had been lifted. On arrival at Blundell's box, Bill found that the signal box had, apparently, been out of use for some time. The clips were removed, and with the help of platelayers the points barred over because of difficulty in getting the locking bar to locate correctly. The train was loaded and made its way back to Bryn Junction, whereupon, it was belled on as a ballast train and propelled into Ince Moss Sidings.

Plate 146. Pemberton Colliery c1930s, previously Blundell's Colliery until 1929 with, left to right, King Pit, Prince Pit and Queen Pit. Around 1,800 miners and surface workers were employed here at this period. Apart from the company's own wagons in view there are those of the L.M.S. for loco coal, Hardman, B.T.B., CORY and at least three other private owner wagons which cannot be fully identified. Middle right, Little Lane runs right to left across the picture towards Billinge Road and is identified by the row of terraced houses. The dark line in front of the terraced houses is the fencing alongside the Lancashire Unions Pemberton Branch as it curves right to left towards Pemberton Junction. *Wigan & Leigh Archives.*

Plate 147. Ex-L.M.S. Fowler designed 0-8-0 No.49586, approaches Pemberton Junction on 1st August 1951 on the Pemberton Loop line with a mixed freight. The now closed Lancashire Union's line from Goose Green Junction to Norley Hall ran across picture at the back of the farmhouse sited alongside the ex Lancashire & Yorkshire's line to Wigan, left, but in front of the terraced housing beyond the farmhouse, passing under the L&Y lines. *John Sloane Collection.*

NORLEY HALL COLLIERIES

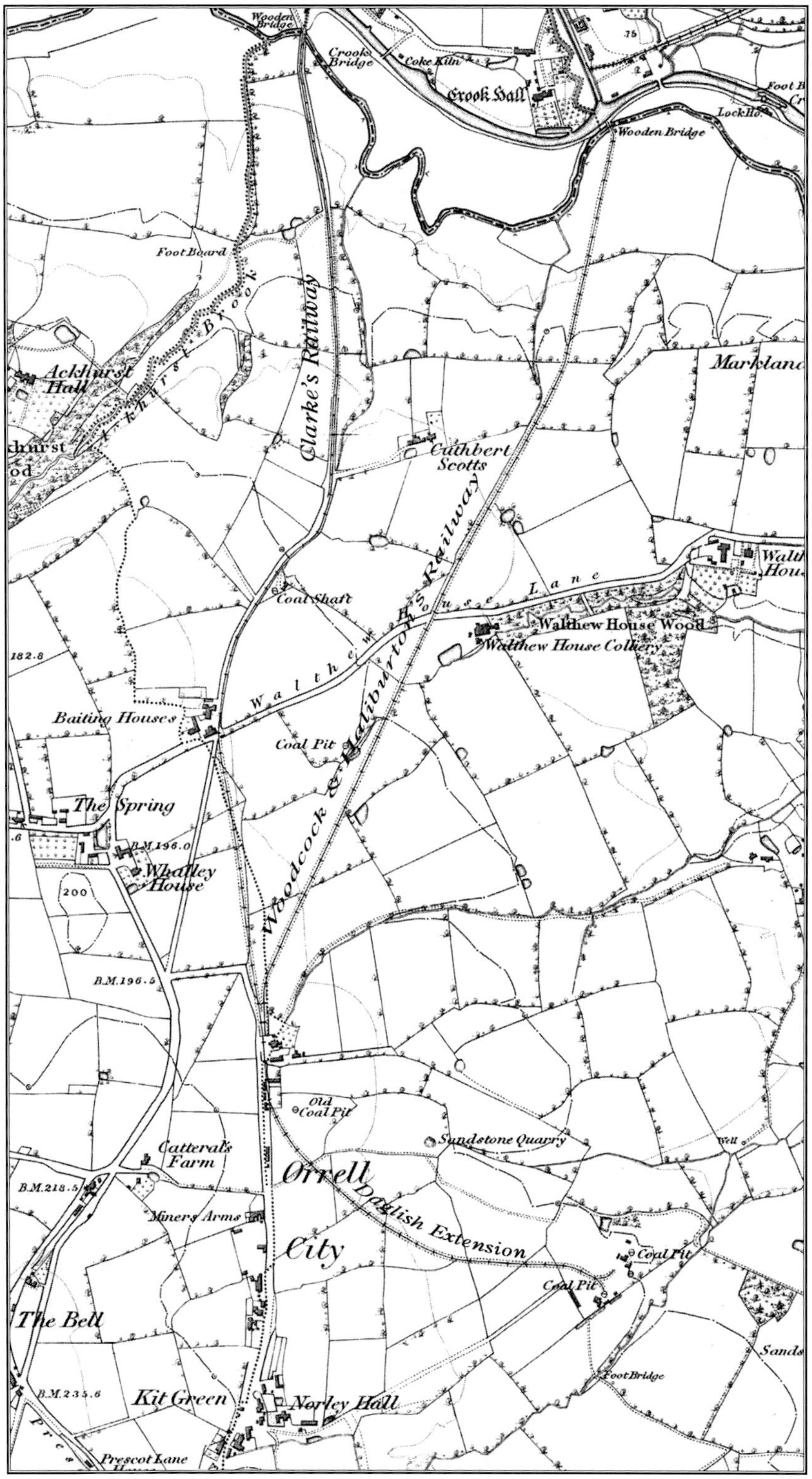

Fig 28. Clarke's colliery railway, Woodcock & Haliburton's railway and the deviation and extension of the former by Robert Daglish to his Norley Hall pits are shown from the first series Ordnance Survey of 1845/7.

The Lancashire Union's Pemberton Branch was to terminate at Norley Hall where it made an end-on connection with the Norley Hall colliery railway in 1871. However, to trace the origins of the latter's railway we must go back to the last quarter of the eighteenth century.

In the area to the North-West of Wigan there had been a number of colliery wagonways or railways which had made connections with, firstly, the River Douglas from the mid 1770s, and later, with the Leeds-Liverpool Canal in the vicinity of Orrell, Crooke and Gathurst. For the most part these are outside the parameters of this work and I will deal only with those that had a bearing on the Lancashire Union's plans, Clarke's railway at Orrell being one of these.

One William Berry constructed a railway in 1780, described in an advertisement of 1781 as a "good and commodious railed or planked road" which ran from his colliery at Orrell to the Leeds-Liverpool Canal at Crooke. William Clarke, together with his brother John and partners, acted as trustees for William Berry's estate from about the same period. Further mines were sunk at Gathurst by William & John Clarke in 1789, and at Pingot, south of Orrell in 1792, the colliery railway being extended as necessary. In 1812 a further extension of the railway was made to Winstanley where new mines were being sunk, giving an approximate line length of 4 miles. This had now become known in the area as Clarke's Railway.

Enter Robert Daglish who, from 1804 had been the manager at Haigh Foundry and, in 1810, was appointed as manager of Clarke's collieries and was destined to have a great influence in the sphere of railway and mining operations in the South Central Lancashire area.

In 1812, Daglish would construct the first steam locomotives in Lancashire for use on Clarke's railway. These would be built at Haigh Foundry, based on the cog and rack system demonstrated by John Blenkinsop on the Middleton Colliery Railway near Leeds a year or two earlier. Daglish obtained Blenkinsop's permission under licence to use his design, with, it is believed, some minor modifications.

Plate 148. Exactly what it says on the tin, or in this case as over-written on the photograph, Union Bridge. It is in fact a view of the Lancashire Union's bridge on Ormskirk Road, as viewed towards Wigan. The photograph is undated but looks to be around 1920. It is now a little difficult to visualise coal trains working over it from Norley Hall Collieries.
Courtesy, Cliff Reeves.

To use these locomotives, Clarke's railway had been relaid with cast-iron, fish-bellied rails but still to the standard Lancashire wagonway gauge of 4ft. Whilst at work on Clarke's railway, these locomotives became known as the 'Yorkshire' or 'Walking Horse'.

In a letter to *Kaleidoscope* in September 1822 Benjamin Hick of Union Foundry, Bolton, wrote that: *three engines were in service on the Orrell Railway, two always in use and another spare. Each locomotive weighed in at 6½ tons and hauled twelve loaded wagons at 3 tons each up an incline of approximately 1:36 at 3mph. On level plane the engine would draw 90 tons!*

Robert Daglish continued as manager of the Orrell Collieries on behalf of the creditors after the owners became bankrupt in 1816, the mines continuing in production until the early 1830s. The mines at Winstanley continued in production until 1852, but the colliery railway system south of Orrell City (now in the vicinity of Kitt Green) was out of use by the early 1840s, only the northern 'original' part of it being shown on the first series Ordnance Survey of 1845/6.

Norley Hall Collieries had been sunk in the early 1840s by Robert Daglish and his brother, John. To work their coals to the canal they had taken over what remained of Clarke's railway, laying an extension from the southern end of this to the Norley Hall pits and it is believed that one of Daglish's locomotives worked over the route until 1852.

This new branch line appears to cross the end of Woodcock & Haliburton's railway alongside what is now City Road. This latter railway had been built in the late 1820s or early 1830s from their pits south of Orrell to the Leeds - Liverpool Canal at Crooke. The working life of these pits was, apparently, quite short, closing about 1840. Again, only the northern part of this railway is shown on the first series Ordnance Survey. By the 1860s there were three pits at Norley Hall and conversion of the railway to standard gauge had taken place.

In replying to a letter from a Mr Jones of Mount Pleasant, Liverpool dated 1st April 1856, Daglish wrote in reference to these locomotives: *I made the first in the County in 1812 and put it on an extensive colliery* (railway) *under my direction, into full action at the beginning of 1813 which was nearly 2 years before Mr. Geo. Stephenson made a Locomotive Engine in Northumberland.* Continuing he adds; (this) *caused a saving of nearly £500 per annum compared to the use of horses, drivers etc, so that I had* (an)*other two at work before the end of 1816 and had them in use for upwards of 36 years when I finished* (at) *the colliery on which they were applied.*

A post-script adds: *I worked two of my locomotove engines on a cog railway by which the resistance was obtained, and one of them by adhesion produced between the surface of the rail and the periphery of the driving wheels.*

A second note from the same date is something of a testimonial under the heading: *To all whom it may concern. This is to testify that I made the first Locomotive Engine in Lancashire in the year 1812, & put it into action in 1813 on a extensive colliery under my direction belonging to the late John Clarke Esquire., in the township of Orrell near Wigan, for the conveyance of coal etc by trains of wagons from his colliery near Orrell Mount to the Leeds & Liverpool Canal, which was upwards of 16 years before any Locomotive Engines were put fairly into action on the Liverpool & Manchester Railway.*

Robert Daglish Senr. M. & C.E.

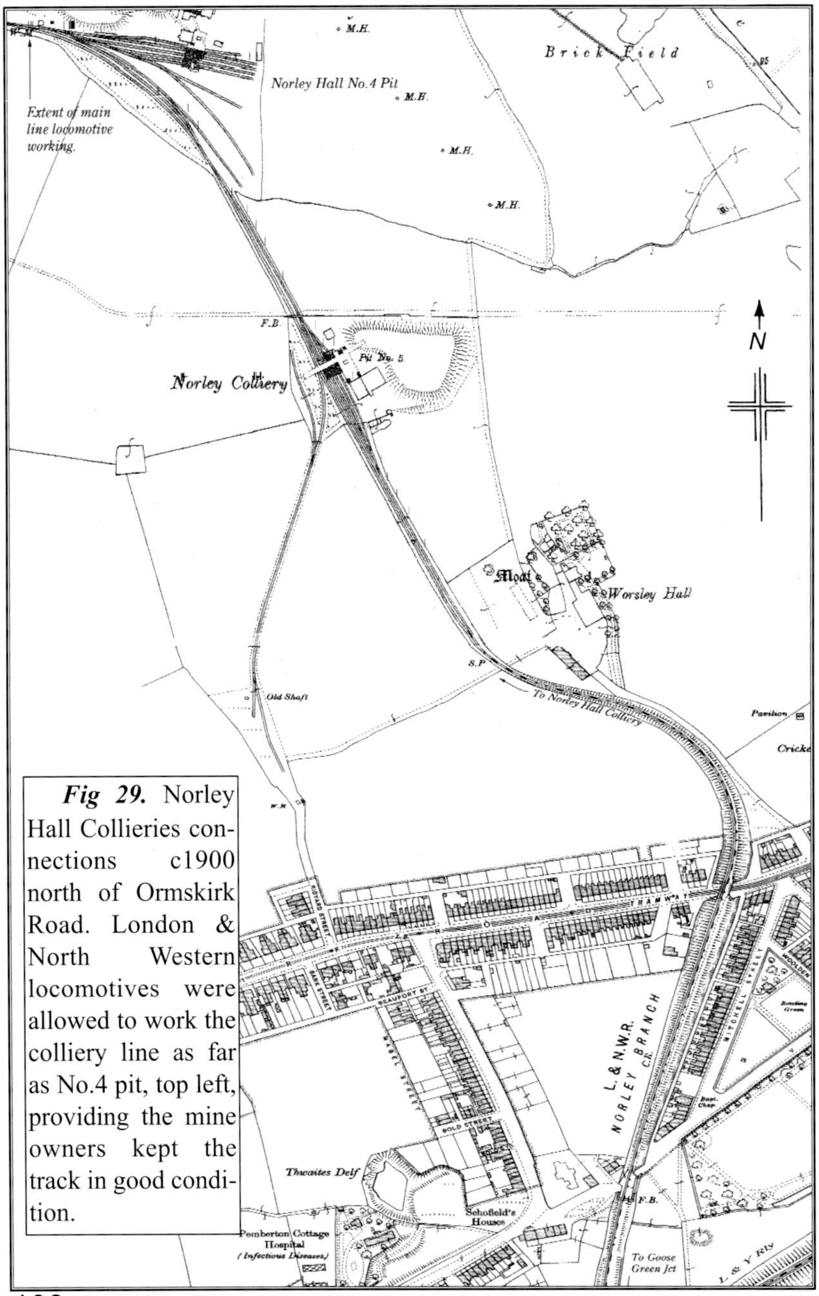

Fig 29. Norley Hall Collieries connections c1900 north of Ormskirk Road. London & North Western locomotives were allowed to work the colliery line as far as No.4 pit, top left, providing the mine owners kept the track in good condition.

The late Mr. Donald Anderson, a well renown authority on mining in the Wigan area, took notes from a Mr. Joseph Hilton, born 1849 who, some 80 years later, recorded that Daglish's locomotive the " Yorkshire Horse" had been installed in the colliery stables (Norley Hall) for hay cutting etc, and was only demolished when the colliery closed in the early 1920s.

In 1827, Robert Daglish had laid out much of George Stephenson's Bolton & Leigh Railway. In so doing, he had deviated from Stephenson's planned alignment as the railway approached Leigh. This aroused Stepenson's wrath and he is on record as commenting unfavourably on Daglish's survey.

Was this the reason why Daglish had no locomotive at the Rainhill Trials in 1829? It seems very strange that so eminent an engineer as Daglish was not involved, his home and works being only a few miles from such a celebrated event.

George Stephenson was a self-taught man, but reputed to be of a stubborn nature. He would certainly not have taken kindly to being usurped by a younger understudy however capable!

After the death of Robert Daglish in 1865, his executors sold out to Thomas Waley and partners who were trading as the Norley Hall Company. Under an agreement with the Lancashire Union Railway dated 1st January 1871, the company extended their colliery railway to make an end-on connection with the Lancashire Union about 1/2 mile north of the Lancashire & Yorkshire's line through Pemberton which had opened in 1848.

In 1874, the Norley Hall Co. sank a fourth shaft followed by a fifth in 1881 and it was agreed that London & North Western locomotives would work along the colliery railway as far as No.4 pit provided that the colliery owners kept the line in good repair, for which the latter were charged 1/4d per ton.

As from 1875, the mines had been trading as the Norley Hall Coal & Cannel Company and, from 1887 as a limited concern. However in the 1890s the company was in some financial difficulty, No.4 pit closing in 1896 and the rest by February 1897. In the latter year, Nos.2 & 3 pits at Norley Hall were reopened by S.W.Higginbotham, passing to H.S.Higginbotham in 1906, finally ceasing production in 1914.

Nos.4 & 5 pits at Norley Hall were purchased by Sharrock & Gaskell, also in 1897 and worked in conjunction with their Orrell Collieries (in what is now the Marsh Green area) which had been acquired in 1895.

These particular Orrell Collieries had been worked by Woodcock & Halliburton and later, by M.Hustler and Wm. Brancker, who used the former owners' railway to reach the Leeds-Liverpool Canal. When the Lancashire & Yorkshire's Wigan - Southport line was opened in 1855, a connection was put in - Brancker's Siding - to serve the collieries which confirms that their railway at Orrell had been converted to standard gauge. With the Brancker family as majority shareholders, the Orrell Coal & Cannel Company Limited was formed on 8th July 1875. The venture, however, was not a success and the company was liquidated in 1895.

It is at this juncture that Sharrock & Gaskell acquired Nos.2&3 pits at Orrell and merged with Norley Hall Nos.4&5 pits, becoming The Orrell Colliery Company.

It was now an appropriate time to update the colliery rail system and the old line from the canal, through the former Norley Hall No.2 pit, was lifted (the northern part of Clarke's railway and Daglish's later extension) and a new line built from their Orrell Collieries to a point near the Norley No.4 shaft, thus allowing the company to work to either the Lancashire & Yorkshire at Brancker's, or the Lancashire Union at Pemberton. That the London & North Western (and Lancashire & Yorkshire locomotives via the Pemberton Branch) were allowed to work over the colliery lines to No.4 pit at Norley Hall as per the previous agreement, was confirmed on 24th November 1918.

The mines lists state that No.5 pit at Norley Hall closed in 1924, No.4 pit having closed in 1922. Orrell No.2 closed about 1900, No.3 closing on 20th October 1924, a brickworks opening on the sites in 1925. Whilst Brancker's Sidings on the former Lancashire & Yorkshire Railway were retained to serve the brick works, the sidings agreement regarding the Lancashire Union connection was cancelled in February 1932 and track lifting completed by late November, but no traffic had worked between Goose Green Junction and Norley Hall since May 1926.

Various dates have been given for the closure of the Pemberton Branch; c1946, 22nd March 1947 and 26th November 1947. However, the photograph of the bridge over the A49, ***Plate 143,*** calls all of these into question, given that Land Rovers were not produced before 1949. Also, Bill Paxford's recollections, ***Page 102,*** adds further doubt to previous closure dates. It may well be that access to the branch via Pemberton Junction had ceased by late 1947 and that some traffic was shunted in from the former Lancashire Union at Bryn Junction, perhaps condemned wagons or cripples awaiting transportation. Either way it seems that at least a part of the branch was open longer than previously thought.

Plate 149. Locomotive *Orrell* is seen in 1914 at either Orrell or Norley Hall after the two companies had merged. It is believed to have been built by Haigh Foundry and purchased by Sharrock & Gaskell in 1895. This locomotive is almost identical to *Arthur*, also taken over by Sharrock & Gaskell in 1895, having 11x14 inch cylinders and known to have been built at Haigh Foundry, whereas *Orrell* had 10x14 inch cylinders. *Wigan & Leigh Archives.*

III. WHELLEY JUNCTION TO STANDISH

In 1874, the London & North Western drew up plans for the widening of the North Union lines between Bamfurlong and Standish. South of Wigan these new lines would have been to the east of the existing North Union main lines and quite independent thereof. However, north of Wigan station they would have been alongside the existing lines.

That the Lancashire Union lines offered a much cheaper alternative to what would have been an expensive undertaking is patently obvious and by extensions at the northern end from Whelley to Standish, and at the southern end from Bamfurlong to Amberswood in the form of the Platt Bridge Junction Railway, the Wigan widenings were negated. The Wigan - Standish section has only ever been double track. Golborne Junction to Springs Branch was eventually widened under an Act of 1883.

The northern section of the through route from a new junction at Whelley to a new junction with the North Union at Standish, south of Standish Station, was authorised by the last Lancashire Union Act of 28th June 1877. This has, in other publications, always been quoted as a single line in the Up direction of 1 mile 30.45 chains, and under this Act a sum of £75,000 was to be raised. The contract was let to Holme & King for £44, 986 on 4th January 1880. It is likely that most of this money was spent on a viaduct of thirteen arches and six iron spans which crossed the Douglas Valley at a height of 50ft. The line from Whelley Junction to Standish passed beneath the Boar's Head route.

A burrowing junction for the Down line was authorised by a separate Act granted to the London & North Western on 18th July 1881, opening on 5th June 1882. I have come to the conclusion that this date refers to both Up and Down lines, being entirely concomitant with the opening of Whelley Junction and Standish Junction Signal Boxes, and that the London & North Western Act was an afterthought. Bearing in mind that the contract for the 1877 Act was not let until 1880, it remains a fact that the viaduct as built under the 1877 Act was wide enough for double track and the culvert bridge, as seen for example, in ***Plate 172*** of '9F' No.92008, would also take a double track arrangement. It begs the question, was the 1881 Act put forward to eliminate a double junction at Standish with the knowledge that on completion of the 'Whelley' as a through route off the W.C.M.L., additional lines would be required north of Standish Junction. I believe so; as on examining the details of the 1881 Act at Preston Records Office - PDR\1142 - the portion of the Down Loop to be constructed is shown in red ink on the accompanying Ordnance Survey map included within, and runs only for a distance of 3 furlongs 7 chains 45 links* south from Standish Station to Whelley at approximately the location shown in ***Plate 174***. Therefore the Act of 1877 must have been planned originally for a double track arrangement throughout.

Under an Act of 1888, quadrupling of lines from Standish to Euxton Junction were completed in the autumn of 1895.

* *823.9 yards*

Plate 150. At Whelley Junction on 13th August 1966, Stanier Mogul No.42986 calls for a photo stop whilst working the 'Wigan Area Railfans Society' (WARS) brake-van railtour.

The Signal Box at Whelley Junction, 1mile 829 yards from Standish Junction, was one of the smaller Type '4s' having an 18 lever frame. It was to close on 19th June 1967. This engine, the sole survivor of its class, is preserved on the Seven Valley Railway.

Brian Taylor, courtesy of the Stanier Mogul Fund.

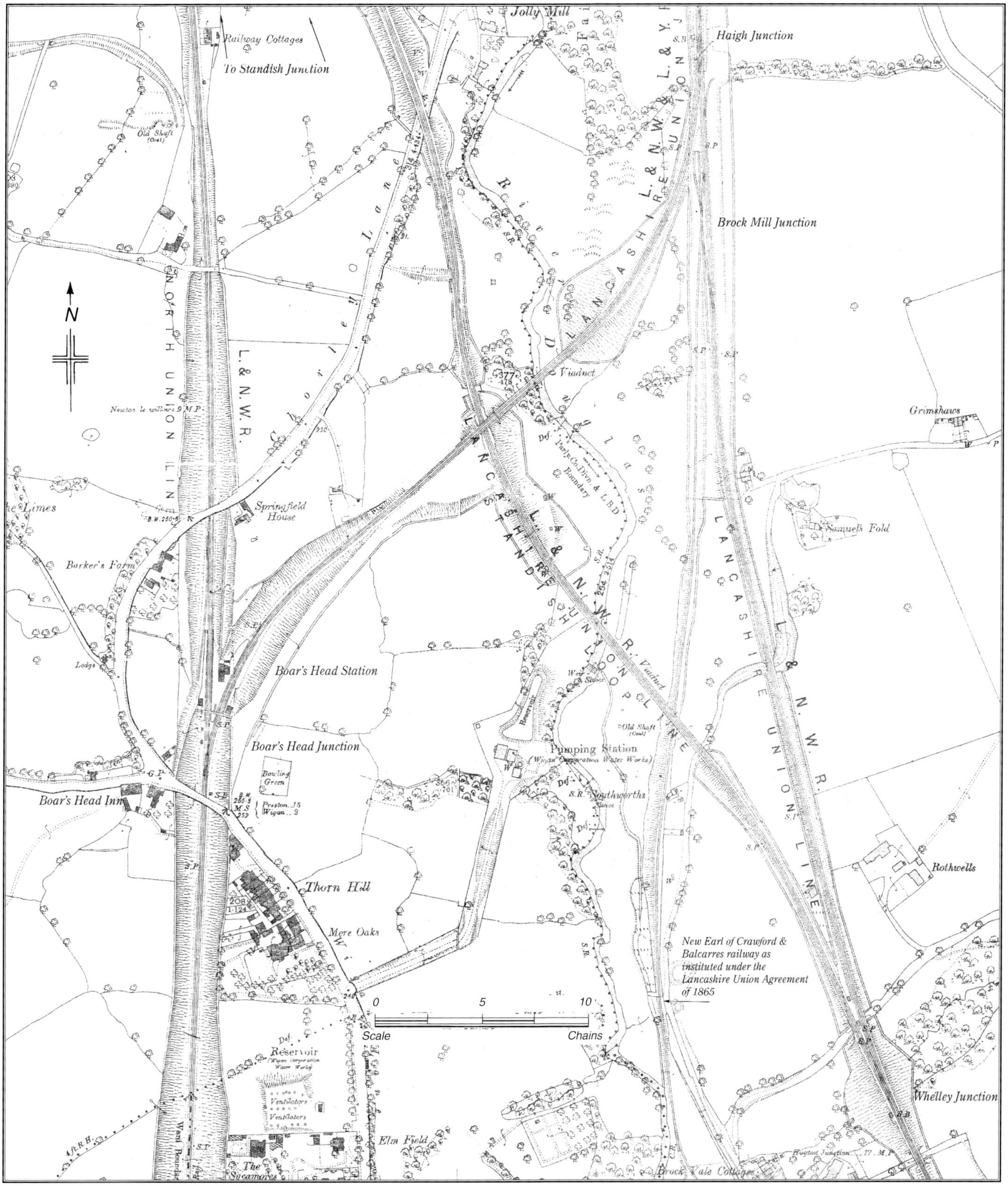

Fig 30. The layout of lines from the second series Ordnance Survey. The joint Lancashire Union/Lancashire & Yorkshire line from Boar's Head passes over the Lancashire Union's Whelley Junction - Standish Junction line instituted under their final Act of 1877.

Plate 151. D342 approaches Whelley Junction from Standish Junction on 8th April 1968 with a van train. Over on the right the abandoned line to Haigh Junction tells its own story. *Courtesy, Kidderminster Railway Museum, John Marshall*

Plate 152. On a gloomy 24th August 1968 the Locomotive Club of Great Britain (LCGB), North West Branch, ran a DMU tour of local lines. The two car unit is seen heading north over the Whelley Viaduct. *Peter Eckersley.*

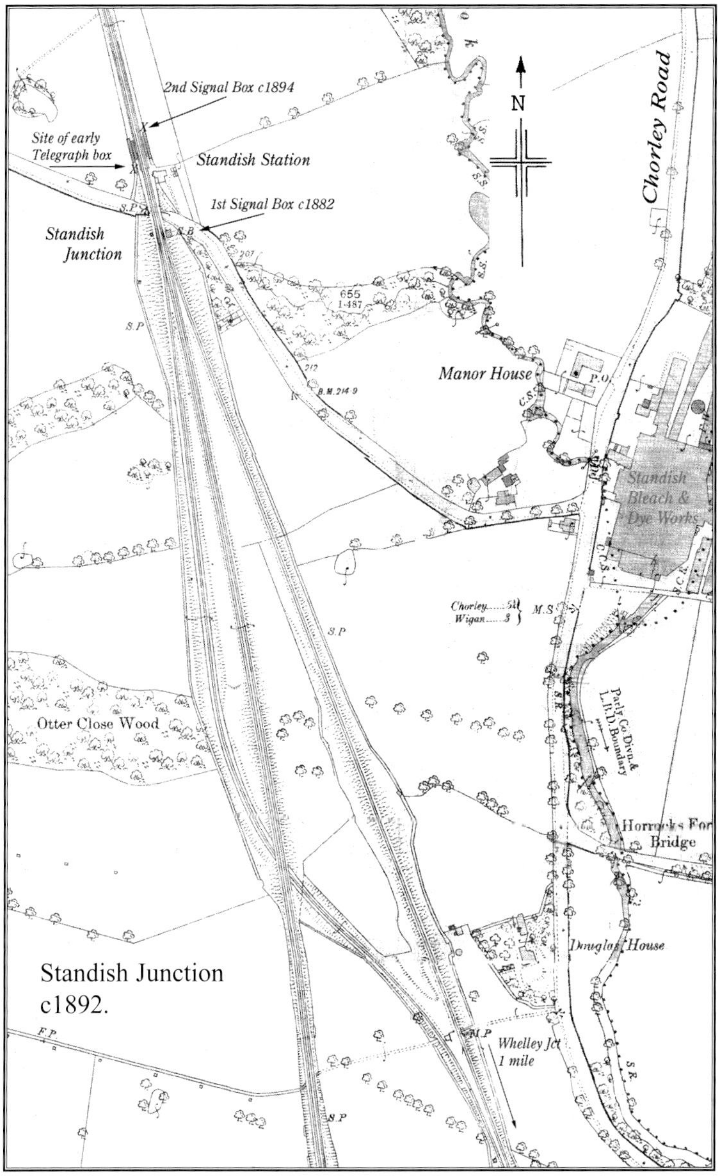

Standish Junction c1892.

Fig 31. The last Lancashire Union Act of 1877, and the London & North Western Act of 1881, had authorised new lines from Standish to Whelley, where new junctions would be made with the existing North Union and Lancashire Union routes. By construction of these lines, and the Platt Bridge Junction Railway's Bamfurlong - Amberswood route authorised in 1883, expensive quadrupling of lines between Wigan and Standish was avoided.

The distance between Standish and Whelley given in the 1877 Act at 1 mile 30.45 chains differs by 160 yards from that given in following appendices at 1 mile 829 yards; exactly 160 yards in difference, due to relocation of signal boxes. It seems certain that the signal box at Whelley Junction, as seen in ***Plate 150,*** is the sole occupant of the post. It is thought that an early telegraph box existed at Standish and appears to be shown on the 1881 plans just south of Standish Station. It is assumed that the original distance is taken from this box. Of the two later boxes at Standish Junction, the first had opened on 5th June 1882 and is concomitant with the opening of the route but was sited further south. This was, in turn, replaced by a second, larger box in December 1894, built at the northern end of the Wigan platform, surviving until 1973. This Ordnance Survey is pre-quadrupling of the lines north of Standish.

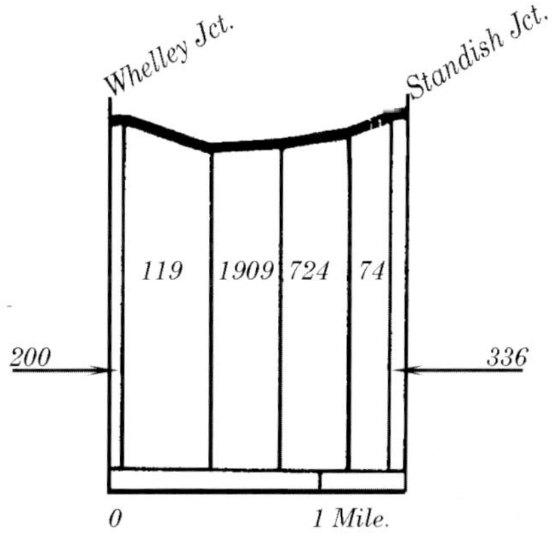

Plate 153. A holiday excursion hauled by an unidentified Hughes 2-6-0 'Crab' traverses Whelley Viaduct about 1960.

Courtesy, Cliff Reeves.

Plate 154. 'Britannia' Class 4-6-0 No.70015 *Apollo*, is about to pass under the WCML en route to Standish Junction on 19th March 1967 with an RCTS special, seen some 6½ hours after starting out from Manchester Victoria at 10.00a.m. *John Ryan.*

Plate 155. Cattle may safely graze on the banks of the River Douglas below the Whelley Viaduct without fear or trepidation from passing trains above! This view looking north east towards Boars Head Viaduct must have been taken around 10a.m-11a.m., as the western side of Whelley Viaduct is in full shadow.

Plate 156. This aeriel view dates from the 1960s. At bottom right is Whelley Junction, the line going off to the right joins with the Boar's Head route at Haigh Junction. The Whelley Viaduct, built under the last Lancashire Union Act of 1877, passes to left of the Boar's Head Viaduct, centre, to join the W.C.M.L. at Standish Junction, running out of picture at top left. The course of the River Douglas was diverted during the construction of the viaduct. The former branch line from Brock Mill Junction to Haigh Foundry, which closed in 1919, is distinctly marked by the line of vegetation which passes beneath the Whelley Viaduct's fourth arch from Whelley Junction. Also of interest is the chimney, upper centre; this is the bleach works at the junction of Rectory Lane and Chorley Road (A5106), recently transformed into housing. Left foreground is Wigan Road (A49). On the extreme left are the remains of Victoria Colliery and, top left, Bradley Mill.

Plate 157. An example of the ex - Lancashire & Yorkshire 0-6-0 Class '27' built by Aspinall in 1889, on the Down Whelley Loop approaching the W.C.M.L. overbridge as seen in ***Plate 154.*** The Up Whelley Loop can be seen in the background. *B.K.B.Green.*

Plate 158. '9F' No.92056 is obviously working hard on the Down Whelley Loop on 23rd September 1967, seen passing below the W.C.M.L. with a through freight. *Peter Eckersley.*

Plate 159. 'Britannia' Class No.70013 *Oliver Cromwell* is seen working a northbound W.C.M.L. passenger train on 4th November 1967 and is about to pass over the Down Whelley Loop.
Peter Eckersley.

Plate 160. An unidentified Caprotti fitted Class '5' at Standish Junction in 1960, with the 'EVEREDS' special to Blackpool from the Midlands area. The Down Loop from Whelley Junction can clearly be seen, right, on the rising gradient as it connects the W.C.M.L. A full array of signals at Standish is also seen in this view. *B.Nichols.*

Plate 161. Type '4' No.D244 approaches Standish Junction on the Down Whelley Loop with a van train on 17th May 1968. Note that the signal arms have been removed from the gantry on the main lines. *John Sloane.*

Plate 162. Stanier 2-6-4T No.42465 is seen on the Down Slow at Standish Junction working the 5.26pm Wigan N.W. - Preston local on 14th May 1951. Note the pill box, extreme right. *B.K.B.Green.*

Plate 163. Stanier '8F' No.48519 is about to take the Up Whelley line with a van train on 29th June 1967. *John Sloane.*

Plate 164. Here's a cracking shot of an original parallel boilered 'Royal Scot' Class 4-6-0 No.6145 *The Duke of Wellington's Regiment (West Riding)* pounding its way through Standish Junction in 1938. In the right foreground is the cross-over for trains working off the Down Whelley onto the Down Fast and, note the station platform also on the right, the station here not closing until 23rd May 1949. L&NW signalling completes the scene. *W.D.Cooper.*

Plate 165. Stanier 'Jubilee' Class No.45684 *Jutland* passes Standish Junction with a Euston - Barrow express on 14th May 1951. This picture gives an illustration of how the Up Slow line crosses over the Down Fast enabling slow freights to access the Up Whelley. Note that the locomotive's tender still has its L.M.S. insignia. *B.K.B.Green.*

Plate 166. Standish Junction box is seen from a passing southbound train on 18th August 1969. Some rationalisation of the track has already taken place here.

This Type '4' cabin opened in December 1894 having a 72 lever frame. It was to be decommissioned on 15th January 1973. *John Sloane Collection.*

Plate 167. D312 passes Standish Junction box having worked 'Whelley' on 13th May 1968 with a Down freight.

John Sloane.

Plate 168. The view through the cab window of a Preston - Wigan DMU on the approach to Standish Junction on the Up Slow line c1968. It is about to cross to the Up Fast line. Again some track has been relocated in preparation for electrification.

John Ryan.

Plate 169. 'Peak' class No.D2 *Helvellyn* is about to take the Up Whelley at Standish Junction c1960. Under the TOPS renumbering scheme this would become 44 002. *B.Nichols.*

Plate 170. Ex L&NWR 'G2A' 0-8-0 No.49025 takes the Up Whelley Loop from Standish Junction in 1957 with a freight and is obviously putting in some effort. *John Sloane*

Plate 171. Stanier Class '5' No.44871 traverses the Up Whelley from Standish Junction on 14th May 1951 with a through fast freight. The houses on the far right are on Chorley Road. 44871, used on the '15 Guinea Special' on the 11 August 1968, has been preserved and is still active on the main line. *B.K.B.Green.*

Plate 172. B.R. Standard '9F' No. 92008, takes the Up Whelley Loop from Standish Junction on 23rd September 1967 working the Up Long Meg to Widnes. Plenty of room here for double track. *Peter Eckersley.*

Plate 173. Ex-L.M.S. Class '5' No. 45279 is but a few yards further south on the Up Whelley Loop also on 23rd September 1967 working an express freight. *Peter Eckersley.*

Plate 174. Type '4' No.381, later 40 181 under TOPS renumbering, is seen on the Up Whelley loop on 24th September 1971. As can be seen, the Down Loop diverges here to pass beneath the W.C.M.L., far left, to rejoin the main lines at Standish Junction. The locomotive had some years life ahead, not being cut up until 1986. *Ian Isherwood.*

Plate 175. On 7th April 1968, a Brush Type '4' in the early B.R. two-tone green livery, approaches on the Up Whelley from Standish Junction with a diversion. The photograph is taken from the elevated Boar's Head route where it passes over the Whelley lines. *Courtesy,Kidderminster Railway Museum, John Marshall.*

IV.THE JOINT LINES: BOAR'S HEAD TO ADLINGTON

At Boar's Head, a junction was made with the North Union's Wigan to Preston line, the former curving away on a north to north east axis where it would meet the Lancashire Union route at Haigh Junction.

That there should be a station at Boars Head was not fully settled until 28th March 1868, and tenders for all seven stations on the joint lines, plus a warehouse at Brinscall, came to £10,677. These were accepted on 25th May 1868.

Abraham Pilling had received the contract for the Boar's Head - Adlington route for £65,836, awarded on 11th December 1866. The station contract at Boar's Head was awarded to Pilling on 27th August 1868, as was the contract for the Ellerbeck branch for £9,000. Contracts for the other two stations on the Boar's Head route, at Red Rock and White Bear, were awarded to Savile & Rosthern. Those stations on the Chorley - Cherry Tree line were awarded to William Hanson.

It was decided, by working agreements of 6th May and 29th June 1866, that the London & North Western would work the passenger trains on the Lancashire Union lines between St. Helens and Wigan, Boar's Head and Adlington, and to jointly work trains to Blackburn with the Lancashire & Yorkshire, whose Wigan to Chorley trains went via Crow Nest Junction at Hindley over the newly constructed route from Hindley to Red Moss. This branch had opened on 15th July 1868 to goods, and to passengers on 14th September 1868. After several inspections of the lines by the Inspecting Officer, Hutchinson, these services began on 1st December 1869.

From 1885, and for the next twenty years thereafter, through carriages were run from Blackburn to Euston via Chorley and Wigan by the London & North Western until re-routed via Bolton and Manchester Victoria. Between 1922 and 1939, a Saturdays only train ran from Colne to Llandudno, also via Chorley and Wigan.

Plate 176. Boars Head Station at the junction with the former North Union line photographed about 1935. The platforms served both the North Union and Lancashire Union joint lines, closing on 31st January 1949. *Author's Collection.*

Plate 177. An ensemble led by 0-6-0 shunter No.12075 passes Boar's Head on the Down line on 20th April 1968. B.R. notes from 12th January state:- 'The facing connection from the Down Main to the Down Branch line to Adlington Junction has been secured out of use pending removal. The Down Main Home and Down Main to Adlington Junction home signals, together with the starting and distant signals for Adlington Junction direction have been taken away. A new facing connection between Up and Down Main lines, 223 yards on the Wigan side of the box has been brought into use controlled by a new ground frame, situated outside the Down Main line 225 yards from the box and released by Annetts key from the box'.

John Sloane.

Plate 178. On 20th May 1967, '8F' No.48648 heads south past Boar's Head with a mixed freight and is seen from an elevated viewpoint on Wigan Lane. *John Sloane.*

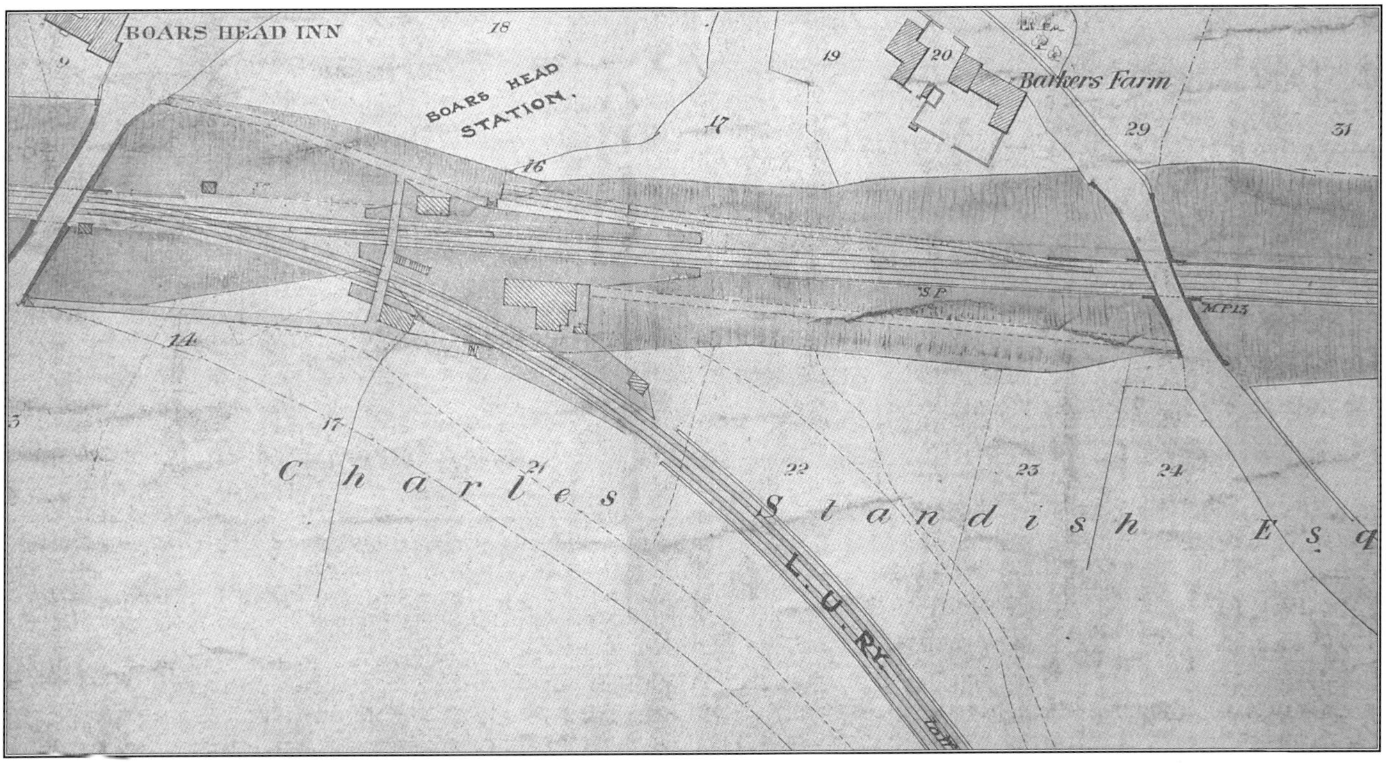

Fig 32. This original 1854 North Union line plan has been updated to include the Lancashire Union Joint line at Boar's Head Junction. An early Telegraph Box, Boar's Head Siding, is listed c1866. A second box, possibly that shown opposite the junction alongside the North Union's Down line, opened following the commisioning of the lines to Adlington. In March 1899, a third box opened here, built in the triangle between the former North Union and Lancashire Union lines and shown in the accompanying photographs. This was a type '4', elevated on a gantry. *Courtesy, John Hall.*

Plate 179. The scene at the former Boar's Head Junction site on 22nd March 2007 as Class '37' No.37 515 heads north on a driver training special. Wigan Lane bridge in the background marks the point of divergence to Adlington. *John Sloane.*

Plate 180. The snow is begining to fall as an unidentified 'Pacific' working the Down 'Royal Scot' passes Boar's Head in the mid 1950s, the locomotive obviously working hard up the bank and is seen to good effect as the hot exhaust gasses meet the cold air.

Author's Collection.

Plate 181. An altogether different view of Boar's Head Station taken on a damp 3rd August 1969 as Type '4' No.D1852 approaches the W.C.M.L with the diverted 10.45 Blackpool - Euston having worked via Chorley. The station had closed on 31st January 1949. The line throughout from Boar's Head to Adlington had closed to passengers on 4th January 1960, except for diversions, closing to all traffic on 5th October 1971.

John Ryan.

Plate 182. A northwards view from Boar's Head Viaduct towards Haigh Junction, the signal box which can be seen upper left is where the route from Whelley Junction comes in. The first signal box at Haigh Junction, probably a Saxby & Farmer type, had opened in 1869. This was to close in December 1897 on the opening of a L&NW Type '4' box having a 35 lever frame, 21 working and 14 spare. This was to close on Sunday 18th June 1967.

Plate 183, below. This is the view southwards back towards Boar's Head. The track of the Whelley Junction - Standish Junction route can be seen on the extreme left hand. *Both, B.R.*

Plate 184. The LCGBs 'Makerfield Miner' special heads north over Boar's Head Viaduct on 24th August 1968. The brick piers of this bridge, at a height of 86 ft above the valley floor, remain intact, a visual testament to the engineering skills required to construct a railway line over the Douglas Valley. The itinerary for this tour was as follows:- Earlestown - Golborne - Bamfurlong Jct, rev., Haydock Branch Jct - Ashton, rev; - Bamfurlong Jct low level - Amberswood Jcts - Whelley Viaduct - Standish Jct, rev; Boar's Head - Adlington Jct, rev; Hindley No.2 Jct - De Trafford Jct - Ince Moss Jct, rev; Fir Tree House Jct - Platt Bridge Jct - Bickershaw Branch, rev; Bickershaw Jct - Howe Bridge East Jct - Hulton's Sidings, rev; Howe Bridge West Jct - Tyldesley, rev; - Leigh - Kenyon Jct - Earlestown - Warrington B.Q., rev; Earlestown.
Peter Eckersley.

Plate 185. Red Rock Station photographed from a passing train on 11th April 1957. The station closed on 26th September 1949, goods facilities being withdrawn on 2nd September 1957. Regular passenger services between Blackburn, Chorley and Wigan ceased on 4th January 1960. A Saxby & Farmer Type '6' box, seen end of platform, was in operation here by the early 1870s. This was replaced in 1899 by a L&NW Type '4' having 9 working levers and 11 spare, seen left. Closure came on Saturday 4th October 1958.
Courtesy, Kidderminster Railway Museum, John Marshall.

RED ROCK

Just beyond the junction at Boar's Head, the Douglas Valley was crossed by an impressive viaduct at a height of 86ft from the valley floor, the viaduct itself consisting of six blue engineering brick pillars on which rest seven wrought iron spans of 55ft. Immediately after crossing this viaduct, Haigh Junction is reached where the line via Whelley joins. At 1 mile beyond Boar's Head, Red Rock Station was reached at approximately 12½ miles from Gerards Bridge Junction. White Bear Station was sited just short of Adlington Junction. The Ellerbeck Colliery Branch, although a part of the joint act, connected with the Lancashire & Yorkshire route between Adlington and Chorley stations

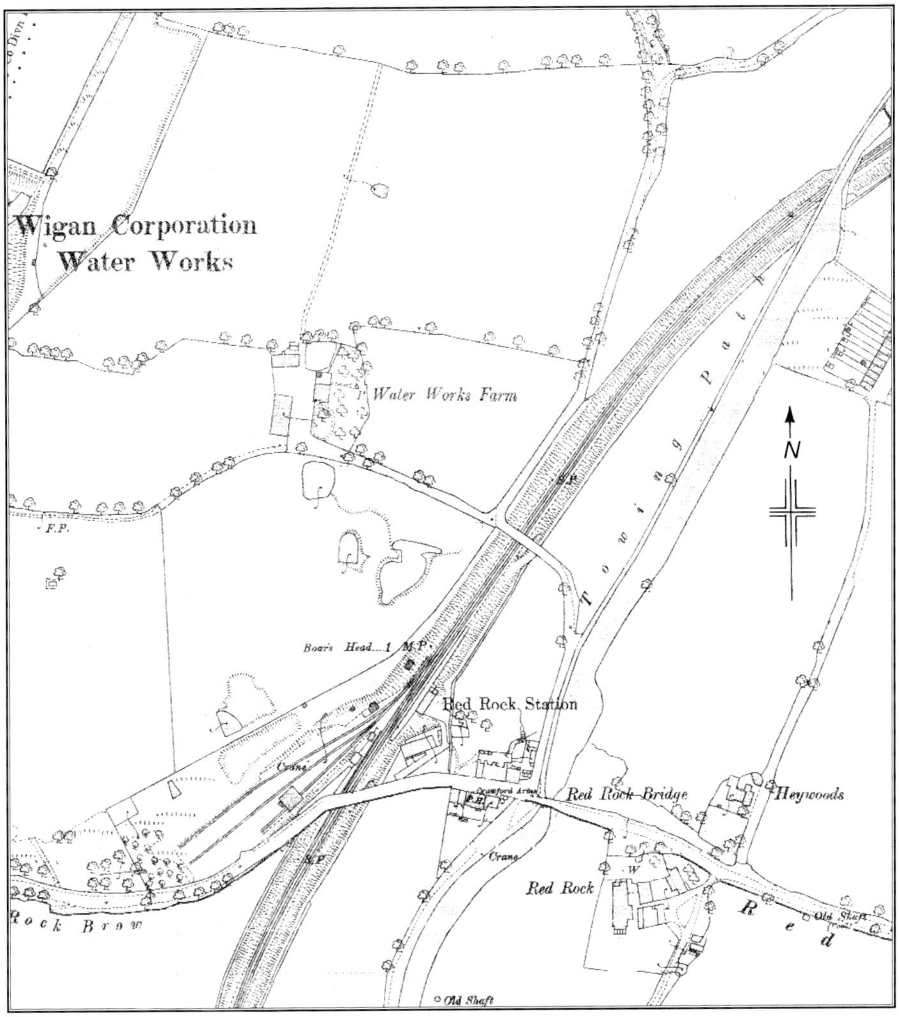

Fig 33. Red Rock Station and the nearby Lancaster Canal are shown on the Ordnance Survey of 1892. Red Rock Lane, the present B5239, passes over railway trackbed and canal, along which bank pleasant countryside walks may be enjoyed.

Plate 186. Just beyond Red Rock the Lancaster Canal passed over the railway and as can be seen from the accompanying photograph the bridge had stone abutments which carried cross-braced girders of considerable depth.

Some 40 years after closure of this route the bridge is worth a look and is only a short walk from the B5239, the impressive masonry as solid as the day it was built.

Courtesy, Kidderminster Railway Museum, John Marshall.

Plate 187. Red Rock Station is viewed from the B5239 overbridge looking north in the 1950s. The bridge in the background carried Arley Lane over the railway and beyond that, out of sight, is the Lancaster Canal overbridge.

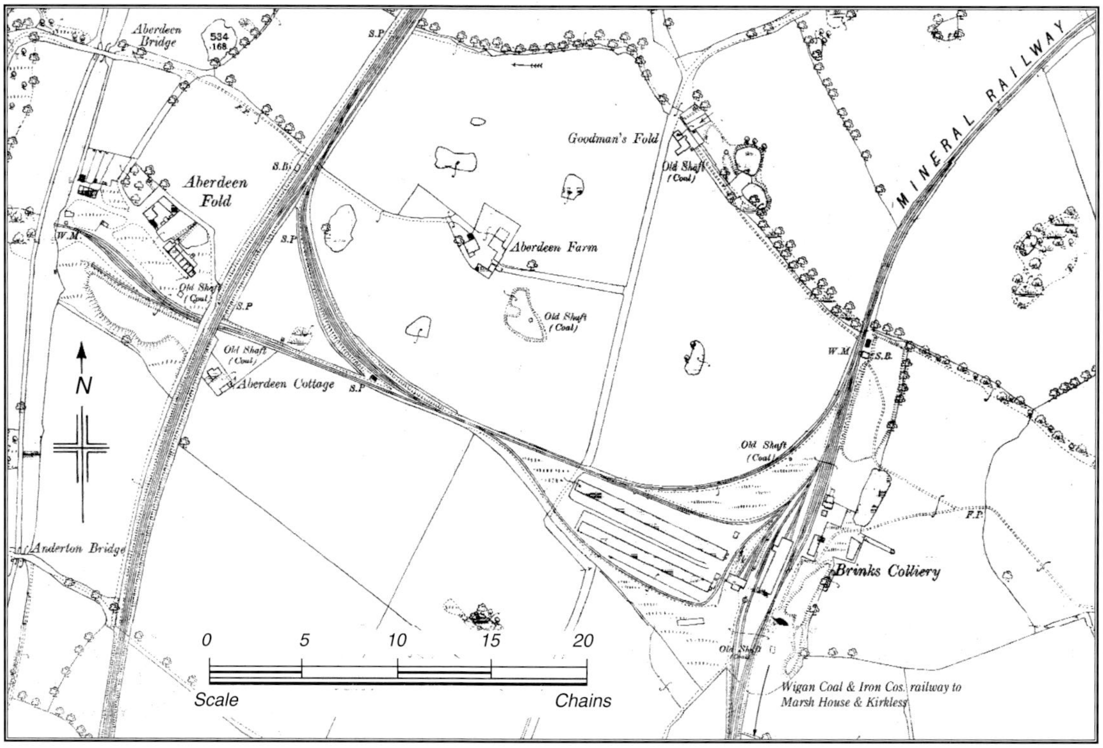

Fig 34. Brinks Colliery & Sidings are shown about 1890. The earlier link to the Lancaster Canal at Aberdeen Wharf is crossed by the main line of railway at its western end. Top right is the Waterhouse Branch to the former Bolton & Preston Railway at Adlington. Running southwards from Brinks Colliery is the Wigan Coal & Iron Co's. railway to Marsh House and Kirkless.

An early signal box at Brinks was replaced by a L&NW Type '4' in 1899.

The Sidings Schedule records that the connection with the Lancashire Union was authorised under the 1864 Act which made provision for the Earl of Crawford and Balcarres to make a junction wherever required.

Brinks Colliery was sited east of the joint line having been established about 1840. In 1845/6 a colliery railway was built running west to a wharf on the Lancaster Canal near Aberdeen Fold. The main lines would have to bridge over this when built and a west to north facing curve connected colliery and main line.

By an agreement of 31st December 1842, between the Bolton & Preston Railway, R.H.Blundell and the Earl, the Bolton & Preston constructed a short branch line - the Waterhouse Branch - from its main line at Adlington approximately 1/2 mile in length, southward towards Brinks Colliery, crossing the Blackrod Estate owned by R.H.Blundell. This, in turn, would connect with an extension of the Earl of Crawford and Balcarres private railway. By this branch, the Earl would work his own traffic to Bolton and Rochdale, in addition to transporting Blundell's traffic.

Workings by colliery locomotives via the Waterhouse Branch to Bolton and beyond ceased about 1860. However, an agreement between the Earl and the inheritors of the Bolton & Preston, namely the Lancashire & Yorkshire Railway, authorised the latter to use Brinks engine shed and work the Earl's traffic to Bolton and further afield. The Earl's locomotives continued to be based at Brinks shed until the formation of the Wigan Coal & Iron Company in 1865, at which point they were based at Kirkless where new facilities had been established for locomotives.

According to the Siding Schedules the connection with the former Lancashire Union/Lancashire & Yorkshire joint line was out of use by 1931, being removed on 20th December 1933. The last working by colliery locomotives off the main line consisted of slack trains for Marsh House Washery. It is believed that the Waterhouse Branch connections with the former Bolton & Preston line were severed about the same period.

The signal box at Brinks Sidings closed between 1933/7 and the block section extended.

The early signal boxes on the route were Saxby & Farmer types, inspected on 21st August 1869. These were replaced between 1875 and 1897.

Signal box locations & line distances, Boar's Head to Adlington Junction.

	Dist to c1933
Boar's Head.	
Haigh Junction.	832yds
Red Rock Sta.	833yds
Brinks Sdg.	1m 693yds
White Bear Sta.	1616yds
Adlington Jct.	431yds

Closure dates

Boar's Head. (3rd box)	1.10.1972
Haigh Junction.	18. 6.1967
Red Rock.	4.10.1958
Brinks Sdg. To G/F	c1933/7
Final closure	1949/53
White Bear.	12.1.1969
Adlington Jct	5. 3. 1972

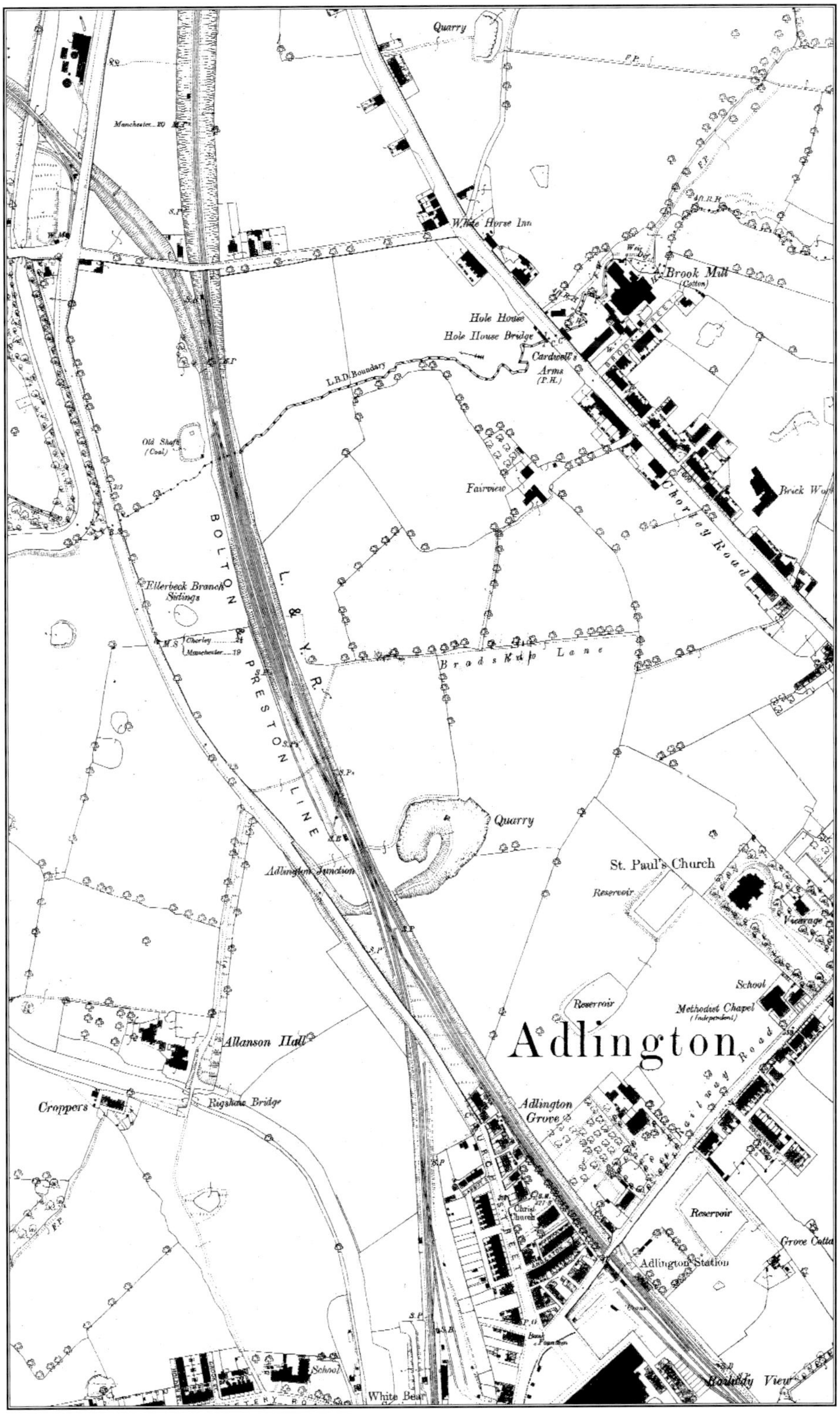

Fig 35. White Bear Station, bottom centre, Adlington Junction and the Ellerbeck Colliery Branch connections and sidings are all shown on this 1892 survey. The first signal box at White Bear is shown alongside the Up platform. This was replaced in 1893 and sited alongside the Down line much nearer to Church Street bridge. Station and Goods Yard closed on 31st January 1949.

WHITE BEAR

Plate 188. White Bear Station is probably better known for its association with the ex-L&Y 0-6-0 Class ' 3F' No.52322, seen here in the old goods yard on 8th April 1961, which had been taken over by Leonard Fairclough. The locomotive had received a 'cosmetic' restoration at Horwich Works and carries a false number plate - 1122, later replaced by No.1300. The locomotive was transferred to Carnforth in April 1976.

Courtesy, Kidderminster Railway Museum, John Marshall.

Plate 189. A view looking towards Adlington Junction on 18th July 1970, the station having closed on 4th January 1960. The route had been reduced to single track the Down line having closed to traffic on 12th January 1969.

On the plus side, the ex-L&Y 0-6-0 has received some rudimentary cover!

Industrial buildings now occupy the site.

John Ryan.

Plate 190. the former waiting room at White Bear, as seen in ***Plate 189***, has been restored into cottage accommodation, the only reminder at this location that the railway once passed this way.

A 15 lever signal box at White Bear is believed to have opened in 1877. This was replaced in 1893 by a L&NW Type '4' having 20 levers. It was to close on 20th March 1965, but actual disconnection did not take place until Sunday 12th January 1969. *Author.*

Plate 191. This view at White Bear dates from pre-Grouping days, viewed in the opposite direction from ***Plate 189,*** that is looking southwards towards Red Rock. The bridge in the background has since been demolished and infilled to allow new roadworks to take place. On the Chorley bound platform, right, is the waiting room, now transformed into a cottage.

Lens of Sutton Association.

Plate 192. Adlington Junction signal box is photographed from a passing Blackburn-Chorley-Wigan train taking the junction c1957. There was a signal box here from 1875, inspected on 27th September 1877 having 15 levers, 13 working and 2 spare. The signal box shown here, an L.M.S Type '11', dates from 1954 and was to close on 5th March 1972.

Courtesy, Kidderminster Railway Museum, John Marshall.

Plate 193. At Adlington Junction on 8th May 1965, Class '8F' No.48535 passes on the main lines with a Brindle Heath - Wyre Dock coal train, the lines to White Bear going off to the right.

B.R. notes of 12th January 1969 state:- 'The facing crossing Down Branch to Down Main opposite the box has been secured out of use pending removal'.

John Sloane Collection.

Plate 194. The scene at Adlington 'Junction' in April 2010, just west of milepost 19. This photo is taken from the extant level crossing as seen in ***Plate 192.***

B.R. notes dated 5th October 1971 state:- 'Between Adlington Junction and Boar's Head the Up line will be taken out of use' and 'the facing connection from the Up Main to the Up Branch will be secured pending removal and associated signal*(ling)* will be taken away. The trailing crossover between the Up and Down Main lines will be secured out of use pending removal'. *Author.*

THE ELLERBECK COLLIERY BRANCH

The Ellerbeck Colliery Branch as planned, was to be some 1500 yards in length, and was intended to connect with the independent Lancashire Union line between Adlington & Chorley as per their original 1863 proposal. In the event, this section of the Company's proposal was not authorised by Parliament under the 1864 Act. Consequently the length of the branch was extended to 1¼ miles and would, instead, connect with the Lancashire & Yorkshire's line north-west of Adlington.

J.S.Perring had been appointed as engineer for the Ellerbeck Branch in September 1867. He also produced an estimate of £330,000 for the joint lines. On 27th August 1868, the contractor Pilling's estimate of £9,000 for construction of the Ellerbeck Branch was accepted.

Construction of the branch proceeded slowly which, apparently, displeased the landowner, Earl Cardwell, and when the joint Lancashire Union/Lancashire & Yorkshire Act of 13th July 1868 came before Parliament the influence of the Earl resulted in a completion date being set under Section 9 of the Act to be no later than 18 months beginning on 25th inst.

The Sidings Schedule quotes an agreement of 13th February 1869 between William Standish Carr Standish and the Lancashire & Yorkshire Railway for a siding some 150 yards long (Standish's Siding) to be built by the railway company at the end of the Ellerbeck Branch. This was, it seems, a 'Quid-pro-Quo' for his support of the company's Blackburn-Chorley-Wigan proposal of 1864. Also, the Lancashire & Yorkshire had undertaken to provide a branch line to Duxbury Park and nearby coalfields.

The branch was reportedly in operation by 29th June 1871. However, the Ellerbeck Colliery itself was not sunk until the mid 1870s. It seems that a number of smaller collieries in the surrounding area of Duxbury Park were carting their coals to the branch for transshipment into railway wagons.The official opening of the branch, according to Lancashire & Yorkshire records, as 6th January 1877, is more in keeping with production from Ellerbeck Colliery coming on stream, as it appears in the mines lists in 1876 under the ownership of the Hilton House & Red Moss Coal Co. Ltd., who used their own locomotives to work the branch free of charge, under an agreement with the railway companies of 30th December 1876.

It seems that Earl Cardwell, his tenants and lessees had been granted rights by the Lancashire Union railway based on the original plan of 1864, whereby the former could make connections with the branch and would be then charged accordingly to the length of line. In the event, being that the amended line was longer, the railway companies had extricated themselves from cartage by quoting the Lancashire Union Act of 1865 whereby the Company were not bound to furnish motive power on the branch! It would now cost the railways 3d per ton to carry the coal over the branch to the main line, against a previously agreed rate of 1½d.

Ownership of the colliery changed hands twice between 1876 and 1879, the Ellerbeck Collieries Company Ltd., formed by 1880. On 20th October 1881, new agreements were made between the colliery owners and the railway companies. Traffic originating on the branch was now charged at 1½d per ton if worked by mainline locomotives. A similar amount was paid by Thomas Whittle's Farnworth House Colliery which had opened in 1877. If, however, traffic was worked by Ellerbeck Colliery engines along the branch to the main line, they in turn received 1½d per ton from the railway companies.

Whittle's colliery, located at the end of the branch, was taken over by the Duxbury Park Colliery Co. Ltd. in 1883, and in 1885 the latter received authorisation to work its own traffic over the branch which came into effect on 1st January 1886.

To avoid conflicting traffic movement over the branch the London & North Western and Lancashire & Yorkshire Joint Committee appointed a pilotman to regulate the traffic of both Duxbury Park and Ellerbeck Collieries. On 29th December 1917, Duxbury Park closed becoming a pumping station for Ellerbeck therefore the pilotman was no longer required.

The Ellerbeck Colliery Company sold out to the Adlington Coal Company in 1928/9. However, in 1932 the colliery was temporarily closed and it is believed at this juncture rail traffic over the branch ceased. In 1933 the colliery was reopened by the Blackrod Colliery Company Ltd, traffic now moving over to road transport which continued from nationalisation in 1947 when the colliery became the property of the N.C.B.

The L.M.S. Traffic Committee authorised removal of part of the branch in January 1936, work being completed in January 1937.

If the mineral train from Long Meg ran at weekend it usually ran as 'Long Meg - Adlington Junction' and was stored in the Ellerbeck Colliery Sidings adjacent to the main lines, seen in ***Fig 35.***

Gradient profile:-
Boar's Head -Adlington Junctions.

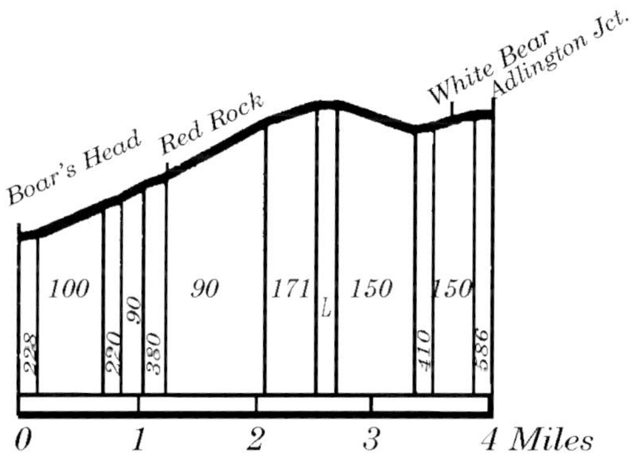

Plate 195. Stanier Class '5' No.45411 is seen approaching Chorley in July 1966 with a Manchester Victoria - Blackpool Central train.
Alex Mann.

CHORLEY TO CHERRY TREE

Chorley and Adlington are located on the Bolton - Euxton Junction route and before continuing with the joint line to Cherry Tree, a brief resume of the Bolton - Euxton route and its origins are as follows:-

The original plan for the Bolton & Preston Railway had been surveyed by the engineer J.U.Rastrick in 1836 and was to be routed from Bolton via Adlington and Chorley to a junction with the Preston and Walton Summit Tramway at its southern terminus at Walton Summit. This tramway had been built to connect the two sections of the Lancaster Canal across the Ribble Valley, opening in 1803 and was to be incorporated into the Bolton & Preston Company, although the latter only followed the course of the tramway for some 1½ miles.

The Bill for the Bolton & Preston Railway was, therefore, presented to Parliament on 10th March 1837, receiving Royal Assent on 15th July the same year. It would make an end-on connection with the Manchester, Bolton & Bury Canal Co's. Railway at Bolton, this line having opened for traffic on 29th May 1838.

The Act as passed, required the canal company to provide the necessary land on the north side of Fishergate at Preston for the railway to be used jointly by the Bolton & Preston and Lancaster Canal Companies and also stipulated that the tramway must be kept open during construction of the railway.

Completion of the Bolton & Preston Railway would reduce the distance between Manchester and Preston by approximately 7 miles, as opposed to the existing route via Parkside and the Wigan Branch Railway (North Union since 22nd May 1834). The North Union raised objections to the Bolton & Preston proposals as the latter's route to Preston from Wigan was then nearing completion. To pacify the North Union, a clause inserted into the Bolton & Preston Act stipulated that construction of the line beyond Chorley could not begin for three years!

Plate 196. Chorley Station looking north from the level crossing on Steele Street controlled by Chorley No.3 box. The former L&Y Goods Yard is on the left.
Courtesy, Kidderminster Railway Museum, John Marshall.

Plate 197. Ex-Aspinall L&Y 2-4-2T No.50850, a 26C Bolton engine, waits to depart from Chorley with the 12.13 Horwich - Blackburn stopper on 2nd January 1960.

50850 was the last working example of the class, withdrawn from Southport in November 1961.

The Transport Treasury, (Alex Swain)

Plate 198. When compared to the 1890s Ordnance Survey, seen overleaf, the railway infrastructure here is but a fraction of what it once was. This photograph is taken from Stump Lane looking towards Chorley Station and the end of the Preston bound platform is in view. Blackburn Junction, giving access to the Cherry Tree route, was situated approximately where the speed restriction sign is positioned. In the left foreground where the caravans stand, was the Lancashire & Yorkshire engine shed which closed in 1922. The lines to/from Blackburn Junction went on the eastern side of these where, also, were more sidings and the London & North Western's goods yard.The latter closed on 4th August 1975, having been a coal depot since 13th September 1965. *Author.*

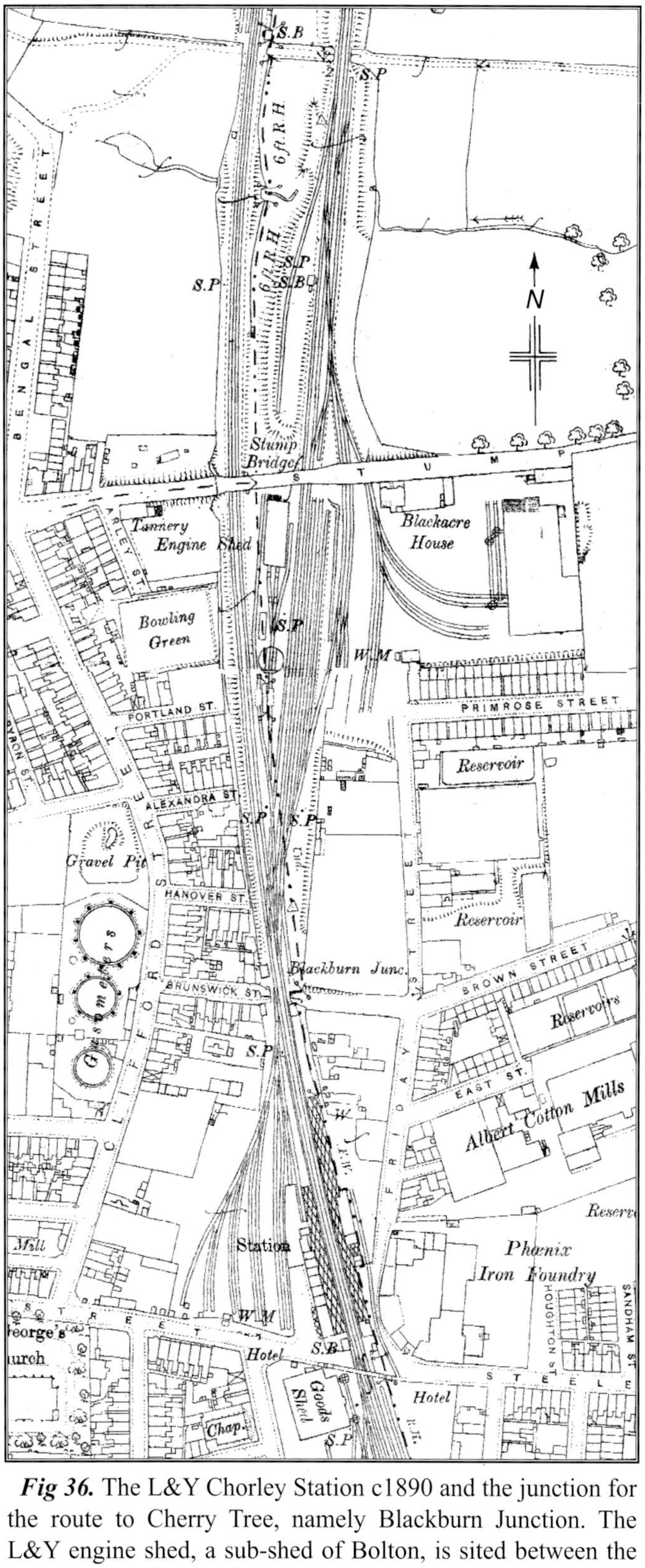

Fig 36. The L&Y Chorley Station c1890 and the junction for the route to Cherry Tree, namely Blackburn Junction. The L&Y engine shed, a sub-shed of Bolton, is sited between the main running lines and the joint lines to Cherry Tree. It was to close after the amalgamation with the L&NW in 1922. The L&NW goods yard is to the right of the engine shed, latterly used only as a coal depot.

A new survey was carried out from Chorley with a view to connecting with the North Union at Euxton. An amended Bill was therefore presented to Parliament on 14th March 1838, receiving Royal Assent on 4th July. Section 17 of this Act repealed the 'three year clause' of the previous Act. The North Union looked upon this plan more favourably as they would gain from tolls charged to the Bolton & Preston Company for use of North Union metals between Euxton and Preston under sections 25-30 of this Act. From Bolton, the new railway was opened to Rawlinson Bridge on 4th February 1841, and to Chorley on 22nd December. After considerable effort to complete construction of the line through some difficult ground west of Chorley, the route to Euxton Junction opened on 22nd June 1843.

Even as the last rails were being spiked, the North Union and Bolton & Preston Railways were at loggerheads over operations between Euxton and Preston, largely brought about by the underhand tactics of the North Union and not finally resolved until 1844 when, in May of that year, the two companies were amalgamated.

On 1st January 1846 the North Union was leased jointly by the Grand Junction Railway and the Manchester & Leeds Railway. However, by the time the relevant Act had been passed on 27th July 1846, the Grand Junction had become a part of the London & North Western Railway.

Under a separate Act of 7th August 1888, the North Union Railway was dissolved, being absorbed by the London & North Western and Lancashire & Yorkshire Railways*. Following on from this, under the London & North Western's Act of 26th July 1889, the route from Parkside to Euxton became the property of the London & North Western; the former Bolton & Preston Railway route from Bolton to Euxton became a part of the Lancashire & Yorkshire, Euxton to Preston remaining in joint ownership. In 1921 the two major concerns were to amalgamate in advance of governmental diktat which saw the formation of the 'Big Four' railway companies, all the lines above becoming a part of the London, Midland & Scottish Railway.

What many thought would be the final 'Act' was played out on 1st January 1948 when the railways were nationalised. All that was undone by the railway privatisation Act of 1993, which took effect in 1996.

* *Lancashire & Yorkshire Railway: successor to the Manchester & Leeds Railway.*

Plate 199. Chorley Station is seen here in the early years of the twentieth century as a trio of station staff pose for the camera. Some ancient stock rest in the Bolton platform awaiting departure.
Lens of Sutton Association.

Plate 200. Ex W.D. No.90281 is seen shunting a wooden bodied wagon near Lyons Lane bridge at Chorley on 23rd May 1967 after working a goods train into the nearby goods yard.
John Sloane.

From Chorley Station, the joint line to Cherry Tree branched off at Blackburn Junction and after a short 1/4 mile declivity began a 1:60 climb to cross the Lancaster Canal by a stone viaduct at Botany Bay made up of nine spans 33ft wide, at a height of 48ft with 4ft 6in thick piers. Total length was 385ft. Stations along the route were at Heapey, Brinscall, Withnell and Feniscowles.

It was not an easy line to construct, having six sections of line between gradients of 1:60 and 1:65 which accounted for 60% of the total route mileage of 7 3/4 miles, taking a meandering course through the pleasant scenery of the locality to reach Cherry Tree.

Some of the embankments were over 80ft high with culverts at 10ft and 18ft diameter to accommodate Stock Clough and Roddlesworth Brooks respectively, which were also at considerable depth beneath rail level. At Blackburn, the London & North Western built an engine shed near to the junction with the Bolton line.

By use of the Lancashire Union and Joint Lines route the distance to Wigan from Blackburn was reduced from 27 miles to 18 miles; Chorley to Wigan from 11 to 8 miles, and St. Helens to Wigan from 13 to 9 miles.

In total, the cost of constructing both the joint lines was £900,000, equating at almost £20,000 per mile of track. (£40,000 per route mile)

Plate 201, *left.* Another shot of '8F' 48750 working the L.C.G.B. brake van special shortly after departing Chorley as the train begins to climb towards Botany Bay viaduct. The railway embankment has been completely removed here. In the foreground, the bridge carried the railway over Harpers Lane. At middle centre, the train will pass beneath the hump-backed bridge which was situated on Thornhill Road. More house building has taken place in the immediate foreground and on the north-west side of Sycamore Road which forms a junction with Thornhill.

Eddie Bellass.

Plate 202, below. As viewed from the bank of the former Lancaster Canal, now a part of the Leeds-Liverpool north-east of Chorley, Botany Bay Viaduct with the mill of the same name, extant, in the background. This viaduct would succumb to explosives on 10th November 1968 to make way for the M61 Motorway. Early signalling notes give a Railway Signalling Co. box here as Chorley Viaduct opening in 1882 and closing in 1888, the exact position of which is uncertain.

The embankment on the right is still in situ and a boat yard carries on its business on the north bank of the canal

Courtesy, Kidderminster Railway Museum,

HEAPEY

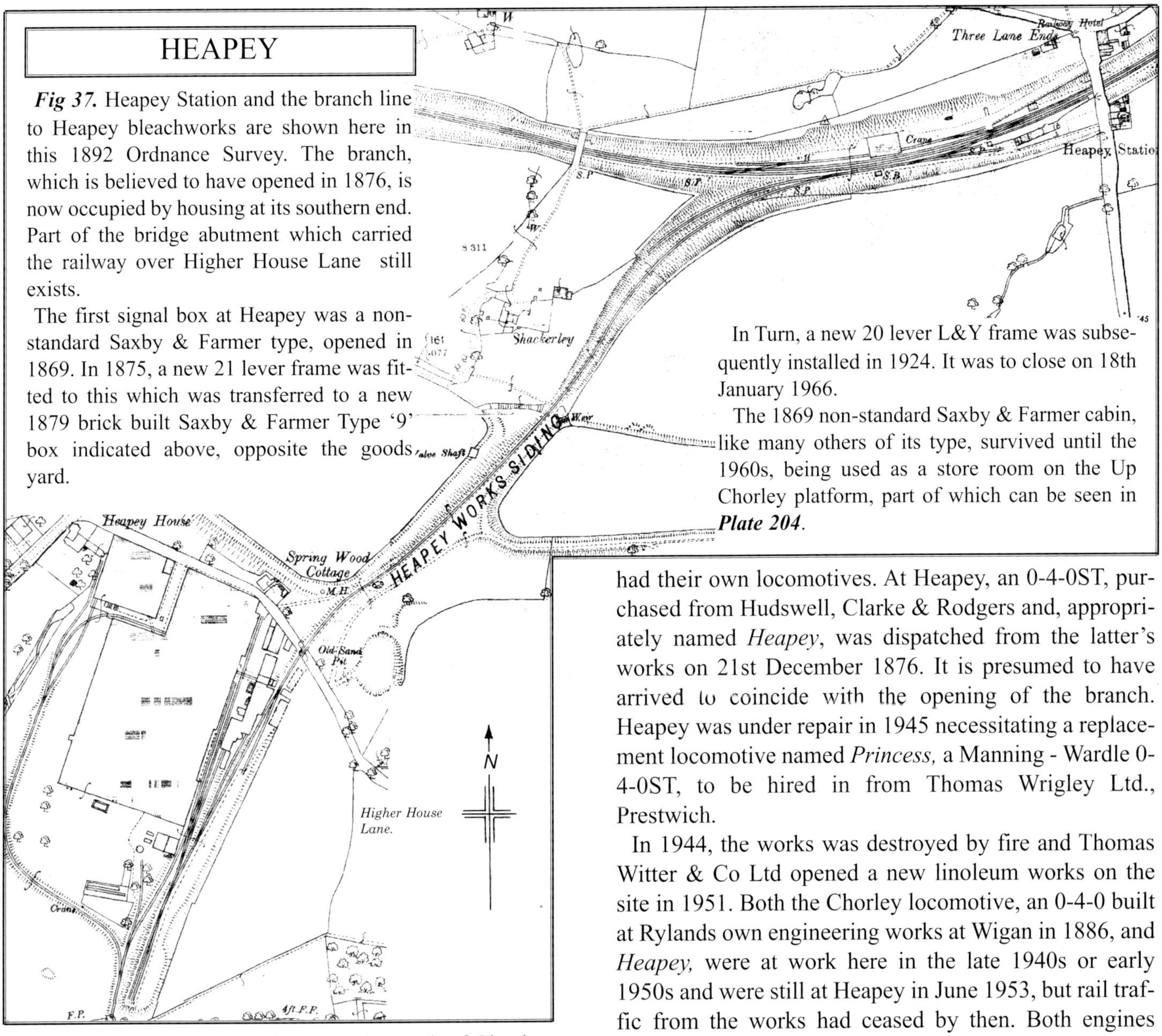

Fig 37. Heapey Station and the branch line to Heapey bleachworks are shown here in this 1892 Ordnance Survey. The branch, which is believed to have opened in 1876, is now occupied by housing at its southern end. Part of the bridge abutment which carried the railway over Higher House Lane still exists.

The first signal box at Heapey was a non-standard Saxby & Farmer type, opened in 1869. In 1875, a new 21 lever frame was fitted to this which was transferred to a new 1879 brick built Saxby & Farmer Type '9' box indicated above, opposite the goods yard. In Turn, a new 20 lever L&Y frame was subsequently installed in 1924. It was to close on 18th January 1966.

The 1869 non-standard Saxby & Farmer cabin, like many others of its type, survived until the 1960s, being used as a store room on the Up Chorley platform, part of which can be seen in ***Plate 204***.

Rylands & Sons had a linoleum works north of Chorley Station. Originally owned by J.Marsden, it had been taken over by Rylands in 1874. By 1884 the works passed to a subsidiary company, the Dacca Twist Co.

In April 1874, Rylands & Sons were granted permission to construct a private branch line to their bleachworks at Heapey. The connection west of Heapey Station was provided by an agreement with the Dacca Twist Co. of 31st January 1877, having been first proposed in an agreement between the landowner, William Standish Carr Standish, and the Lancashire & Yorkshire Railway on 29th January 1864, to secure his support for their Blackburn-Chorley 1864 Act.

The Heapey bleachworks and Chorley linoleum works had their own locomotives. At Heapey, an 0-4-0ST, purchased from Hudswell, Clarke & Rodgers and, appropriately named *Heapey*, was dispatched from the latter's works on 21st December 1876. It is presumed to have arrived to coincide with the opening of the branch. Heapey was under repair in 1945 necessitating a replacement locomotive named *Princess,* a Manning - Wardle 0-4-0ST, to be hired in from Thomas Wrigley Ltd., Prestwich.

In 1944, the works was destroyed by fire and Thomas Witter & Co Ltd opened a new linoleum works on the site in 1951. Both the Chorley locomotive, an 0-4-0 built at Rylands own engineering works at Wigan in 1886, and *Heapey,* were at work here in the late 1940s or early 1950s and were still at Heapey in June 1953, but rail traffic from the works had ceased by then. Both engines were broken up in 1954. The works were closed in 1982 and sold to Wm. Ainscough for storage. Most of the site is now covered by housing.

Signal box locations & line distances c.1960.

Chorley No.4 (Blackburn Jct).	To	
Heapey.	2m	185yds
Heapey Sidings (ROF).		637yds
Brinscall Station.	1m	993yds
Withnell Station.		1410yds
Brick & Tile Cos. Sidings.		1092yds
Feniscowles Station.		1739yds
Cherry Tree Junction.	1m	292yds
	7m	1068yds

Plate 203. A view from a special working on 17th September 1960. After crossing the former Lancaster Canal the train is climbing towards Heapey. Passenger services between Blackburn, Chorley and Wigan via Boar's Head ceased on 4th January 1960, goods services by this route ceasing in 1966.

Courtesy, Kidderminster Railway Museum, John Marshall.

Plate 204. A view at Heapey as an unidentified Stanier tank engine waits to depart with a Chorley bound train composed of three coaches plus one van c1957. As in other locations along this route the Saxby & Farmer telegraph boxes survived, even after replacement by more modern signal boxes, being put to other uses, as in this example here, extreme right, the non-standard box of 1869 which had been used as a store room. The main station building on the Chorley platform has been preserved and incorporated into a much larger residence.

John Ryan.

Plate 205. Heapey Station is seen here in this view looking North-East (towards Cherry Tree) c1957. It will be seen from the accompanying photographs of stations along this route that the main buildings were of almost identical construction, having been built by the same contractor, William Hanson. It is presumed that the stone for these stations was quarried locally, complementing the moorland scenery of the route.

The goods yard here closed on 25th January 1965.

John Ryan.

Plate 206. A present day view at Heapey photographed in the opposite direction to ***Plate205*** from the road-overbridge. The original station building has been preserved and tastefully incorporated into more lavish accomodation. *Author.*

Plate 207, above. At the western end of Heapey station the new owners have constructed dog kennels and a cattery. Having been allowed to view the premises it was found to be pleasantly laid out, complete with lawned areas, beyond which the cuttings of the main lines, and the branch to the linoleum site are still clearly visible. The original cobbled way to the former goods yard has also been preserved and is in good order. *Author.*

Plate 208. The branch line to Heapey linoleum works crossed Higher House Lane by an overbridge. Today, only the northern buttress remains to give any clue to the casual observer that there was once a railway here. *Author.*

Plate 209. In the opposite direction to ***Plate 204,*** but on the same day, a four-coach Blackburn bound train calls at Heapey. The onlookers admire the cameraman's technique. *John Ryan.*

HEAPEY R.O.F. SIDINGS

Royal Ordnance Factory (ROF) Chorley was planned in the late 1930s as a part of Government strategy to expand the capacity of the existing ROFs, the prime object being to disperse the manufacture of armaments and ammunition away from the south of England which would be particularly vulnerable to air raids.

The two largest of these new manufacturing plants, which were known as 'filling factories', on account that they filled the shell casings with explosives, were to be at Chorley and Bridgend. In total, some twenty World War II sites were selected for the construction of filling factories.

As was to be expected, a great deal of emphasis had to be given to safety and various precautionary features were incorporated into their design, construction and general site layout. Reinforced concrete blast walls, surface buildings separated by generous open spaces, high grassed embankments and extensive underground bunkers, all connected by an internal road and railway network. High security fencing surrounded the entire site, some of it electrified.

Chorley ROF was the largest filling factory in the country occupying some 928 acres and at its peak of production during hostilities, employed 28,000 personnel. Security was paramount and for that reason these sites were never shown on Ordnance Survey maps until quite recently. The site even had its own railway station, Chorley Halt, last used on 27th September 1965 when the passenger service was withdrawn.

It was of course realised that the major industrial towns and cities of the North-West of England would be on the receiving end of bombing raids and therefore a storage facility was constructed at Heapey, the site being compulsorily purchased in 1937.

The site, to the north-east of Chorley, was well chosen, the surrounding Pennine Hills offering protection against accidental explosions or the stray bomb. In fact you could probably hide an army here! Train loads of munitions would be transferred from the main production facility at Chorley, most likely carried out during the hours of darkness, away from prying eyes. The rail entrance to the site was north of Heapey Station, but south of bridge 13. Five sidings accommodated the munitions trains before they were shunted to underground bunkers deep into the hillside for unloading.

Plate 210. Photographed in May 1959 are ex-Lancashire & Yorkshire 2-4-2 No.50712 and 0-6-0 No.51546. The security fencing can be seen in the foreground, and on the rising ground, which at the higher level formed the embankment alongside the main lines. *John Sloane Collection.*

Plate 211. This line-up of dumped locomotives at Heapey ROF dates from 22nd May 1959. Working left to right are:- 43890, 52237, 51404, 50647, 51457, 52268, 51415, 52216, 51423 & 51512. *John Sloane Collection.*

Plate 212. The following views at ROF Heapey are taken from the opposite side to ***Plates 210 & 211.*** Ex-L&Y 2-4-2 No.50712 and an unidentified ex-MR '4F' 0-6-0 are seen on 26th December 1959. *Bob Maxwell.*

Plate 213. The ex-L&Y 0-6-0 saddle tanks were rebuilds of former Barton -Wright Class '23' 0-6-0s of 1877 vintage. Again on 26th December 1959 0-6-0ST No.51404 is dumped in front of an ex-MR '4F' 0-6-0 tender engine. At lower level one of the two reservoirs can be seen and whilst these are still intact, they are difficult to see through the proliferating vegetation. *Bob Maxwell.*

Plate 214. Ex L&Y saddle tank No.51512 at Heapey also in December 1959. Note the water tower on the hillside and also the reservoir appearing to be in front of the smokebox but actually at a lower ground level.
Bob Maxwell.

Plate 215. The farmhouse as seen in ***Plate 214*** above, is relatively easy to find but to get a similar photographic angle a bit of tramping about was necessary. The barn, as seen above on the extreme left, is almost a complete ruin but the shell of the farmhouse survives, as does the fencing around it. This shot is from a point near the site gate using a short telephoto lens. *Author.*

Today (2010), there are still visible signs of the site's former use; concrete pill boxes, a typical M.o.D. designed reinforced concrete bridge, miles of security fencing which in places has recently seen repairs, shiny new bolt-heads sticking out like sore thumbs from the rusting W.W.II. ones. Some fencing still has the electrical insulators in place. Two lodges, at lower level than the sidings, are suggestive of an emergency water supply, a valuable prerequisite in case of the foreseeable fire following on from any explosion. The lodges, adjacent to the former rail sidings are separated by a walkway and all seem to be in good order.

Royal Ordnance are said to have abandoned part of the site after the cessation of hostilities and many of the outbuildings were demolished. Some remained and are still in use whilst others are in a dilapidated state.

Intriguingly, at least two, possibly three, of the original four underground bunkers at Heapey appear to be still in use by BAE Systems. Presumably, armaments are still stored here.

Privatisation of Royal Ordnance occurred in the 1990s, at which juncture, the headquarters of Royal Ordnance Plc was moved to the Chorley site, although their registered office remained in London. Some 400 acres of the Chorley site were declared surplus in the early 1990s. Production at Chorley had ceased by 2007 and although some evidence of its former past remains, the new Buckshaw Village occupies much of the site. A new railway station, Buckshaw Village, is scheduled to open on the old Chorley Halt site.

The sidings at Heapey and connections to the main lines were also kept intact, and in the late 1950s were used to store redundant locomotives, a sort of overspill dump from Horwich Works where space was at a premium. The first engines are reported to have arrived in December 1958, being removed by 20th October 1960, except, that is, for Stanier 2-6-2T No.40178, which was not officially withdrawn from service. It was still in the sidings on 23rd June 1961.

The following is a list of engines known to have been stored at Heapey but may not be complete.

Ex-LMSFowler 3P 2-6-2T. Nos.40061 & 40068.

Ex-LMSStanier 3P 2-6-2T No.40178.

Ex MR Johnson 3F 0-6-0 Nos.43398, 43538, 43660, 43711 & 43753.

Ex MR Fowler 4F 0-6-0 Nos.43890 & 43984.

Ex L&Y Aspinall 2P 2-4-2T Nos.50643, 50644, 50705 & 50712.

Ex L&Y Aspinall 2F 0-6-0ST (rebuilds of Barton-Wright Class 23 of 1877) Nos.51316, 51404, 51415, 51423 ,51457, 51512.

Ex L&Y Aspinall 1F 0-6-0T No. 51546.

Ex L&Y Aspinall 3F 0-6-0 Nos.52120, 52216, 52237, 52360, 52387, 52427 & 52432.

At least half of those engines as listed here were scrapped at Central Wagon Co., Ince.

Plate 216.This is a south-easterly view at Heapey on 22nd May 1959. Out of shot on the right was the gated entrance to the ROF site and the main line ran on the far side of the embankment which rises in height from south to north and topped by a stone wall. The line to the bunkers can be seen between security fencing and the locomotives. Left to right are:- 52268, 51415, 52216, 51423 & 51512. *John Sloane.*

Plate 217. A view looking towards Heapey Station with the ROF Sidings entrance on the right. From here, a long head-shunt ran towards the distant overbridge which is that seen when looking north-east from Station Road, Heapey. *Author.*

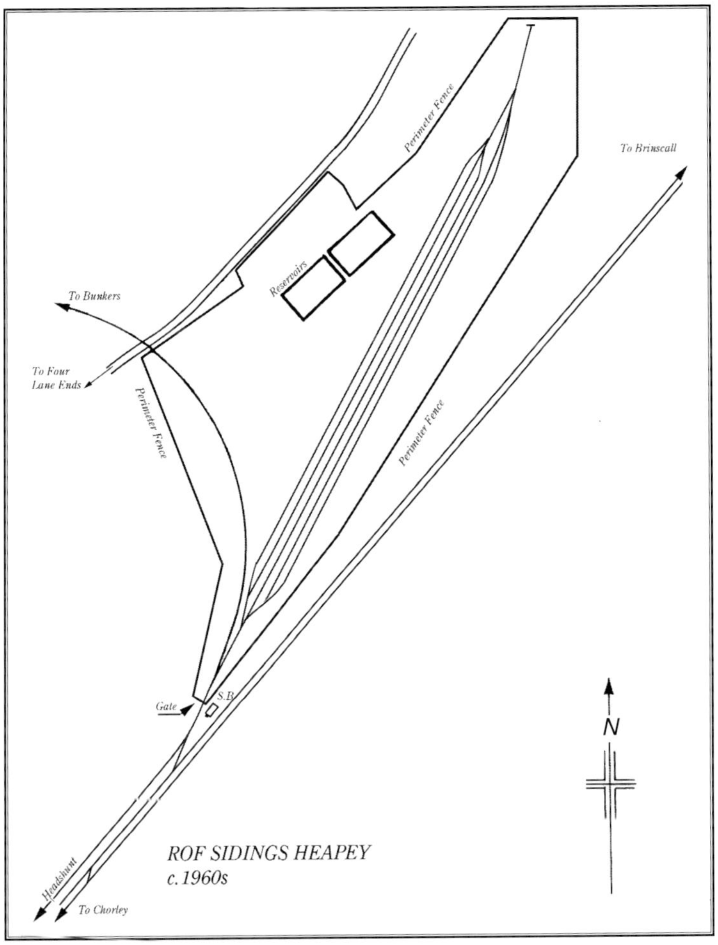

Fig 38. R.O.F Sidings, Heapey about 1960. The length of sidings were approximately 350 yards from the gate. Between the sidings and the main lines an embankment, wider and higher at its northern end than the south, shielded viewing from passing trains and also accounts for the angle of alignment. As traffic entered the site through the gate a north to west curve allowed the loaded vans to be shunted towards the underground bunkers for unloading and storage, the empty vans then shunted in reverse back through the gate into a long headshunt and propelled into the sidings awaiting return to Chorley. The headshunt ran southwards for some 280 yards, ending on the northern side of an occupation bridge near the Station Hotel.

In 1938, a 'new' signal box was installed at the gate entrance to control the ROF traffic, some 637 yards north-east of Heapey Station. In fact, it was not new at all, having come from a previous location on the Lancashire & Yorkshire lines, possibly from Dunlop Sidings, Castleton and fitted with a 16 lever frame. It was to close on 1st October 1967.

Fig 39, Below. To the north of Heapey R.O.F. was Woods Sidings, alongside the Up, Chorley line. Here a Gloucester Wagon Co. signal box was built having 14 levers, opening in 1879. Evidently, in its early days it had served the local gas works. In 1925, a new L&Y frame having 12 levers was fitted to this box. During W.W.II. the sidings were used by the M.o.D. for non-munitions storage. The box closed in 1956.

Plate 218. This is the entrance to the former ROF Sidings c2010. The gates have long gone but the metal posts from which they were hung still remain in situ. These and the trackbed are viewed in a northwards direction towards bridge No.13. The signal box was situated on the railway side of the gate here, alongside the Down line. *Author.*

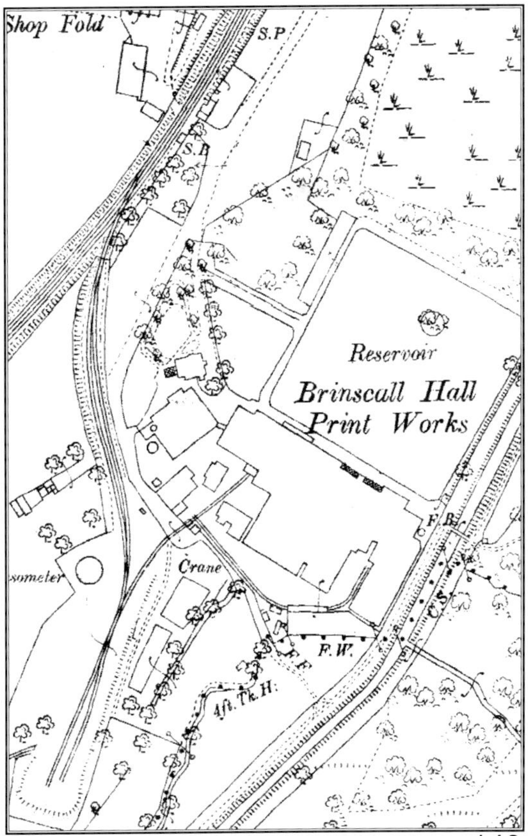

BRINSCALL

Plate 219. Brinscall Station as viewed towards Withnell. Here, the main station buildings were on the Up, or Chorley platform. Nothing of the station or line remains here to give any indication that a railway once passed by, the buildings long since demolished and the bridge and associated embankments which carried the railway over School Lane having been swept away and new housing built upon the lowered trackbed adjacent to School Lane with a meandering footpath running North-Eastwards.

John Ryan.

Plate 220. A close up view of the main station buildings at Brinscall c1912 with some period Lancashire & Yorkshire advertising for the Continent on the gable end. The station clock, in the window next to the lamp says 4.30p.m., a moment in time frozen in perpetuity. Two staff pose for the photographer as, presumably, a couple of locals lurk in the doorway! *Lens of Sutton Association.*

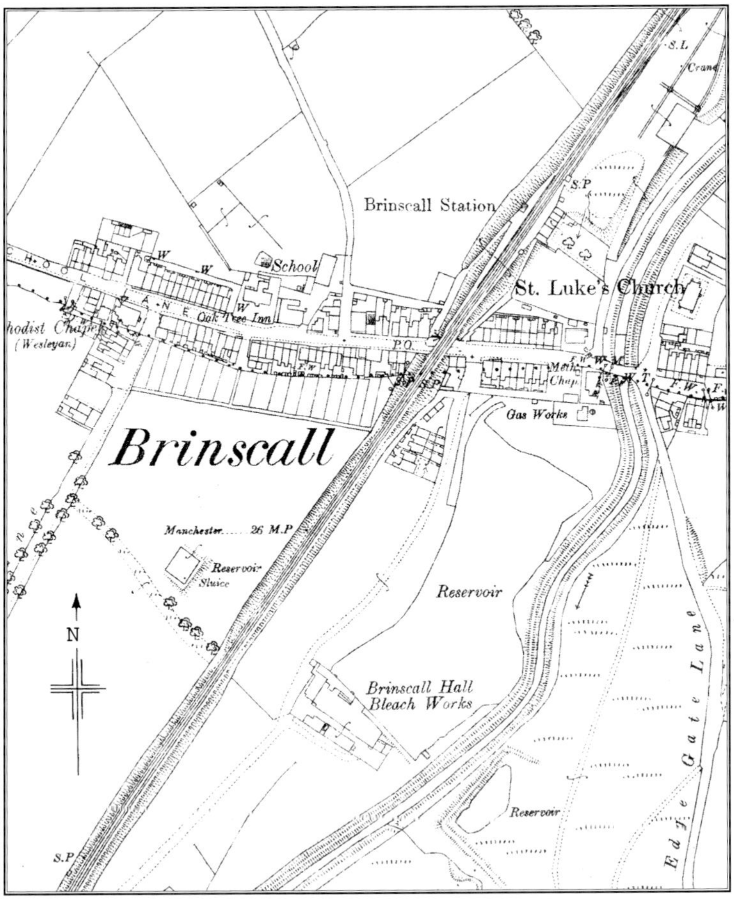

Fig 40. Brinscall rom the second series Ordnance Survey. School Lane is prominent running left to right across picture. The goods yard at Brinscall closed on 4th January 1961 but traffic to private sidings continued a little longer.

Plate 221. An unidentified Blackburn service, possibly hauled by Stanier 2-6-4T No.42544, arrives at Brinscall Station c1957. *John Ryan.*

Plate 222. A wider angled view of Brinscall Station in the South-West direction towards Chorley. The steepness of Brinscall Bank is obvious and the heavier freight trains or passenger excursions would have a bank engine attached to assist. Note that the distant arm has been removed from the Up line signal post near School Lane bridge.

Brinscall originally had a non-standard Saxby & Farmer box, opened in 1869. On Sunday 22nd February 1874 this was replaced by a Saxby & Farmer, brick built, Type '6' cabin having 20 levers. Rather late in the day, a BR/LMR Type '15' box opened in 1958, also having 20 levers. This was to close on Sunday 1st October 1967. *John Ryan.*

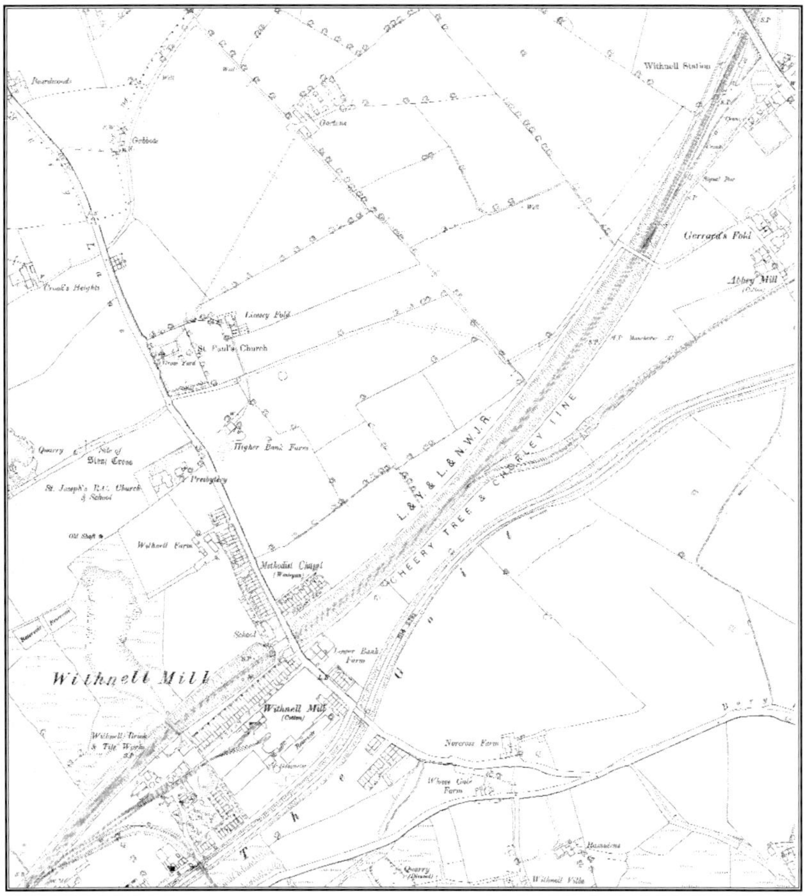

WITHNELL

Fig 41. Withnell Mill and sidings were just beyond Brinscall, and nearer to the latter than to Withnell. At first glance, one could be forgiven for thinking that Withnell should have been named Abbey Village being sited close to it. However, the parish boundary clearly shows that the railway company correctly named the station as it is just inside the boundary line. Abbey Mill Sidings, between Brinscall and Withnell, appear to have been operated by a Saxby & Farmer 2 lever ground frame, opened in 1878 which remained in situ until closure of the sidings in1954. Withnell Brick & Tile Co's Sidings would later be re-sited between Withnell and Feniscowles with connections off the Down line.

Plate 223, below. This view at Withnell is said to be c1912, and a first look gives the impression of it being earlier but for one factor, the poster for the White Star Line on the platform depicting a four funnelled liner - Titanic or sister ship? The fencing on the perimeter, station platforms and goods yard look to be in immaculate condition, as though it was put up the week before. There are at least two identifiable L&NW wagons in a yard full of traffic.

Lens of Sutton Association.

Plate 224 . Withnell Station in Post-Grouping days with L.M.S. and private owner wagons in the yard, one of which is possibly C.W.S. Withnell Station was also provided with a Saxby & Farmer non-standard signal box in 1869, seen here on the Up Chorley platform. It was still in situ c1960. In 1879, a new Gloucester Wagon Co., 18 lever box was opened here and is seen at the far end of the goods yard. A new L&Y 16 lever frame was fitted to this in 1927, surviving until closure of the cabin on Tuesday 13th October 1962. *Lens of Sutton Association.*

Plate 225. A second shot of Aspinall L&Y 2-4-2T No.50850 at Withnell with the 12.13 Horwich - Blackburn train on 2nd January 1960. The period gas lamp to the right adds photogenically to the scene.
The Transport Treasury, (Alex Swain).

Plate 226. Withnell Station has been lovingly preserved in its original state having been purchased by the owner from British Rail in 1969. *Author.*

A visit to Withnell Station in April 2010 was to reveal a pleasant surprise. The former station buildings are still intact, along with up and down platforms which, although grassed over, all of the edge stonework remains and is in excellent condition. I and my associates were kindly shown around site by the owners on a beautiful spring day. We would not have needed much persuasion to linger awhile.

For many years a narrow gauge railway was in operation around the site and it was often a full time job keeping the visitors supplied with tea and biscuits whilst the railway engines ran round the circuit, carried over the old trackbed by specially constructed miniature bridges between the platforms.

On the northern edge of the property a bridge of stone and girder construction carried the main road over the railway. The powers that were tried to persuade the then prospective purchasers to buy the trackbed over which it spanned, as well as the station site. You would have had to be a shilling short of a pound to agree to that and my guess is that in the not too distant future it will need expensive repair. At the southern end of the station the trackbed is walkable, a part of Withnell Nature Reserve, and has been well set out with informative photographs and text on entering the reserve.

I have withheld the owners name for obvious reasons and would urge any enthusiasts to respect their privacy and not to trespass on the property.

Plate 227. This is the bridge mentioned in the text, ***Page 154.*** It has been rusting away since closure of the route and bits of it often come loose and drop off. The stonework, however, is still sound. *Author.*

Plate 228. Stanier Class '8F' No.48756 climbs the bank near Withnell with a mineral train from Huncoat to Bamfurlong on 27th May 1964. The banker is 'Crab' No.42722. *Courtesy, Kidderminster Railway Museum, John Marshall.*

FENISCOWLES

Plate 229. Feniscowles Station about 1957 showing the main station buildings and beyond these the goods shed. Goods facilities remained operative here until closure of the route itself on 22nd April 1968. The former goods yard site is now a caravan park.

John Ryan.

Fig 42, below. Feniscowles station and goods yard are shown from the second series Ordnance Survey. Distance to Cherry Tree Junction was 1 mile 292 yards.

Plate 230. This impressive viaduct carried the railway between Feniscowles and Cherry Tree over the A674 and remains a testament to the stone masons art.

Author.

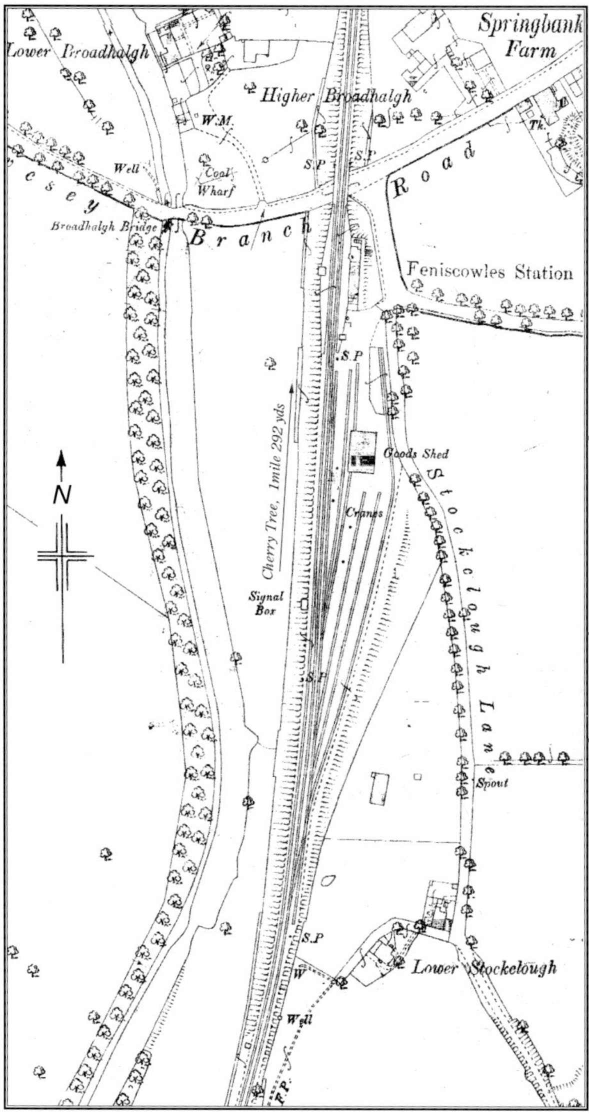

Plate 231. On the Blackburn or 'Down' platform the buildings were of timber and at least provided shelter from the driving rain and gales which could be quite strong in this exposed location.

The first signal box at Feniscowles was, again, a non-standard Saxby & Farmer type opening in 1869, serving what was to become a busy goods yard. In 1879 this was replaced by a Gloucester Wagon Co., all timber, 18 lever cabin until 1st October 1927, at which date a new L&Y 16 lever frame was fitted, finally closing on Sunday 1st October 1967. It is seen in ***Plate 232,*** below. *John Ryan.*

Plate 232. Although Chorley to Cherry Tree closed as a through route on 3rd January 1966, Feniscowles - Cherry Tree remained open until 22nd April 1968. In the intervening period, 'Britannia' Class 4-6-2 No.70015 *Apollo* traversed the soon to close section with the Railway Correspondence and Travel Society (R.C.T.S) *Lancastrian Railtour* which had left Manchester Victoria at 10.a.m., arriving Feniscowles about 13.00 where the participants had a short break allowing the opportunity to photograph a big 'Pacific' in unusual surroundings. The tour still had a good mileage to cover before arriving at Manchester Piccadilly only 10 minutes down at 17.44 after running almost 169 miles. *Apollo* is seen running round before departing for Blackburn. The locomotive appears to be in excellent condition and was worked with gusto by the Newton Heath and Lostock Hall crews. The signal box also appears to be well maintained but the rusting trackwork and single wagon in the goods shed tell their own story. *John Ryan.*

Plate 233. Another R.C.T.S. special 'The Rebuilt Scot Commemorative Railtour' hauled by Class '5' No.44822 and 'Royal Scot' No.46115 *Scots Guardsman,* had traversed the branch on 13th February 1965 and are seen here approaching Cherry Tree.The special will run parallel with the Preston-Blackburn route before joining the latter at Cherry Tree Junction just before the station. The train should have been hauled by sister engine No.46160 *Queen's Westminster Rifleman* which had been failed after running a hot axle earlier in the week. The tour also allowed a visit to Hellifield shed to view a number of locomotives which were a part of the National Collection. Upper right, the footbridge has been replaced with a more modern concrete construction from where the recent photograph below is taken. Housing development has swallowed up all the land on the right. *Bob Maxwell.*

Plate 234, below. The junction at Cherry Tree was west of the station, that is on the Preston side and for a couple of hundred yards the main Preston - Blackburn, and the branch lines, ran side-by-side, the branch from Chorley turning east towards Cherry Tree just beyond the footbridge seen in ***Plate 233*** above, approximately where the iron fencing is on the left. On 4th August 2010, Stanier '8F' is seen hauling the outward leg of 'The Fellsman' railtour from Lancaster via Hellifield to Carlisle. *Ian Pilkington.*

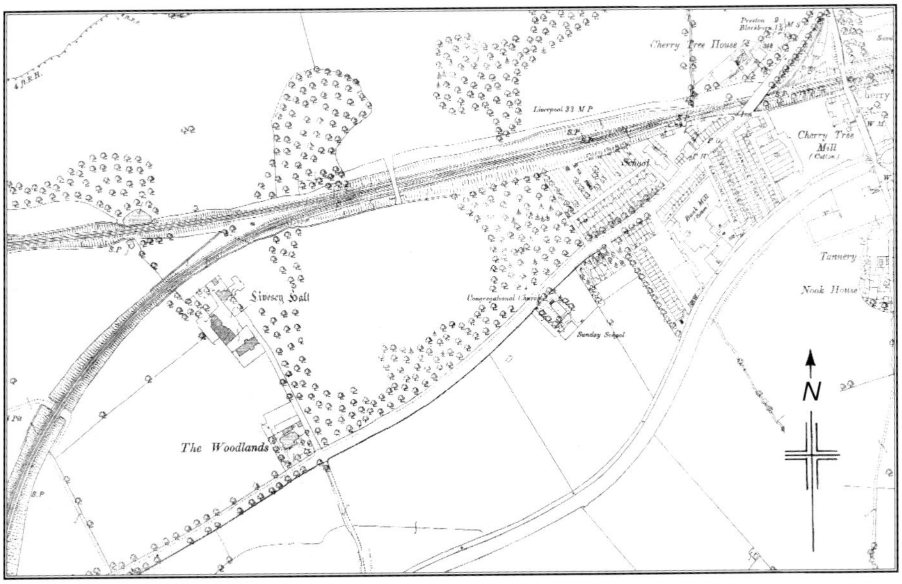

Fig 43 . The junction at Cherry Tree with the Blackburn - Preston line c1892. The branch lines and main Preston-Blackburn lines can be seen to converge on the Preston side of Cherry Tree Station.

Plate 235. And, finally, the L.C.G.B. Brakevan Special of 4th April 1964 hauled by '8F' No. 48750, has arrived at Blackburn, the end of the line as far as the participants were concerned. Nevertheless, this was a unique trip, taking in scenes of industry now long gone and some very pleasant country-side en route. In those days, brakevan trips for the enthusiast were not uncommon but to be allowed on a scheduled freight working was something else. *Eddie Bellass.*

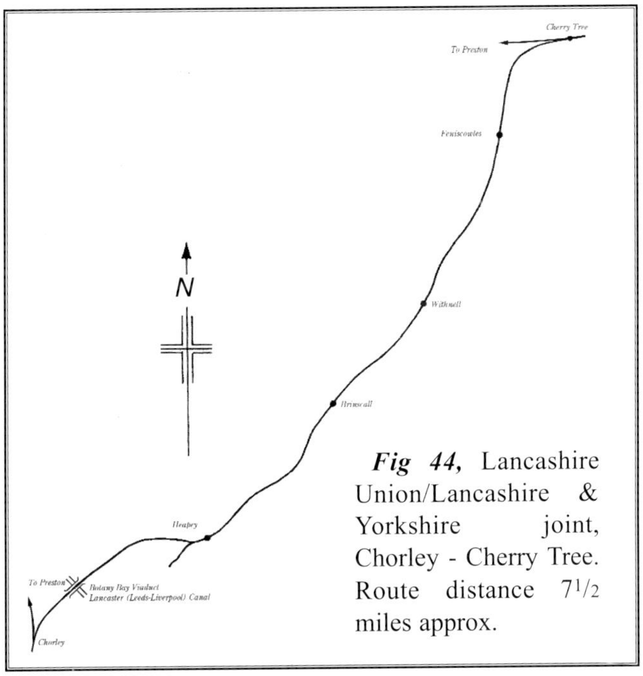

Fig 44, Lancashire Union/Lancashire & Yorkshire joint, Chorley - Cherry Tree. Route distance 7½ miles approx.

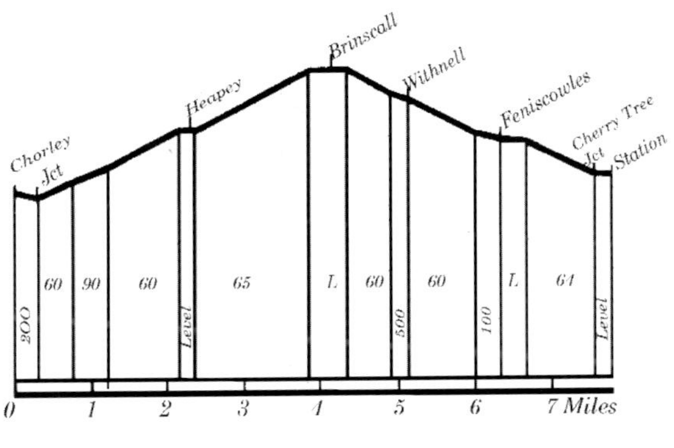

Left, Gradient Profile, Chorley - Cherry Tree. The highest point on the route was Brinscall at 588 feet. The railway then descended 249 feet in 3½ miles to Cherry Tree Junction. In the opposite direction, descent was almost 300 feet to Blackburn Junction at Chorley.

EXTRACTS FROM WORKING TIME TABLES

L&NW Northern Division July 1885:- Wigan Coal & Iron Co. engines

Lindsay Sidings	6.45am	10.30am
Brinks Colly Sidings	7.05am	10.45am
Adlington Jct (L&Y)	7.15am	10.50am
Adlington Jct (L&Y)	7.40am	11.40am
Brinks Colly Sidings	8.10am	11.50am
Lindsay Sidings	8.25am	12.05pm

Harry Townley

L&NW Northern Division 2/1892 & 5/1892:- Wigan Coal & Iron Co. engines

Lindsay Sidings	6.46am	1.45pm	
Whelley Jct	6.50am	1.50pm	
Haigh Jct	6.59am	1.56pm	
Brinks Colly Sidings	7.00am	2.00pm	
Adlington Jct L&Y	7.05am		
Adlington Jct L&Y	7.40am		
Brinks Colly Sidings	8.15am	11.55am	2.45pm
Haigh Jct	8.23am	12.03pm	2.48pm
Whelley Jct	8.27am	12.05pm	2.50pm
Lindsay Sidings	8.32am	12.10pm	2.55pm

John Ryan

L&NW Northern Division July 1906:- Wigan Coal & Iron Co. engines

From Kirkless	11.00am	4.30pm
Rose Bridge Jct	11.03am	4.32pm
Lindsay Sidings	11.09am	4.40pm
Lindsay Sidings	11.25am	6.10pm
Rose Bridge Jct	11.32am	6.18pm
	To Kirkless	To Kirkless
Lindsay Sidings	6.46am	1.30pm
Whelley Jct	6.50am	1.35pm
Haigh Jct	6.59am	1.40pm
Brinks Colly Sidings	7.25am	1.45pm
Adlington Jct (L&Y)	7.32am	
Adlington Jct (L&Y)	7.40am	
Brinks Colly Sidings	8.15am	11.55am
Haigh Jct	8.23am	12.03pm
Whelley Jct	8.27am	12.05pm
Lindsay Sidings	8.32am	12.10pm

Harry Townley

LNWR Northern Division 12.7 to 30.9.1913 Wigan Coal & Iron Co. Engines

From Kirkless	11.00am	4.30pm
Rose Bridge Jct	11.15am	4.32pm
Lindsay Siding	11.20am	4.40pm
Lindsay Siding	11.35am	6.10pm
Rose Bridge Jct	11.40am	6.18pm
	(To Kirkless)	
Lindsay Siding	1.30pm	
Whelley Jct	1.35pm	
Haigh Jct	1.40pm	
Brinks Colly Sdg	1.45pm	
Brinks Colly Sdg	11.55am	2.50pm
Haigh Jct	12.03pm	3.00pm
Whelley Jct	12.05pm	3.05pm
Lindsay Siding	12.10pm	3.10pm

John Ryan

L&NW Northern District October 1922 Wigan Coal & Iron Co. engines

Kirkless	4.30pm	
Rose Bridge Jct	4.32pm	
Lindsay Sidings	4.40pm	
Lindsay Sidings	11.35am	6.10pm
Rose Bridge Jct	11.40am	6.18pm
	To Kirkless	To Kirkless
Brinks Colly Sdg	11.55am	2.50pm
Haigh Jct	12.03pm	3.00pm
Whelley Jct	12.06pm	3.06pm
Lindsay Sidings	12.10pm	3.10pm

Harry Townley

LMSR WTT 7th July To 21st September 1930 Wigan Coal & Iron Co. engines

Lindsay Sidings	11.35am	2.50pm
Rose Bridge Jct	11.40am	6.18pm
	Minerals to Kirkless	
Brinks Colly Sdgs	11.55am	2.50pm
Haigh Jct	12.03pm	3.00/3.20pm
Whelley Jct	12.06pm	3.25pm
Lindsay Sidings	12.10pm	3.30pm
	Mineral	Mineral

John Ryan

Distance from	Week Days. STATIONS.	1	2	3	4	5	6	7	8	9	10	11	12	13	14	15	16	17	18	19	20	21	22	Sundays. 1	2	3	4
		Goods and Coal to Pagefield		Goods & Coal.	Goods & Coal for Wigan.	Goods & Coal for Wigan.	Goods & Coal for Wigan.	Mineral Empties from Aintree Siding.		Engine and two Vans.	Coal to Brindle Heath	Mineral		Mineral to Lostock Junct.		Mineral to Astley Bridge.		Mineral to Westhoughton.	Fast Coal Empties from Aintree Sidings	Mineral to Westhoughton.	Mineral to Astley Bridge.				Goods and Coal to Pagefield.		
		S M		S M	M O	M	M	S		S	S O	S				S		S	S	S	S						
		a.m.		a.m.	a.m.	a.m.	a.m.	a.m.		a.m.	p.m.	p.m.		p.m.		p.m.		p.m.	p.m.	p.m.	p.m.				a.m.		
...	Long Lane Colly. Sidings dep	...	...	...	...	...	...	...	...	...	...	...	...	...	...	...	...	...	...	7 5	...	...	...	...	...	...	...
...	Cross Tetley's ,,	...	...	...	...	...	...	...	...	...	...	1 35	...	...	...	...	...	...	...	7 23	...	...	...	...	...	...	...
...	Bamfurlong Junction ,,	...	...	...	...	...	...	...	...	...	...	...	...	...	...	...	...	...	...	...	...	...	...	...	...	...	...
...	Bamfurlong Sidings arr	...	...	...	...	...	...	...	...	...	...	1 45	...	...	...	...	...	...	...	...	...	...	...	...	...	...	...
...	Bamfurlong Sidings dep	...	...	...	...	...	...	...	...	...	...	1 48	...	...	...	...	...	...	...	...	...	...	...	...	...	...	...
...	Garswood ,,	...	...	...	...	...	...	...	...	...	...	...	...	Runs Engine and Two Vans, Pemberton to Park Lane.	...	...	...	...	...	...	...	...	...	...	...	...	...
...	Ashton Pit Siding ,,	...	...	...	...	...	...	...	...	...	...	...	...		...	...	...	...	...	...	...	...	...	...	...	...	...
...	Bryn Junction arr	...	...	...	...	...	...	...	...	...	...	...	...		...	...	...	...	...	...	...	...	...	...	...	...	...
...	Bryn Junction dep	...	...	...	...	...	...	...	...	...	...	...	...		...	...	...	...	...	...	...	...	...	...	...	...	...
...	Pemberton Junction ,,	...	...	8 0	...	...	...	9 30	...	11 50	...		...		...	...	...	...	8 30	...	...	...	...	...	...	...	...
...	Blundell's Siding	...	...	...	...	...	...	...	...	12 0	...		...	2 50	...	...	...	...	8 35	...	...	...	...	...	...	...	...
...	Orrell Colliery Siding arr	...	...	...	...	...	...	...	...	...	...		...	...	...	...	...	...	8 40	...	...	...	...	...	...	...	...
...	Norley Colliery Siding arr	...	...	...	...	...	...	...	...	12 10	...		...	...	...	...	...	...	8 45	...	...	...	...	...	...	...	...
...	Park Lane Colliery dep	...	...	8 15	...	...	...	X	...	...	...	For Lostock Junction.	...	3 0	...	...	...	6 30	...	...	...	...	...	...	...	...	...
...	Bryn Junction arr	...	...	8 20	...	...	...	9 55	...	...	...		...	3 5	...	...	...	6 35	...	...	...	...	...	...	...	...	...
...	Bryn Junction dep	...	...	8 30	...	...	...	10 6	...	...	...		...	3 10	...	...	...	6 40	...	...	...	...	...	...	...	...	...
...	Garswood Hall arr	...	...	8 35	...	...	...	...	...	...	...		...	3 15	...	...	...	6 45	...	...	...	...	...	...	...	...	...
...	Garswood Hall dep	...	...		...	...	...	X	...	...	...		...	3 30	...	...	...	7 10	...	...	...	...	...	...	...	...	...
...	Bryn Hall Sidings arr	...	...	..	...	...	...	10 12	...	...	...		...	3 35	...	...	...	7 15	...	...	...	...	...	...	...	...	...
...	Bryn Hall Sidings dep	...	...	...	...	...	...		...	...	...		...	3 45	...	...	...	7 25	...	...	...	...	...	...	...	...	...
...	Ince Moss Junction arr	...	...	5 10 a.m. from Horwich.	...	...	...	...	...	...	...	...	...	...	...	...	...	...	...	...	...	...	...	...	...	...	...
...	Ince Moss Junction dep	. .	...		...	...	...	...	...	...	...	...	...	3 50	...	...	...	7 30	...	...	...	...	...	...	...	...	...
...	Bamfurlong Sidings arr	...	...		...	...	...	...	...	...	...	...	...	...	...	...	...	...	...	7 28	...	...	...	...	...	...	...
...	Bamfurlong Sidings dep	1 0	...		6 15	6 25	8 40	...	...	...	...		...	...	...	...	...	...	...	7 45	...	...	...	...	1 0	...	...
...	Springs Branch dep	1 5	...		6 20	6 30	8 45	...	...	...	...	Starts from Long Lane when required.	...	...	...	...	...	...	...	...	...	...	...	...	1 5	...	...
...	Wigan arr	1 10	...		6 25	6 35	8 50	...	...	...	...		...	...	...	...	...	...	...	...	...	...	...	...	1 10	...	...
...	Amberswood J. West ,,		...	...				...	...	...	...		...	...	...	4 0	...	...	...	X	10 30	...	...	...		...	...
...	Bickershaw Junction ,,	...	...	...	...	...	...	...	...	...	...		...	...	...	...	...	...	...	...	...	...	...	...	...	...	...
...	Amberswood J. East ,,	...	...	...	...	...	...	...	...	...	...		...	...	...	...	...	...	...	...	...	...	...	...	...	...	...
...	Lindsay Siding ,,	...	...	...	...	...	...	...	...	...	12 20		...	...	...	...	...	...	...	...	...	...	...	...	...	...	...
...	Round House Junc. ,,	...	...	...	...	...	...	...	...	...	...	...	...	...	...	...	...	...	...	...	...	...	...	...	...	...	...
...	De Trafford Jnc. arr	...	...	...	...	...	...	...	...	...	...	2 0	...	4 X 0	...	4 X 10	...	7 45	...	7 55	10 X 35	...	...	...	...	...	...
...	De Trafford Jnc. dep	...	...	...	...	...	...	...	...	...	...	2 5	...	4 X 5	...	4 X 15	..	8 0	...	8 5	10 X 45	...	...	...	...	...	...
...	Hindley Junction arr	...	...	...	...	...	...	...	...	...	12 40	2 8	...	4 8	...	4 18	...	8 3	...	8 7	10 50	...	...	...	...	...	...

No. 7—Runs to Bamfurlong Sidings when required.

No. 18—Works traffic for Park Lane Siding if required.

Distance from	STATIONS.	Week Days. 1	2	3	4	5	6	7	8	9	10	11	12	13	14	15	16	17	18	19	20	21	22	Sundays. 1	2	3	4
			Express Coal and Empties.				Goods and Coal.		Mineral Empties	Coal.	Coal Empties.	Mineral for Sandhills.	Mineral.	Engine and two Vans.	Express Coal to Sandhills.	Express Coal Empties.		Coal Empties from Hindley Junction.			7.17 p.m Fast G'ds Miles Platting to Round House.	Coal Empties from Blackburn (King Street).	Fast Empties from Halliwell.				
			S M				M		M O	S M	S O	S	M O	S		S		S				S	S				
			a.m.				a.m.	...	a.m.	a.m.	a.m.	a.m.	noon	p.m.	p.m.	p.m.		p.m.	...	...	p.m.	p.m.	p.m.				
...	Hindley Junction dep	...	2 35	...	...	...	...	...	...	...	11 35	...	12 0	...	...	2 55	...	5 0	...	...	8 23	8X27	8 40	...	...	...	...
...	De Trafford Jun. arr	...	2 40	...	...	...	...	...	...	...	11 40	...	...	...	...	3 0	...	5 5	...	...	...	8 30	8 43	...	...	...	...
...	De Trafford Jun. dep	...	2 50	...	...	...	...	...	...	...	11 50	...	...	...	...	3 10	...	5 15	...	...	8 25	8 35	8 50	...	...	...	...
...	Round House Junc... dep		...	...	...	...	...	...	...	...	...	...	...	...	...	...	...	...	...	...	8 27	...	...	...	...	...	...
...	Lindsay Siding arr	...	...	...	...	...		...	...	...	12 0	...	...	...	...	...	...	...	...	...		...	...	...	...	...	...
...	Amberswood J. East... ,,	...	X	...	...	...	6.0 a.m. Bamfurlong Sidings to Aintree	...	...			...	...	...	...	3 20	...	...	...	...	...	...	9 5	...	...	...	...
...	Bickershaw Junction pass	...	...	...	...	...		...	...		...	...	...	...	...		...	...	...	...	...	...	...	...	...	...	...
...	Amberswood J. West dep	...	X	...	...	...		...	...		...	...	12 10	...	...	...	...	...	...	...	...	X	9 10	...	...	...	...
...	Wigan ,,	...	...	...	...	...		...	5 40		...	...		12 55	...	...	...	...	...	...	...	...		...	...	...	...
...	Springs Branch ,,	...	...	...	...	...		...	...			...	...	...	...		...	...	...	...	...	...	...	...	...	...	...
...	Bamfurlong Sidings arr	...	3 10	...	...	...		...	5 50			...	...	...	...		...	5 25	...	...	...	8 50	...	...	...	...	...
...	Bamfurlong Sidings dep	...		...	...	...	...	...				...	...	...	...		...		...	...			...	...	...	...	...
...	Bamfurlong Junction ,,	...	...	...	...	...	...	...	...	To Winstanley Colliery Siding (S) To Wigan Shed (S O).	From Bullfield.	...	...	...	...	From Bromley Cross.	...	...	...	...	Engine and Van returns to Wigan District	...	...	...	...	...	...
...	Cross Tetley's ... arr	...	...	...	...	...	...	...				...	...	1 15	...		...	...	...	...		...	...	...	...	...	...
...	Long Lane Colliery Siding ,,	...	...	...	...	...	...	...				...	...		...		...	...	...	...		...	...	...	...	...	...
...	Bamfurlong Sidings dep	...		...	...	...	6 0	...				...	...	...	...		...	...	...	...		...	...	...	...	...	...
...	Ince Moss Junction arr	...	From Ramsbottom.	...	...	...	...	...	From Wigan.		...	..	...	...	...		...	...	...	...	...	...	...	...	...	...	...
...	Ince Moss Junction dep	...		...	...	...	6 5	...			...	...	...	...	...		...	...	...	...	...	...	...	...	...	...	...
...	Bryn Hall Sidings arr	...		...	...	...	...	...			...	...	...	...	...	...	...	...	...	...	...	...	...	...	...	...	...
...	Bryn Hall Sidings dep	...		...	...	...	...	...	...	...	...	11 10	...	...	...	...	...	...	...	...	...	...	...	...	...	...	...
...	Garswood Hall Sidng.... arr	...		...	...	...	...	...	...	...	...	...	...	...	...	...	...	...	...	...	...	...	...	...	...	...	...
...	Garswood Hall Sidng.... dep	...		...	...	...	...	...	...	9 30	...	...	...	...	...	...	...	...	...	...	...	...	...	...	...	...	...
...	Bryn Junction arr	...		...	...	...	6 12	...	...	9 35	...	11 15	...	...	...	...	...	Runs engine and van Bamfurlong to Long Lane.	...	...	...	...	...	...	...	...	...
...	Bryn Junction dep	...	...	...	...	...	6 20	...	...	9 42	...	11 20	...	...	...	...	...		...	...	...	...	...	...	...	...	...
...	Park Lane Siding arr	...	...	...	...	...	...	...	...	...	...	11 25	...	...	...	...	...		...	...	...	...	...	...	...	...	...
...	Park Lane Siding dep	...	...	...	...	...	...	...	...	9 55	...	11 30	...	...	...	...	...		...	...	...	...	...	...	...	...	...
...	Norley Colliery Siding ... dep	...	...	...	...	...	...	...	...	...	...	...	...	...	12 30	...	...		...	...	...	...	...	...	...	...	...
..	Orrell Colliery... dep	...	...	...	...	...	...	...	...	...	...	...	...	...	12 45	...	...	...	...	...	...	...	...	...	...	...	...
...	Blundells Siding arr	...	...	...	...	...	...	...	...	...	...	...	...	...	12 58	...	...	...	...	...	...	...	...	...	...	...	...
...	Pemberton Junction ...... arr	...	...	...	...	...	6 30	...	...	10 8	...	11 40	...	...	1 2	...	...	...	...	...	...	...	...	...	...	...	...
...	Garswood ,,	...	...	...	...	...	...	...	...	...	...	...	...	...	...	...	...	...	...	...	...	...	...	...	...	...	...

No. 11—Engine and Van returns Sandhills to Brynn Hall or Ashton Colliery, as required.

c1909

Up line

Dist. from Liverpool	Week Days.—Up. STATIONS.	1	2	3	4	5	6	7	8	9	10	11	12	13	14	15
			Exp. Goods	Minra Empts	Minra Empts.		Minra Empts	Empt. Cattle Wagns	Expres Gd		Mineral Empts.	Minral Empts		Exp. Gd		
	Up. (See Note A.)	...	MO	M	SM		M	MO	M		M	280 M		199 M		
	Wigan to Preston, see pages to 69)	...	a.m.	a m	a m		a m	a.m.	A.M.		a m	a.m.		A.M.		
...	LIVERPOOL L. St. dep	...	...	11.15 p.m. from Garston.	12.10 a.m. from Garston.	...	...	...	...	...	...	...	...	...	...	...
1¼	LIVERPOOL Edge Hill	...	12 1			...	12 40	1 20	1 40	...	...	...	...	2 40	...	...
2¾	Olive Mount Junction	...	For Kendal.			...	...	...	For Kendal.	...	...	...	...	For Blackb'rn	...	...
3¾	Broad Green	...				...	...	...		...	...	...	...		...	...
5¼	Roby	...				...	...	...		...	...	...	...		...	...
5¾	Huyton	...				...	...	...		...	1.5 a.m. from Garston.	...	...		...	...
6¼	Huyton Junction	...	12 15			...	12 56	1 33	1 52	...		...	...	2 53	...	...
7½	Prescot dep	...	...	...	...	...	...	...	...	...		...	...	...	...	...
8¾	Eccleston Park	...	...	...	...	...	...	...	...	...		...	...	...	...	...
9⅞	Thatto Heath	...	...	...	...	...	...	...	...	...		...	...	...	...	...
11½	St. HELENS arr	...	12 31	...	...	...	...	...	2 7	...		2 15	...	...	...	...
	St. HELENS dep	...	12 36	...	...	...	...	1 47	2 18	...	...	2 30	...	3 7	...	...
11⅞	Pocket Nook Jun. arr	...	...	...	...	...	1 15	...	...	...	...	...	...	3 10	...	...
	Pocket Nook Jun. dep	...	...	...	...	...	1 35	...	...	...	...	...	...	3 25	...	...
12⅛	Gerard's Bridge Junction	...	...	...	...	...	...	...	...	...	...	...	...	...	...	...
13	Carr Mill	...	...	...	...	...	...	...	...	...	...	...	...	...	...	...
13¾	Carr Mill Junction	...	12 41	12 37	1 20	...	1 40	...	2 24	...	2 25	2 38	...	3 32	...	...
15¼	Garswood	...	...	...	...	...	...	...	...	...	...	...	...	...	...	...
16	Ashton Colliery Siding	...	...	...	...	...	...	...	...	...	...	...	...	...	...	...
16½	Bryn (for Ashton-in-Makerfield)	...	...	...	...	...	...	...	...	...	...	...	...	...	...	...
16⅞	Bryn Junction arr	...	12 54	12 53	1 32	...	2 0	2 5	2 34	...	2 43	2 51	...	3 45	...	...
17⅜	Pemberton and Norley Branches: Bryn Junction dep	...	...	...	...	...	...	...	...	...	...	2.5 a.m. from Marshs Siding.	...	...	...	...
18¼	Park Lane Colliery arr	...	...	...	...	...	...	...	...	...	...		...	...	...	...
19⅜	Blundell's Pembrtn Col	...	...	...	...	...	...	...	...	...	...		...	...	...	...
19⅝	Pemberton J. (L.&Y.)	...	...	C	C	...	C	C	...	...	...		...	...	...	...
	Norley Colliery arr	...	...			...			...	...	...		...	...	...	...
...	Norley Colliery dep.	...	...	...	...	...	...	...	...	...	...		...	...	...	...
...	Pemberton J. (L.&Y.) ,,	...	...	...	...	...	...	For Carlisle.	...	...	...		...	...	...	...
...	Blundell's Pembrtn Col	...	...	...	...	...	...		...	...	...		...	...	...	...
...	Park Lane Colliery ,,	...	...	...	...	...	...		...	...	...		...	...	...	...
	Bryn Junction arr	...	...	...	...	...	...		W	...	...	...	...	...	...	...
16⅞	Bryn Junction dep	...	12 54	12 53	1 32	...	2 0	2 5	2 34	...	2 43	2 51	...	3 45	...	...
17⅜	Garswood Hall Siding	...	...	...	...	...	...	...	...	...	...	...	...	...	...	...
17¾	Bryn Hall Siding	...	...	...	...	...	...	...	...	...	...	...	...	...	...	...
18½	Ince Moss Junction arr.	...	...	1 0	1 40	...	2 10	...	2 40	...	2 50	...	...	3 50	...	...
19	Springs Branch	...	1 7			...		2 12	...	...		3 0	...	4 3	...	...
20¼	WIGAN	...	1 40	...	...	...	...	2 17	...	...	...		...	4 8	...	...

Dist. from Liverpool	Week Days.—Up. STATIONS.	16	17	18	19	20	21	22	23	24	25	26	27	28	29	30
		Mineral	Mineral	Minral Empty		Minral Empts.	Minral Empts.	Gd	Emp. W'g'ns	PAS	PAS	Minral Emp'y	Minral Empt.	Minral Empty	L. & Y. Goods & Coal	
	Up. (See Note A.)	SM	390 SM	M		SM	MO	1	116				M 2m		SM	
	Wigan to Preston, see pages to 69)	A.M.	a m	A.M.		a m	a m	a m	a.m.	A.M.	a m	A.M.	a	a m	a.m.	
...	LIVERPOOL L. St. dep	...	For Maudlands.	3.10 a.m. from Garston.	...	4.10 a.m. from Garston.	4 30 a m from Garston.	...	...	6 6	...	6.15 a.m. from Garston.	...	...	5.10 a.m. from Horwich.	...
1¼	LIVERPOOL Edge Hill	...			...			5 5	5 40	6 10	...		6 20	6 30		...
2¾	Olive Mount Junction	...			...			...	...	...	...		...	...		...
3¾	Broad Green	...			...			...	...	6 15	...		...	...		...
5¼	Roby	...			...			...	...	6 19	...		...	...		...
5¾	Huyton	...			...			...	...	6 22	...		...	...		...
6¼	Huyton Junction	...			...			5 18	5 50	6 25	...		6 35	6 45		...
7½	Prescot dep	...		...	...	...	...	5 40	...	6 28	...	...	...	...	...	...
8¾	Eccleston Park	...	...	...	...	...	...	...	...	...	...	...	...	...	...	...
9⅞	Thatto Heath	...	...	...	...	...	...	...	...	6 35	...	...	...	...	...	...
11½	St. HELENS arr	...	...	...	...	...	...	...	6 10	6 40	...	...	6 50	...	...	...
	St. HELENS dep	...	...	...	...	...	5 40	5 50	6 30	6 42	...	...	7 0	...	...	...
11⅞	Pocket Nook Jun. arr	...	...	...	...	...	5 42	5 52	...	...	...	...	...	7 5	...	...
	Pocket Nook Jun. dep	...	...	...	...	...	5 53		...	...	...	...	...	7 30	...	...
12⅛	Gerard's Bridge Junction	...	...	...	...	...	...	Calls at Prescot daily (M) to detach Wagons.	...	...	...	...	...	...	...	...
13	Carr Mill	...	...	...	...	...	...		...	...	...	...	...	...	...	...
13¾	Carr Mill Junction	...	...	4 45	...	5 30	6 0		6 38	6 45	...	7 30	For Haydock Jct.	7 35	...	...
15¼	Garswood	...	...	...	...	...	...		...	6 51	7 30	...		7 43	...	...
16	Ashton Colliery Siding	...	...	...	...	...	...		...	...	...	...		...	...	...
16½	Bryn (for Ashton-in-Makerfield)	...	...	...	...	...	...		...	6 55	7 35	...		...	...	...
16⅞	Bryn Junction arr	...	...	5 2	...	5 57	6 17		6 50	...	...	7 46		7 51	...	...
17⅜	Pemberton and Norley Branches: Bryn Junction dep	...	...	...	...	...	...		Will carry Exp. Signals when conveying Wgns for Wigan Warehouse.	...	...	...	...	...	...	...
18¼	Park Lane Colliery arr	...	...	...	...	...	...			...	...	...	...	...	...	...
19⅜	Blundell's Pembrtn Col	...	...	...	...	...	...			...	...	...	...	...	...	...
19⅝	Pemberton J. (L.&Y.)	C	...	C	...	C	C			...	...	C	...	C	...	...
	Norley Colliery arr		...		...					...	...		...		...	...
...	Norley Colliery dep.	...	...	...	...	...	...	...		...	...	...	...	...	...	...
...	Pemberton J. (L.&Y.) ,,	...	W	...	...	...	...	...		...	...	...	...	...	8 0	...
...	Blundell's Pembrtn Col	...	3 20	...	...	...	...	...		...	...	...	...	...	...	...
...	Park Lane Colliery ,,	4 0	3 40	...	...	...	...	...		...	...	...	...	...	8 15	...
	Bryn Junction arr	4 5	3 45	...	...	...	...	...	...	...	...	...	...	...	8 20	...
16⅞	Bryn Junction dep	4 15	3 57	5 2	...	5 57	6 17	...	6 50	...	...	7 46	...	7 51	8 30	...
17⅜	Garswood Hall Siding	...	4 32	...	...	...	...	...	...	...	...	...	...	...	8 35	...
17¾	Bryn Hall Siding	...	...	...	...	...	...	...	...	...	...	...	...	...		...
18½	Ince Moss Junction arr.	4 23	4 40	5 10	...	6 5	6 25	...	7 0	...	...	7 55	...	8 0	...	...
19	Springs Branch	4 25	...	...	...	...	...	...	...	...	...	...	...	...	...	...
20¼	WIGAN		...	...	...	...	...	...	...	7 5	7 45	...	...	...	...	...

A. Trains from Liverpool to Wigan run on to and travel over, the Down Line from Springs Branch No. 1 Junction Box.

Week Days—Up. STATIONS.	31	32	33	34	35	36	37	38	39	40	41	42	43	44	45
	PAS	Exp Goods			Minral Empty	PAS	Minral		PAS		Minral	Minral Empty	PAS	L. & Y. Minral Empty	PAS
	MO	235 SM			SM		141 S				103	117 S	20	S	
(Wigan to Preston, see pages to	a.m.	a m			a.m.	a.m.	a.m.		A.M.		A.M.	A.M	a.m.	A.M.	A.M.
LIVERPOOL L. St. dep	7 45		...	...		7 50	...	...	8 20	...	...	...	9 0	...	9 10
LIVERPOOL Edge Hill	7 50	7.20 a.m. from Widnes.	...	...	7.5 a.m. from Garston.	7 56	...	...	8 25	...	...	8.0 a.m. Garston to Hul on Siding.	9 6	...	9 15
Olive Mount Junction	...		...	...		...	...	...	...	...	...		...	...	...
Broad Green	...		...	...		8 1		...	8 30	...	...		...	...	9 20
Roby	...		...	...		8 5		...	8 34	...	...		...		9 24
Huyton	...		...	...		8 8	Arrives Bamfurlong 9.0 a.m.	...	8 37	...	...		...	L. & Y. Co.'s Train From Aintree Sorting Sidings.	9 27
Huyton Junction	7 58		...	...		8 9		...	8 38	...	...		...		9 28
Prescot dep	...		...	...	...	8 14		...	8 43	...	...		9 18		9 33
Eccleston Park	...		...	...	...	8 17		...	8 47	...	...		...		9 36
Thatto Heath	...	...	...	...	...	8 21		...	8 50	...	...	...	...		9 40
St. HELENS arr	8 8	...	...	...	...	8 26		...	8 55	...	...	...	9 25		9 45
St. HELENS dep	8 10	...	...	...	...	8 28		...	8 58	...	...	...	9 27		
Pocket Nook Jun. arr	...	...	...	...	...	...		...	...	...	...	...	...		...
Pocket Nook Jun. dep	For Preston.	...	...	...	...	...		...	...	...	...	...	For Blackpool.		...
Gerard's Bridge Junc.		...	...	...	...	...		...	...	...	...	...			...
Carr Mill		...	...	...	...	8 32		...	...	...	...	...			...
Carr Mill Junction		8 18	...	...	8 30	...		...	...	...	...	9 20			...
Garswood		...	...	...	C	8 38		...	9 7	...	...	...			...
Ashton Colliery Siding	...	...	...	...		...		...	...	...	...	...			...
Bryn (for Ashton-in-Makerfield)	...	...	...	...	...	8 42		...	9 12	...	...	...			...
Bryn Junction arr	...	8 35	...	...	8 45	...		...	...	...	...	9 37		...	...
Pemberton and Norley Branches: Bryn Junction dep	...	See	...	...	Runs to Bamfurlong Sdgs when required.	...	...	...	...	...	...	...	...	...	...
Park Lane Colliery arr	...	note.	...	...		...	...	...	...	...	...	...	...	...	...
Blundell's Pembrtn Col	...	8 45	...	...		...		...	...	...		...	Arrives Prescot 9.15 a.m.	...	...
Pemberton J. (L&Y) ,,	...		...	...		...	C	...	...	...	C	...		...	...
Norley Collr'y. arr	...		...	...		...	...	...	...	...	...	...		...	...
Norley Collr'y. dep	...	...	...	...		...	...	...	...	...	...	...		...	...
Pemberton J. (L&Y) ,,	...	...	...	...		...	...	...	...	...	...	...		9 30	...
Blundell's Pembrtn Col	...	...	...	...		...	...	...	...	...	9 0	...	...	...	...
Park Lane Colliery ,,	...	...	...	...		...	...	...	...	...	9 25	...	...	X	...
Bryn Junction ... arr	...	...	...	...		...	...	...	...	...	9 30	W	...	9 45	...
Bryn Junction dep	...	8 35	...	...	8 46	...	...	...	...	...	9 45	9 37	...	10 6	...
Garswood Hall Sid.	...	...	...	...	...	...	8 50	...	...	...	...	...	...	X	...
Bryn Hall Siding	...	...	...	...	...	...	...	...	...	...	...	...	...	10 12	...
Ince Moss Junction	...	8 43	...	...	8 50	...	...	...	...	...	9 55	9 45	...		...
Springs Branch arr	...	9 0	...	...		...	8 55	...	...	...		...	...	...	...
WIGAN	8 28		...	...	...	8 50	...	...	9 20	...	...	...	9 44	...	...

Week Days—Up. STATIONS.	46	47	48	49	50	51	52	53	54	55	56	57	58	59	60	61
	Goods	Minral Empty	PAS	PAS	Minral		Minral Emp'y	Goods	Minral Empty	Fast Minral Empts	PAS	Minral Empty	PAS	Goods		Goods.
	263 S	224			141 S		161 MO	281		167 M				254 SO		
(Wigan to Preston, see pages to	a.m.	A.M.	A.M.	a.m.	a m.		a.m.	a.m.	A.M.	a.m.	A.M.	a.m.	a m	a.m.		a.m.
LIVERPOOL L. St. dep	...	...	9 50	...	...	...	...	...	...	...	10 25	...	11 12	...	...	...
LIVERPOOL Edge Hill	...	...	9 57	...	...	...	...	...	9.25 a.m. from Garston.	...	10 30	...	11 17	...	...	...
Olive Mount Junction	...	...	...	...	...	...	9.0 a.m. from Garston.	...		...	...	...	...	...	...	10.45 a.m., Garston to Hulton's Siding.
Broad Green	...	...	...	...	...	...		...		...	10 35	...	...	...	...	
Roby		9.10 a.m. Widnes, to Fleetwood.	...	...	...	...		...		...	10 39	...	...	...	...	
Huyton			...	...	...	...		...		...	10 42	...	...	...	...	
Huyton Junction	...		10 4	...	...	...		...		...	10 43	...	11 24	...	...	
Prescot dep	...		...	...	...	...		10 30	...	...	10 48	10.10 a.m. from Garston.	...	...	...	
Eccleston Park	...		...	...	Arrives Bamfurlong at 10.45 a.m.	...	...	...	...	...	10 51		...	...	...	
Thatto Heath	...		...	...		...	...	...	...	...	10 55		...	...	...	
St. HELENS arr	...		10 12	...		...	...	...	...	...	11 0		11 32	...	...	
St. HELENS dep	...		10 14	10 20		...	...	10 45	...	...	11 3		11 34	...	...	
Pocket Nook Jun. arr	9 50		...	...		...	...	...	...	...	...		...	...	...	
Pocket Nook Jun. dep		...	...	...		...	...	...	...	...	...		...	11 45	...	...
Gerard's Bridge Junc.	9 55	...	...	...		...	...	...	...	...	...		...		...	...
Carr Mill		...	...	...		...	...	...	...	...	11 8	...	...	11 50	...	...
Carr Mill Junction	...	10 15	...	...		...	10 20	...	10 50	11 5	...	11 27	...	...	...	11 51
Garswood	...	...	...	10 28		...	...	...	C	...	11 14	...	...	...	...	...
Ashton Colliery Siding	...	...	...	...		...	...	...		...	...	...	...	...	...	...
Bryn (for Ashton-in-Makerfield)	...	...	...	10 32		...	...	...	...	...	11 18	...	...	...	...	...
Bryn Junction arr	...	10 27	...	...	...	...	10 38	...	11 2	11 20	...	11 45	...	...	...	12 2
Pemberton and Norley Branches: Bryn Junction dep	...	...	...	...	...	...	...	...	Runs to Bamfurlong S'd'gs when required.	8.30 a.m. Garston to Green's Siding.	...	...	...	...	...	...
Park Lane Colliery arr	...	Is "C" on Sats.	...	...	...	...	...	...			...	...	...	...	...	...
Blundell's Pembrtn Col	...		...	...		...	...	...			...		...	...	...	
Pemberton J. (L&Y) ,,	...		...	...	C	...	...	...			...	C	...	...	...	C
Norley Collr'y. arr	...		...	...		...	...	...			...		...	...	...	
Norley Collr'y. dep	...		...	...	...	...	...	...			...	...	...	...	...	...
Pemberton J. (L&Y) ,,	...		For Carlisle.	...	...	...	...	...			For Wigan.	...	For Carlisle.	...	...	...
Blundell's Pembrtn Col	...			...	...	...	...	...				...		...	...	...
Park Lane Colliery ,,	...	...		...	...	...	...	...				...		...	...	...
Bryn Junction ... arr	...	...		...	...	...	...	...		W		...		...	...	W
Bryn Junction dep	...	10 27	...	...	...	...	10 38	...	11 2	11 20	...	11 45	...	...	...	12 2
Garswood Hall Sid.	...	...	...	...	10 30	...	...	...	...	...	...	...	...	...	...	...
Bryn Hall Siding	...	...	...	...	...	...	...	...	...	...	...	...	...	...	...	...
Ince Moss Junction	...	10 40	...	...	10 35	...	10 45	...	11 10	11 30	...	11 55	...	...	...	12 10
Springs Branch arr	...	10 50	...	...	...	...		...		...	...		...	...	...	...
WIGAN	...	1 25	10 28	10 39	...	...	...	...	...	...	11 25	...	11 50	...	...	...

No. 32.—Will run to Blundells Colliery when required. Is "C" Bryn Jctn. to Blundells.

No. 44—Runs to Bamfurlong Sidings when required.

London & North Western c.1909

Week Days. Up.

STATIONS	62	63	64	65	66	67	68	69	70	71	72	73	74	75	76
	Minr'l	Empty Carriages	Minral		Engine & Van	PAS	Minral Empty	Eng'ne & Van	Gd	Cattle.	Minral Empty	Minral Empty	PAS	Minr'l	
			103				173	274		6	262	227			
		SO			S			S		MO		SO			
(Wigan to Preston, see pages 7 to 69)	p m	a.m.	A.M.		p.m	A.M	p m	p m	p m	p m	p m	p.m.	p m	p.m.	
LIVERPOOL Lime St. dep	...	11 25	...	...	...	11 40	...	...	...	...	...	...	1 10	...	...
LIVERPOOL Edge H. "	...	11 32	...	...	...	11 45	...	...	...	...	...	...	1 15	...	...
Olive Mount Junction	...	...	...	...	...	...	...	...	...	...	...	...	...	...	...
Broad Green	...	...	...	...	...	11 50	11.15 a.m., from Garston.	12.30 p.m. from Sutton Oak Junction.	...	12 36	...	...	1 20	...	...
Roby	...	...	...	...	...	11 54			...	...	10.40 a.m. from Clock Face.	...	1 24	...	...
Huyton	...	...	...	...	...	11 57			...	...		...	1 27	...	...
Huyton Junction	...	11 41	...	...	...	11 58			...	12 46		...	1 29	...	...
Prescot	...	...	To Ince Hall via Bamfurlong & Springs Branch.	...	12.0 noon from Sutton Oak Jct.	12 2			...	...		...	1 33	...	...
Eccleston Park	...	...		...		12 6			...	...		12.20 p.m. from Widnes	1 37	2.0 p.m. from Marsh's Siding	...
Thatto Heath	...	...		...		12 10			...	...			1 41		...
St. HELENS arr	...	11 55		...		12 14			...	...			1 45		...
St. HELENS dep	...	...		...		12 15			...	1 X 0	...		1 47		...
Pocket Nook Junc arr	...	...		...		...	...		...	...	C		...		...
Pocket Nook Junc dep	...	...		...		...	...	...	...	...			...		...
Gerard's Bridge Junc.	...	...		...	...	...	...	...	...	...	...	...	...		...
Carr Mill	...	...		...	...	12 19	...	...	...	...	...	...	1 51		...
Carr Mill Junction	...	...		...	12 10	...	12 20	12 33	12 55	1 5	1 6	1 12	...	2 10	...
Garswood	...	...		...	12 15	12 24	...	12 45	1 10	...	...	1 30	1 57	...	...
Ashton Colliery Siding	...	...		...	...	...	...	...	1 25	...	...	...	...	...	...
Bryn (for Ashton-in-Mak'field)	...	...		...	...	12 28	...	...	...	...	...	...	2 1	...	...
Bryn Junction arr.	...	...		...	...	...	12 32	...	1 30	1 17	1 20	1 40	...	2 25	...
Pemberton and Norley Branches: Bryn Junction dep	...	...	...	...	...	...	...	...	...	...	...	...	...	...	...
Park Lane Colliery arr	...	...	...	...	...	...	...	...	1 35	...	1 25	1 50	...	...	...
Blundell's Pembrtn Col	...	...	...	...	...	...	...	...	1 45	12.30 p.m. from Stanley.	1 40	1 55	...	...	...
Pemberton J. (L&Y) "	C	...	...	...	...	...	...	C	C		...	...	...	C	...
Norley Colliery arr.	For Bamfurlong Sidings.	...	...	...	...	...	...	...	...		1 55	2 0	...	...	...
Norley Colliery dep.		...	11 40	...	...	...	...	...	...		...	...	...	...	...
Pemberton J. (L&Y) "		...	...	...	...	...	...	...	11.40 a.m. from Widnes.		...	...	...	...	...
Blundell's Pembrtn Col		...	11 55	...	...	...	...	...			...	...	...	...	...
Park Lane Colliery "		...	12 5	...	...	...	...	...			...	...	...	...	...
Bryn Junction arr		...	12 10	...	...	...	...	...			...	...	...	...	...
Bryn Junction dep	...	...	12 20	...	...	...	12 32	...		1 17	...	...	...	2 25	...
Garswood Hall Siding	12 20	...	12 50	...	...	...	...	...		...	...	...	...	...	...
Bryn Hall Siding	12 30	...	1 5	...	...	...	...	...		...	...	...	...	...	...
Ince Moss Junction arr	12 35	...	1 7	...	...	...	12 40	...		1 22	...	...	...	2 34	...
Springs Branch	12 50	...	...	...	...	...	...	...		...	...	...	...	2 45	...
WIGAN	...	...	...	...	...	12 35	...	...	See col. 81.	1 30	...	...	2 10	...	...

STATIONS	77	78	79	80	81	82	83	84	85	86	87	88	89	90	91	92
	Minr'l			PAS	Gd	Minral Empty	Minral	Minral Empty		L. & Y. Minr'l	PAS	Gd	Minral Empty	Gd		Minral Empty
	141					163						103	162	281		
							S	MS						SO		MO
(Wigan to Preston, see pages 7 to 69)	p m			P.M.	P	P M.	p m	p.m.		p m	P.M.	p m	p m	p m		p.m.
LIVERPOOL Lime St. dep	...	...	...	1 45	...	...	...	...	...	...	2 30	...	...	...	...	...
LIVERPOOL Edge H. "	...	...	...	1 50	...	...	...	2 15	...	...	2 35	...	2.20 p.m. from Garston	...	...	3 35
Olive Mount Junction	...	...	...	...	See col. 70.	...	...	...	...	Engine and 2 vans leaves Pemberton at 2.50 p.m. for Park L.	...	...		...	...	...
Broad Green	...	...	...	...		1.40 p.m., Garston to Carnforth.	...	...	...		2 40	...		...	...	...
Roby	...	...	...	...			...	...	...		2 44	For Bamfurlong.		...	...	...
Huyton	...	...	...	...			...	...	...		2 47			...	...	...
Huyton Junction	...	...	...	1 57	...		...	2 29	...		2 49		...	...	...	3 50
Prescot	...	...	...	...	...		...	...	...		2 53		...	3 25	...	...
Eccleston Park	...	...	...	...	...		For Preston (Maudlands)	...	...		2 57		...	...	...	...
Thatto Heath	...	...	...	...	...			...	...		3 1		...	...	...	...
St. HELENS arr	Arrives Bamfurlong 3.0 p.m.	...	...	2 5	...	...		...	...		3 6		...	...	...	...
St. HELENS dep		...	...	2 7	...	...		2 43	...		3 8		...	3 37	...	4 10
Pocket Nook Junc arr		...	...	...	11.40 a.m. from Widnes.	...		...	...		...	...	...	3 40	...	...
Pocket Nook Junc dep		...	...	...		...		...	...		...	...	...	...	...	...
Gerard's Bridge Junc.		...	...	...		...		...	...		...	...	...	...	...	...
Carr Mill		...	...	...		...		...	...		3 12	...	...	...	...	...
Carr Mill Junction		...	...	2 10		2 38		2 58	...	...	...	...	3 37	...	...	4 20
Garswood		...	...	...		...		3 15	...	...	3 17	...	...	...	...	...
Ashton Colliery Siding		...	...	...		...		...	...	...	...	...	...	...	...	...
Bryn (for Ashton-in-Mak'field)	...	...	...	...	...	...		...	...	...	3 21	...	...	...	...	...
Bryn Junction arr.	...	...	...	...	...	2 51	...	3 26	...	...	...	...	3 50	...	...	4 35
Pemberton and Norley Branches: Bryn Junction dep	...	...	...	...	...	...	...	...	...	For Lostock Junc.	...	...	...	...	...	...
Park Lane Colliery arr	...	...	...	For Preston.	...	...	...	3 35	...		...	...	...	...	...	4 40
Blundell's Pembrtn Col	...	...	...		...	...	...	3 50	...		...	...	...	...	...	4 45
Pemberton J. (L&Y) "	...	...	...		C	...	...	...	...		...	C	...	...	...	C
Norley Colliery arr.	...	...	...		...	...	...	...	...		...	...	...	...	...	...
Norley Colliery dep.	...	...	...	...	...	...	...	...	...	...	...	...	...	...	...	...
Pemberton J. (L&Y) "	...	...	...	...	...	...	...	See note.	...	W	...	...	...	...	...	...
Blundell's Pembrtn Col	1 35	...	...	...	2 10	...	...		...	...	...	3 0	...	...	...	...
Park Lane Colliery "	1 45	...	...	...	2 20	...	...	...	...	3 0	...	3 10	...	...	...	...
Bryn Junction arr	1 50	...	...	...	2 25	...	...	...	...	3 5	...	3 15	...	...	...	...
Bryn Junction dep	1 55	...	...	...	2 40	2 51	...	3 25	...	3 12	...	3 20	3 50	...	...	...
Garswood Hall Siding	2 10	...	...	...	2 50	...	3 10	...	...	3 30	...	...	...	...	...	...
Bryn Hall Siding	2 50	...	...	...	3 5	...	3 25	...	...	3 45	...	...	...	...	...	...
Ince Moss Junction arr	2 55	...	...	...	3 10	3 0	3 0	3 35	...	3 50	...	3 30	4 0	...	...	...
Springs Branch	...	...	...	...	3 15	3 35	3 45	...	...	...	...	3 35	...	...	...	...
WIGAN	...	...	...	2 24	...	5 45	4 40	...	...	...	3 28	...	...	...	...	...

No. 81—Run to Bamfurlong Sidings when required.
No. 84—Is "C," Bryn Junction to Ince Moss, and runs to Pemberton or Ince Moss as required.

WEEK DAYS. UP.

STATIONS	93	94	95	96	97	98	99	100	10	102	103	104	105	106	107
	PAS	Minral Empty	Minral	Minral	PAS	Gd	Minral	Coal Wgns.		PAS	Minral	Expre Gd	PAS	Gd	L & Y Minral
		175		135		277								107	
		SO		S		S	S	•		SO		S O			S
Wigan to Preston, see pages 37 to 69.	p.m.	p.m.	p.m.	P.M.	P.M.	p. m.	p.m.	p m		p.m.	p.m.	P.M.	P M.	p m	p m
LIVERPOOL Lime S. dep	4 5	...	...	...	4 20	...	...	...	...	...	...	...	5 27	...	...
LIVERPOOL Edge H. "	4 12	3.40 p.m. from Garston.	...	...	4 25	...	...	4 42	...	...	...	4.40 p.m. from Widnes.	5 32	...	...
Olive Mount Junction	...		...	4.0 p.m. from Marsh's Siding.	...	...	...	...	...	...	...		...	...	...
Broad Green	...		...		4 30	...	...	...	...	...	...		5 37	...	...
Roby	...		...		4 34	...	...	...	...	...	...		5 41	...	...
Huyton	...		...		4 37	...	...	...	...	...	To work a trip from Ince Moss to Bound House when required.		5 44	...	...
Huyton Junction	...		...		4 38	...	...	4 57	...	...			5 45	...	...
Prescot	4 21	...	...		4 43	4 55	...	...	...	...		...	5 50	...	...
Eccleston Park	...	...	...		4 47	...	...	...	...	...		...	5 53	For Bamfurlong Sidings.	For Westhoughton
Thatto Heath	...	...	...	Is regular on Mondays.	4 51	...	...	...	...	...		...	5 57		
St. HELENS arr	4 28	...	...		4 55	5 5	...	5 15	...	...		...	6 3		
St. HELENS dep	4 30	...	...		4 57		For Rochdale via Kenyon.	5 25	...	5 50		5 33	6 5		
Pocket Nook Junc arr	...	...	...		...	...		...	...	...		5 35	...		
Pocket Nook Junc dep	...	...	...		...	...		...	...	...		5 55	...		
Gerard's Bridge Junction	...	...	...		...	...		...	...	...		...	...		
Carr Mill	...	...	...		5 1	...		...	...	...		...	6 9		
Carr Mill Junction	4 33	4 42	...	4 45	...	...		5 30	...	...		6 0	...		
Garswood	...	...	4 30	5 0	5 7	...		...	...	5 58		...	6 14		
Ashton Colliery Siding	...	...	4 35	5 25	...	...	...	...	...	...		...	...		
Bryn (for Ashton-in-Makerf'd)	...	...	...	...	5 11	...	...	...	...	6 2		...	6 18	...	...
Bryn Junction arr	4 39	4 55	4 45	5 30	...	...	...	5 50	...	...	...	6 12	...	...	...
Pemberton and Norley Branches: Bryn Junction dep	...	...	...	...	...	...	...	...	...	...	...	...	...	...	...
Park Lane Colliry arr	...	...	...	...	...	...	...	...	...	...	...	...	...	...	...
Blundell's Pembrtn Col	...	...	...	...	...	...	...	...	...	...	...	6 22	...	...	...
Pemberton J. L&Y "	...	...	...	C	Arrives Prescot at 4.41 p.m.	...	...	C	...	...	C	C	...	...	...
Norley Colliery arr	...	...	...	...		...	...	...	...	...			...	...	...
Norley Colliery dep	...	...	...	...		...	...	...	...	...	...	...	...	...	...
Pemberton J. L. & Y.	For Wigan.	...	...	...		...	...	...	...	...	...	...	...	5 40	...
Blundell's Pembrtn Col		...	...	...		...	...	...	...	...	5 15	6 50	...	5 55	...
Park Lane Coll'y "		...	...	...		...	5 0	...	...	...	5 30	...	...	6 5	6 30
Bryn Junction arr		...	...	...	...	...	5 15	...	...	...	5 35	6 55	...	6 10	6 35
Bryn Junction dep	4 39	4 55	4 45	5 30	...	...	5 35	5 50	...	...	5 40	7 0	...	6 20	6 40
Garswood Hall Siding	...	...	5 15	5 53	...	...	6 5	...	...	...	6 5	...	...	...	7 10
Bryn Hall Siding	...	...	5 30	6 15	...	...	6 20	...	...	...	...	...	...	...	7 25
Ince Moss Junction arr	...	5 5	...	6 20	...	...	6 25	5 57	...	...	6 10	7 7	...	6 30	7 20
Springs Branch	...	...	5 40	6 45	...	...	...	6 0	...	...	6 20	7 10	...	...	...
WIGAN	4 45	...	...	...	5 20	...	...	...	...	6 9	...	...	6 28	...	W

STATIONS	108	109	110	111	112	113	114	115	116	117	118	119	120	121	122	123
	PAS	Meat.	Minral	PAS	Minral	Exp Gd	Minral Empty	PAS		Express Gd	Minral Empty		PAS		PAS	Minral Empty
						126	271									
				S	SO	S	S			S						SO
Wigan to Preston, see pages 37 to 69.	p m	p m	p m	P M.	p.m.	p m	p.m.	P.M.		P.M.	P.M.		P.M.	...	p.m.	p.m.
LIVERPOOL Lime S. dep	5 50	...	...	6 15	...	...	...	6 35	...	...	...	...	7 15	...	7 45	...
LIVERPOOL Edge H. "	5 55	...	...	6 21	...	...	...	6 40	...	6 55	6.35 p m from Garston.	...	7 21	...	7 50	7.30 p.m., Garston to Hulton Siding.
Olive Mount Junction	...	For Carlisle.	...	...	...	...	...	...	...	...		...	...	...	...	
Broad Green	6 0		...	6 25	...	...	...	6 45	...	...		...	7 25	...	7 55	
Roby	6 4		...	6 29	...	...	...	6 49	...	...		...	7 29	...	7 59	
Huyton	6 7		...	6 32	...	...	...	6 52	...	...		...	7 32	...	8 2	
Huyton Junction	6 8		...	6 33	...	...	...	6 53	...	7 7		...	...	...	8 3	
Prescot	6 13	...	...	6 38	...	...	4.50 p.m. from Farnworth and Bold.	6 58	...	...	...	...	7 38	...	8 8	
Eccleston Park	6 16	...	...	6 41	...	5.40 p.m. from Widnes.		7 1	...	...	...	...	7 41	...	8 11	
Thatto Heath	6 20	...	For Warrington	6 45	...			7 5	...	...	...	...	7 45	...	8 15	
St. HELENS arr	6 25	...		6 50				7 10	...	...	...	...	7 50	...	8 20	...
St. HELENS dep	...	...		...	For Preston (Maudlands).			7 11	...	7 18	...	...	...	...	8 22	...
Pocket Nook Junc arr	...	...		...				...	...	7 20	...	...	...	...	...	...
Pocket Nook Junc dep	...	6 40		...				...	...	7 30	...	...	...	...	...	...
Gerard's Bridge Junction	...	...		...				...	...	...	...	...	...	...	...	...
Carr Mill	...	...		...		...	...	7 15	...	...	...	...	...	...	8 26	...
Carr Mill Junction	...	6 43		...		6 22	7 0	7 18	...	7 34	7 43	...	...	...	...	8 35
Garswood	...	...		...		...	...	7 21	...	...	...	...	...	...	8 32	...
Ashton Colliery Siding	...	...	...	...		...	...	...	...	...	...	...	...	...	...	...
Bryn (for Ashton-in-Makerf'd)	...	...	...	...	...	...	...	7 25	...	...	...	...	...	...	8 36	...
Bryn Junction arr	...	6 50	...	...	...	6 35	7 13	...	...	7 45	7 54	...	...	...	...	8 48
Pemberton and Norley Branches: Bryn Junction dep	...	...	...	...	...	6 40	...	...	...	...	...	...	...	...	...	...
Park Lane Colliry arr	...	...	...	...	...	...	...	...	...	For Carlisle.	...	...	...	...	...	...
Blundell's Pembrtn Col	...	...	...	...	...	6 45	...	...	...		...	...	...	...	...	...
Pemberton J. L&Y "	...	C	C	...	...	C	...	...	...		C	...	...	...	...	C
Norley Colliery arr	...	...	...	...	...	...	...	...	...		...	...	...	...	...	...
Norley Colliery dep	...	...	...	...	...	...	...	...	...	...	...	...	...	...	...	...
Pemberton J. L. & Y.	...	...	...	...	...	...	...	...	...	...	...	...	...	...	...	...
Blundell's Pembrtn Col	...	...	...	...	7 0	7 20	...	...	...	...	...	...	...	...	...	...
Park Lane Coll'y "	...	...	...	...	7 10	...	...	...	...	...	...	...	...	...	...	...
Bryn Junction arr	...	...	...	...	7 15	7 30	...	...	...	...	...	...	...	...	...	...
Bryn Junction dep	...	6 50	...	...	7 20	7 38	7 13	...	...	7 45	7 54	...	...	...	...	8 48
Garswood Hall Siding	...	...	7 5	...	7 35	...	...	...	...	...	...	...	...	...	...	...
Bryn Hall Siding	...	...	...	...	7 45	...	...	...	...	...	8 10	...	...	...	...	...
Ince Moss Junction arr	...	6 54	7 10	...	7 50	7 45	7 20	...	...	7 50	8 15	...	...	...	...	8 55
Springs Branch	...	...	...	...	...	7 47	7 25	...	...	...	...	...	...	...	...	...
WIGAN	...	W	...	...	W	...	...	7 35	...	W	...	...	...	...	8 45	W

No. 110—Leaves Ince Moss 7.35 p.m. and arrives Bamfurlong Sidings 7.40 p.m.

No. 113—Runs to Bamfurlong Sidings when required.

No. 117—Is limited to a load of 35 and van from Pocket Nook

London & North Western c.1909

Liverpool to Wigan and Pemberton Branch. 159

WEEK DAYS. UP. STATIONS.	Week Days.																			Sundays.											
	124	125	126	127	128	129	130	131	132	133	134	135	136	137	138	139	140	141	142	1	2	3	4	5	6	7	8	9	10	11	12
	Express Gd	Minra. Empty	Fast Gd		PAS	Minral	Fast Gd	Express Gd		Minral	Minral		Express Gd		PAS	PAS			Exp. Gd	Express Gd	Minral Empty		Minral Empty		Minral Empty		Minral Empty		PAS	PAS	
		175					198	435			107								435	127											
		S	SO			SO		S O		S			S						S	*	*										
Wigan to Preston, see pages 37 to 9.	P.M.	P.M.	P.M.		P.M.	p m	P M	P.M.		p.m.	P.M.		p m		p m	p.m.			p. m.	A.M.	A.M.		A.M.		A.M.		A.M.		A.M.	P.M.	
LIVERPOOL L. St. dep	...	...	...	...	9 30	...	...	...	...	...	...	...	...	...	10 55	11 40	...	...	...	11.30 p.m., from Widnes	11.15 p.m. from Garston.	...	...	...	1.5 a.m. from Garston.	...	3.10 a.m. from Garston.	...	8 10	6 45	...
LIVERPOOL Edge Hill	8 10	7.10 p.m. Garston. to Fleetwood	8 25	...	9 35	...	9 45	10 0	...	...	...	...	10 45	...	11 0	11 45	...	...	11 50			...	12 45	...		...		...	8 15	6 50	...
Olive Mount Junction	...		...	...	...	...	...	...	...	...	...	...	...	...	...	...	...	...	...			...	...	...		...		...	...	...	...
Broad Green	...		...	...	9 40	...	...	...	...	...	...	...	See note.	...	11 5	...	...	...	...			...	...	...		...		...	8 20	6 55	...
Roby	...		...	...	9 44	...	...	...	...	...	...	...		...	11 10	...	...	...	...			...	...	...		...		...	...	6 59	...
Huyton	...		...	...	9 47	...	...	...	...	...	...	...	...	...	11 13	...	...	...	...			...	...	...		...		...	8 27	7 2	...
Huyton Junction	8 30	...	8 35	...	9 48	...	9 57	10 12	...	...	...	...	11 0	...	11 14	11 51	...	...	...			...	...	...		...		...	8 28	7 3	...
Prescot dep	...	...	...	...	9 53	...	...	...	...	For Bamfurlong. Arrives Bamfurlong 11.30 p.m.	...	...	For Carlisle.	...	11 19	...	...	...	...	...	...	...	...	...	...	...	...	...	8 34	7 8	...
Eccleston Park	...	...	...	...	9 56	...	...	...	...		...	...		...	11 21	...	...	...	...	...	...	...	...	...	...	...	...	...	8 37	7 11	...
Thatto Heath	...	...	...	...	9 59	...	...	...	...		...	...		...	11 24	...	...	...	...	...	...	...	...	...	...	...	...	...	8 40	7 14	...
St. HELENS arr	...	...	...	...	10 4	...	...	...	...		...	...		...	11 28	11 59	...	...	...	...	...	...	...	...	...	...	...	...	8 44	7 18	...
St. HELENS dep	...	...	...	...	10 6	...	...	10 27	...		For Bamfurlong Sidings.	...		...	11 29	12 0	...	...	12 11	12 2	...	...	...	...	...	...	...	...	8 45	7 20	...
Pocket Nook Jct. arr	8 35	...	9 0	...	...	...	10 13	...	...			...	11 15	...	...	...	...	...	...	12 5	...	...	1 20	...	...	...	...	...	...	...	...
Pocket Nook Jct. dep	8 45	...	9 5	...	...	...	10 50	...	...			...	11 35	...	...	...	...	...	...	12 25	...	...	1 30	...	...	...	...	...	...	...	...
Gerard's Bridge Junction	...	...	...	...	...	...	...	...	...			...	...	...	...	...	...	...	...	...	...	...	...	...	...	...	...	...	...	...	...
Carr Mill	...	...	...	...	10X10	...	...	...	...			...	...	...	...	...	...	...	...	...	...	...	...	...	...	...	...	...	...	...	...
Carr Mill Junction	8 50	8 55	9 10	...	...	10 12	10 55	...	...			...	11 40	...	...	...	...	...	...	12 30	12 37	...	1 37	...	2 25	...	4 45	...	...	...	...
Garswood	...	...	...	...	10 16	...	...	...	...			...	...	...	11X35	...	...	...	...	...	...	...	...	...	...	...	...	...	8 52	7 29	...
Ashton Colliery Siding	...	...	...	...	...	...	...	...	...			...	...	...	...	...	...	...	...	...	...	...	...	...	...	...	...	...	...	...	...
Bryn (for Ashton-in-Makerfield)	...	...	...	...	10 19	...	...	...	...		...	...	-	...	11X39	...	...	...	...	...	...	...	...	...	...	...	...	...	8 56	7 33	...
Bryn Junction arr	9 0	9 7	9 20	...	...	10 25	11 3	10 42	...		...	...	11 50	...	...	Will not convey Passengers for beyond Wigan.	...	...	12 27	12 43	12 53	...	1 59	...	2 42	...	5 2	...	...	...	...
Pemberton and Norley Branches. Bryn Junction dep	For Carlisle.	...	...	...	Calls at Carr Mill on Sats. only	10.0 p.m. from Marsh's Siding	...	For Blackpool.	...		Is "C" on Saturdays.	...	Runs to Tebay on Fridays.	...	Calls at Garswood & Bryn on Sats. only.		...	...	...	...	...	...	...	...	...	...	...	...	...	...	...
Park Lane Colliery ar		...	...	...			...		...			...		...			...	...	...	...	...	...	...	...	...	...	...	...	...	...	...
Blundell's Pembrtn Col		...	C	...			C		...	...		...		...			...	...	For Blackpool.	...	C	...	C	...	C	...	C	...	...	...	...
Pemberton J. L.&Y. ,,		...		...					...	...		...		...			...	...		...		...		...		...		...	...	...	...
Norley Colliery arr		...		...			...		...	...		...		...			...	...		...	...	...	...	...	...	...	...	...	...	...	...
Norley Colliery dep	...	...	For Tebay	...			For Blackburn	...	...	...		...		...			...	...		...	...	...	...	...	...	...	...	...	...	...	...
Pemberton J. L.&Y.	...	...		...				...	...	...	...	...		...			...	...		...	...	...	...	...	...	...	...	...	...	...	...
Blundell's Pembrtn Col	...	...		...				...	...	10 30	11 0	...		...			...	...		...	...	...	...	...	...	...	...	...	...	...	...
Park Lane Coll'y ,,	...	...		...				...	...	10 50	11 10	...	...	...			...	...		...	...	...	...	...	...	...	...	...	...	...	...
Bryn Junction arr	...	...		...		...		...	...	10 55	11 15	...	...	...			...	...	...	...	...	...	...	...	...	...	...	...	...	...	...
Bryn Junction dep	9 0	9 7	9 20	...	...	10 25	11 3	10 42	...	11 0	11 20	...	11 50	...	...		...	...	12 27	12 43	12 53	...	1 59	...	2 42	...	5 2	...	...	...	...
Garswood Hall Siding	...	X	...	...	...	...	...	...	...	X	...	...	-	...	...	...	...	...	...	...	...	...	...	...	...	...	...	...	...	...	...
Bryn Hall Siding	...	X	...	...	...	...	...	...	...	X	...	...	...	...	...	...	...	...	...	...	...	...	...	...	...	...	...	...	...	...	...
Ince Moss Junction arr	9 10	...	9 25	...	...	-	11 6	10 47	...	11 20	...	...	11X55	...	...	...	...	...	12 32	12 50	1 0	...	2 5	...	2 50	...	5 10	...	...	...	...
Springs Branch	...	9 20	...	...	...	10 35	11 10	10 50	...	...	11 30	...	...	...	...	...	...	...	12 35	1 0	—	...	—	...	—	...	—	...	...	...	...
WIGAN	W	11 20	W	...	10 30	—	11 25	11 5	...	...	—	...	W	...	11 48	12 17	...	...	12 50	—	...	...	...	...	...	...	...	...	9 5	7 42	...

No. 130—This train must always convey not less than two breaked vehicles next to the engine,

No. 136—Calls at Ince Moss when required to pick up Meat traffic from Birkenhead. To follow 138 from Pocket Nook Jct. Is "C" Tebay to Carlisle,

Down Line

Wigan and Pemberton Branch to Liverpool. 160

Dist. from Wigan.	Week Days. Down. STATIONS.	1	2	3	4	5	6	7	8	9	10	11	12	13	14	15	16	17	18	19	20	21	22	23	24	25	26	27	28	29	30
		Minral	Minral	Minral		Minral	Mail	Minral Empt.		Minral		PAS	Minral	Minral	Minral	PAS	Minral	Minral	Exp. Gd	Minral	Minral	PAS		PAS		Minral	Minral	Express Gd		Minral	L.&Y. G.&C
		116						390					276				118									118	119				
		S M	S M			S M		S M		S M		M	S M	M	M	M O	S M	M O	M	M	M	M				MO	M	S M		M	M
	Preston to Wigan, see p. 4 to 36	a.m.	a.m.	a.m.	...	a.m.	A.M.	a.m.		A.M.		A.M.	a m	a.m.	a.m.	a.m.	A.M.	a m	A.M.	a.m.	a.m.	a.m.		a.m.		a m	A.M.	A M		a.m.	a m
...	WIGAN dep	12 20	...	...	...	...	1 35	1 20	...	...	...	3 0	1X53	...	...	3 20	...	...	W	...	...	4 50	...	...	...	...	...	5 25	...	...	...
1¼	Springs Branch	12 25	...	...	...	...	...	...	...	...	...	...	...	...	W	...	...	...	...	...	...	...	...	...	...	...	...	5 40	...	...	...
1¾	Ince Moss Junction	12 30	12 50	1 0	...	1 25	...	1 50	...	2 10	...	...	2 15	3 0	3 20	...	3 25	3 30	3 X 43	3 50	4 0	...	...	...	...	5 25	5 30	See note.	...	6 0	6 5
2¼	Bryn Hall Siding	12 45	...	...	...	...	...	...	...	...	...	...	...	...	...	...	...	...	...	...	...	...	...	...	...	...	...		...	...	...
2¾	Garswood Hall Sid.	1 0	...	...	...	...	...	...	...	...	...	...	2 40	...	...	...	...	...	...	4 25	...	...	...	...	...	...	...	...	...	...	...
3¼	Bryn Junction arr.	1 5	12 58	1 7	...	1 33	...	1 57	...	2 17	...	...	2 45	3 8	3 26	...	3 30	3 35	3 48	4 28	4 8	...	...	...	...	5 33	5 37	5 49	...	6 8	6 12
	Pemberton and Norley Branches. Bryn Junction dep	...	...	...	...	...	...	2 3	...	...	...	12.15 a.m. from Carlisle.	11.40 p.m., Carnforth to Clock Face	...	...	...	...	...	9.35 p.m. from Kendal.	...	4 13	...	...	...	...	...	...	12.20 a.m. from Carlisle.	...	...	6 20
	Park Lane Colliery ... arr.	Arrives Brynn Hall 12.35, Garswood Hall 12.50, and Garswood 1.10 a.m.	...	...	...	...	...	2 10	...	...	...			...	...	...	...	...		...	...	...	...	...	...	...	...		...	...	...
	Blundell's Pembrtn Col ,,		...	...	...	...	...	2 15	...	...	...			...	...	...	...	...		...	...	...	...	...	...	...	...		...	...	...
	Pemberton J. (L. & Y.) ...		...	...	...	...	...	—	...	...	...			...	...	...	...	...		...	4 18	...	...	...	...	...	...		...	...	6 30
	Norley Colliery ... arr.		...	...	...	...	...	...	...	...	...			...	...	...	Arrives Garswood 3.38 a.m.	...		...	...	...	...	...	...	...	...		...	...	...
	Norley Colliery ... dep.		...	...	...	...	...	...	...	...	...			...	...	...		...		...	...	...	...	...	...	...	...		...	...	...
	Pemberton J. (L. & Y.) ,,		C	C	...	C	...	Arrives Ince Moss 1.30 a.m.	...	C	...			C	C	12.10 a.m. from Carlisle.	C	C		C	4 40	...	...	...	...	C	C		...	C	...
	Blundell's Pembrtn Col ,,				...		...		...		...										...	...	...	...	...				...		...
	Park Lane Colliery ... ,,		...	...	...	...	...		...	...	...			...	...			...		...	4 50	...	...	...	...	...	...		...	...	...
	Bryn Junction arr.		...	...	...	...	...		...	...	...			...	...			...		...	...	...	...	...	...	...	...	...	...	...	...
3¼	Bryn Junction dep.	1 5	12 58	1 7	...	1 33	...	...	...	2 17	...	...	2 45	3 8	3 28		3 30	3 35		4 28	4 55	...	...	...	...	5 33	5 37	5 49	...	6 8	6.0 a.m., Bamfurlong Siding, to Aintree
3¾	Bryn (for Ashton-in-Makerfield)	...	...	...	...	...	...	...	...	...	...	...	...	...	...		...	...		...	C	...	...	...	...	...	...	...	...	...	
4¼	Ashton Colliery Siding	...	...	...	...	...	...	...	...	...	...	...	...	...	...		...	...		...		...	...	...	...	...	...	...	...	...	
5	Garswood	1 25	...	...	...	...	...	11.45 p.m. from Preston.	...	...	...	...	3 0	...	...	...	4 0	4 0		...	...	...	...	...	...	...	...	X	...	...	
7¼	Carr Mill Junction	1 34	1 15	1 20	...	1 52	...		...	2 30	...	...	3 15	3 20	3 40	...	4 7	4 7	3 58	4 40	5 7	...	...	...	...	5 45	5 50	6 2	...	6 25	
7½	Carr Mill	...	...	...	...	...	...		...	...	...	...	...	For Garston.	1.45 a.m. Hulton Siding to Garston.	...	...	...	...	...	...	...	...	...	...	...	...	"C" on Tues.	...	...	
8⅛	Gerard's Bridge Junction	...	...	...	...	For Garston.	...		...	...	...	...	...			...	...	...	...	For Widnes.	...	...	...	...	...	...	...		...	...	
8⅜	Pocket Nook Jun. arr	...	...	...	...		...		...	...	...	...	...			...	...	...	...		...	...	...	...	...	...	...		...	...	
	Pocket Nook Jun. dep	...	...	1 25	...		...		...	...	...	...	...			...	...	...	...		...	...	...	...	...	...	...		...	6 30	
8¾	St. HELENS arr	1 40	...	...	...		1 50		...	...	...	3 15	...			3 35	4 12	4 12	4 3		...	5 5	...	...	...	5 50	...	6 7	...	...	
	St. HELENS dep	2 0	...	1 27	...		1 51	...	...	...	...	3 16	...			3 36	4 25	4 25	4 10		...	5 10	...	5 45	...	6 0	...	6 20	...	6 33	
10¼	Thatto Heath	...	...	...	...		...	...	...	...	...	...	Runs to Ince Moss only on Tuesday mornings.			...	...	...	...		...	...	...	5 49	...	...	...	...	...	...	
11¼	Eccleston Park	...	...	...	...		...	...	...	...	...	...				...	...	...	...		...	...	...	...	...	...	...	...	...	...	
12¼	Prescot	...	...	...	...	...	...	...	...	...	...	...				...	...	...	...		...	...	...	5 54	...	...	...	...	...	...	
14	Huyton Junction	2 20	...	1 46	...	...	2 1	...	...	...	...	...		...	...	3 47	For Garston.	4 44	4 25	...	To Clock Face.	...	...	5 57	...	...	...	6 32	...	6 45	...
14½	Huyton	...	To Garston.	...	...	...	...	...	...	For Garston.	...	...		...	...	...		...	...	...		...	...	5 59	...	For Garston.	For Garston.	...	...	...	...
15	Roby	...		...	...	...	...	...	...		...	...		...	...	...		...	PL	...		...	...	...	...			PL	...	...	...
16⅝	Broad Green	...		...	...	...	...	...	...		...	...		...	...	...		...	...	...		...	...	6 3	...			...	...	...	...
17½	Olive Mount Junction	2 27		1 55	...	...	...	...	...		...	...		...	...	...		4 55	4 35	...		...	...	...	...			6 42	...	6 55	...
18⅞	LIVERPOOL Edge H. arr	2 30		2 0	...	...	2 10	...	...		...	3 34		...	...	3 55		5 0	4 40	...		5 25	...	6 10	...		...	6 45	...	7 0	...
	LIVERPOOL ,, ,, dep	—	...	—	...	...	2 11	...	...	...	...	3 36		...	...	3 56	...	—	—	...		5 30	...	6 11	...	...	...	—	...	—	...
20¼	LIVERPOOL Lime St. arr	...	...	...	...	...	2 15	...	...	...	...	3 40		...	...	4 0	...	...	...	...		5 35	...	6 15	...	...	...	...	...	...	...

No. 1—Calls at Ince Moss to attach only.

Nos. 16 and 26—Start from Bamfurlong Sidings when required.

No. 27—Calls at Garswood to set down Cattle when required.

London & North Western c.1909

Wigan and Pemberton Branch to Liverpool. 161

Week Days. STATIONS.	31	32	33	34	35	36	37	38	39	40	41
			Exp. Gd	PAS	Emp. Coachs	Minrl	PAS	Minral	Minral	Gd	Fast Gd
Down—(See Note A)								103	141	281	
Preston to Wigan, see pages 4 to 36.			SM a.m.	A.M.	a m	a m	A.M.	A.M.	a.m.	a.m.	a m
WIGAN ...dep	...	...	6 21	7 0	7 5	...	7 55	...	...	...	...
Springs Branch	...	...	6 30	...	...	...	...	...	...	...	...
Ince Moss Junction	...	...	6 34	...	...	7 30	...	7 40	8 10	...	8 25
Bryn Hall Siding	...	...	...	...	...	...	...	7 50	8 25	...	8 30
Garswood Hall Sid.	...	...	...	...	...	...	...	8 5	8 30	...	8 35
Bryn Junction ...arr	...	...	6 40	...	...	7 38	...	8 10		...	8 40
Pemberton and Norley Branches: Bryn Junction ...dep	...	...	...	...	...	...	...	8 15	...	...	...
Park Lane Colliery ar	...	...	...	...	...	...	...	8 20	...	...	C
Blundell's Pembrtn Co	...	...	...	...	...	C	...	8 35	...	...	...
Pemberton Jun. L.&Y	...	...	...	...	...	...	...		...	...	...
Norley Colliey arr	...	...	...	...	...	...	...	...	...	...	...
Norley Colliey dep	...	...	2.25 a.m. from Carlisle.	...	...	...	...	...	...	Shunts as required at Prescot, from 8.40 a.m. to 10.10 a.m.	For Widnes.
Pemberton Jun. L.&Y	...	...		...	...	...	...	...	...		
Blundell's Pembrtn Co	...	...		...	...	...	...	...	...		
Park Lane Colliery...	...	...		...	...	...	...	...	...		
Bryn Junction ...arr	...	...	...	...	...	...	...	...	...		...
Bryn Junction ...dep	...	...	6 40	...	...	7 38	...	...	...		8 40
Bryn (for Ashton-in-Makerfld)	...	...	...	7 7	...	...	8 2		...		...
Ashton Colliery Siding	...	...	...	...	...	...	...		...		...
Garswood	...	...	...	7 11	7 15	...	8 6		...		8 50
Carr Mill Junction	...	...	6 57	...	...	7 50	...				8 58
Carr Mill	...	...	...	7 15	...	...	8 10	7.35 a.m. from Bamfurlong Sidings.	8.0 a.m. from Bamfurlong.		...
Gerard's Bridge Junc	...	...	...	...	...	...	...				...
Pocket Nook Jct. arr	...	...	...	...	...	...	...			...	...
Pocket Nook Jct. dep	...	...	...	...	...	7 55	...		...	...	...
St. HELENS arr	...	...	7 3	7 20	...	...	8 15		...	...	...
St. HELENS dep	...	...	7X10	7 21	...	7 57	8 17		...	8 30	...
Thatto Heath	...	...	...	7 25	...	...	8 23		...	...	...
Eccleston Park	...	...	...	7 28	...	...	8 26	...	...	...	...
Prescot	...	...	...	7 31	...	...	8 30	...	...	8 40	...
Huyton Junction	...	...	7 25	7 34	...	8 10	8 33	...	...		...
Huyton	...	...	...	7 36	...	...	8 35	...	...	...	...
Roby	...	...	PL	7 39	...	...	8 38	...	...	...	...
Broad Green	...	...	...	7 44	...	...	8 43	...	...	...	...
Olive Mount Junction	...	...	7 35	...	...	8 20	...	...	...	...	...
LIVERPOOL EdgeH. ar	...	...	7 40	7 49	...	8 25	8 49	...	...	...	...
LIVERPOOL ,, dp	...	...		7 51	...		8 51	...	...	...	...
LIVERPOOL LimeS. ar	...	...	...	7 55	...	...	8 55	...	...	...	...

Week Days. STATIONS.	42	43	44	45	46	47	48	49	50	51
	PAS	Minral	PAS	Minral	Minrl	Minral	L.&Y. Coal	Minral	PAS	PAS
Down—(See Note A)		224						141		
Preston to Wigan, see pages 4 to 36.	A.M.	SM a.m.	a.m.	M a.m.	MO a.m.	A.M.	SM a.m.	a. m.	a.m.	A.M.
WIGAN ...dep	8 58	W	...	...	...	...	...	...	10 10	...
Springs Branch	...	...	...	8 45	...	...	...	...	...	...
Ince Moss Junction	...	8 45	...	9 5	9 5	9 20	...	9 48	...	...
Bryn Hall Siding	...	8 55	...	...	...	...	...	10 10	...	...
Garswood Hall Sid.	...	9 18	...	...	...	...	9 30	10 15	...	...
Bryn Junction ...arr	...	9 22	...	9 17	9 17	9 28	9 35		...	...
Pemberton and Norley Branches: Bryn Junction ...dep	...	...	...	...	...	...	9 42	...	...	...
Park Lane Colliery ar	...	...	...	...	...	...	9 47	...	...	...
Blundell's Pembrtn Co	...	...	...	C	...	C	...	C	...	...
Pemberton Jun. L.&Y	...	...	...	...	...	...	10 8	...	...	...
Norley Colliey arr	...	...	...	...	...	...	...	...	...	...
Norley Colliey dep	...	...	...	...	...	...	...	...	...	...
Pemberton Jun. L.&Y	...	...	...	...	...	...	...	...	...	...
Blundell's Pembrtn Co	...	...	...	...	...	...	...	...	...	...
Park Lane Colliery...	...	...	...	...	...	...		...	...	...
Bryn Junction ...arr	...	...	...	...	...	...		...	...	...
Bryn Junction ...dep	...	9 22	...	9 17	9 17	9 28		...	...	...
Bryn (for Ashton-in-Makerfld)	9 5	...	...	...	...	...		...	10 19	...
Ashton Colliery Siding	...	...	...	...	...	...		...	...	...
Garswood	9 9	...	...	...	...	...			10 23	...
Carr Mill Junction	...	9 35	...	9 30	9 30	9 40			...	...
Carr Mill	...	...	...	...	...	...	To Winstanley Colliery Siding (S). To Wigan Shed (SO).	9.40 a.m. from Bamfurlong.	...	...
Gerard's Bridge Junc	...	...	...	...	...	...			...	...
Pocket Nook Jct. arr	...	...	...	...	...	...			...	...
Pocket Nook Jct. dep	...	...	...	...	...	...			...	...
St. HELENS arr	9 17	...	...	9 35	9 35	...			10 30	...
St. HELENS dep	9 18	...	9 45	9 55	9 55	...		...	10 35	10 50
Thatto Heath	9 23		9 49	...	...	...		...	...	10 55
Eccleston Park	9 26		9 53	...	...	...		...	...	10 58
Prescot	9 29		9 56	...	...	...		...	...	11 1
Huyton Junction	9 33		9 58	10 20	10 20			...	...	11 4
Huyton	9 34		...	...	...			...	...	11 6
Roby	...	4.15 a.m., Fleetwood to Widnes.	...	...	...	For Garston.	...	...	...	11 9
Broad Green	9 38		...	...	...		...	...	...	11 13
Olive Mount Junction	...		...	...	...		...	...	...	...
LIVERPOOL EdgeH. ar	9 44		10 5	10 35	10 35		...	...	10 52	11 18
LIVERPOOL ,, dp	9 46		10 6			...	...	...	10 54	11 20
LIVERPOOL LimeS. ar	9 50		10 10	...	...	...	...	...	10 58	11 25

Week Days. STATIONS.	52	53	54	55	56	57	58	59	60	61
		Gd	Minral	PAS	Gd	L.&Y. Minral	L.&Y. Eng. & 2 Vans	Minral	Minral	Minral
Down—(See Note A)			103		281			225	161	141
Preston to Wigan, see pages 4 to 36.		A.M.	A.M.	A.M.	SO a m	S a.m.	S a.m.	M a.m.	MO noon	p.m.
WIGAN ...dep	...	...	...	11 5	...	...	...	...	...	...
Springs Branch	...	...	...	...	...	...	...	...	...	...
Ince Moss Junction	...	10 40	10 50	...	...	...	...	11 30	12 0	12 8
Bryn Hall Siding	...	...	10 55	...	...	11 10	...	...	...	12 12
Garswood Hall Sid.	...	...	11 0	...	...	...	...	11 55	...	12 25
Bryn Junction ...arr	...	10 48	11 5	...	...	11 15	...	12 0	12 5	12 30
Pemberton and Norley Branches: Bryn Junction ...dep	...	...	11 10	...	...	11 25	...	...	...	12 35
Park Lane Colliery ar	...	...	11 15	...	...	11 30	...	...	...	12 40
Blundell's Pembrtn Co	...	C	11 25	...		...	...	...	...	1 0
Pemberton Jun. L.&Y	...	...	...	...		11 40	11 50	...	...	
Norley Colliey arr	...	...	11 35	...			12 10	...	...	...
Norley Colliey dep	...	...		...	Does Shunting at Prescot as required.	...	...	...	...	...
Pemberton Jun. L.&Y	...	...	...	...		...	...	...	...	...
Blundell's Pembrtn Co	...	...	...	...		...	...	...	...	...
Park Lane Colliery...	...	...	...	...		...	...	...	...	...
Bryn Junction ...arr	...	...	...	...	...	...	...	...	...	...
Bryn Junction ...dep	...	10 48	...	...	...	...	...	12 0	12 5	...
Bryn (for Ashton-in-Makerfld)	...	...	...	11 12	...	...	...	...	...	...
Ashton Colliery Siding	...	...	...	...	...	...	...	...	...	...
Garswood	...	...	...	11 17	...	...	...	...	...	
Carr Mill Junction	...	11 0	...	...	...		...	12 12	12 17	
Carr Mill	...	...	...	11 21	...		...	...	...	
Gerard's Bridge Junc	...	...	...	...	...		...	...		
Pocket Nook Jct. arr	...	...	...	...	...	For Sandhills.	...	...		11.50 a.m. from Bamfurlong.
Pocket Nook Jct. dep	...	...	...	...	...		...	...	For Garston	
St. HELENS arr	...	...	...	11 27	...		...	...		
St. HELENS dep	...	11 6	...	11 30	11 50		...	...		
Thatto Heath	...	...	...	11 35	...	...	...	...		...
Eccleston Park	...	...	...	11 38	...	...	...	...		...
Prescot	...	...	...	11 41	12 0	...	...	...	...	...
Huyton Junction	...	11 24	...	...		...	...	...	...	...
Huyton	...	...	...	11 46	...	...	...		...	...
Roby	...	...	...	11 49	...	...	...	For Widnes.	...	...
Broad Green	...	...	...	11 54	...	...	...		...	...
Olive Mount Junction	...	...	...	...	...	...	...		...	...
LIVERPOOL EdgeH. ar	...	11 40	...	12 3	...	...	...		...	...
LIVERPOOL ,, dp	...		...	12 5	...	...	...	...	...	...
LIVERPOOL LimeS. ar	...	...	...	12 10	...	...	...	...	...	...

A.—Trains from Wigan to Liverpool run over the Up Line to Springs Branch No. 1 Junction Box, and from that point over the down line to Liverpool.

No. 33 (X)—Calls at St. Helens when required to detach perishable traffic from the North only.

162 Wigan and Pemberton Branch and Liverpool.

Week Days. DOWN. STATIONS.	62	63	64	65	66	67	68	69	70	71	72
	PAS	Gd	Exp Gd	Minral	Minral	L.&Y. Minral	PAS	Gd	Minral	PAS	Gd
		107	2		277			135	345		277
Preston to Wigan, see p. 4 to 36	p.m.	P.M	a.m.	p.m.	SO p.m.	p m	SO p m	S p.m	S p.m.	P.M.	S p m
WIGAN	12 3	...	11 40	...	...	...	...	...	W	1 15	...
Springs Branch	...	...	11 45	...	...	...	...	12 20	...	...	...
Ince Moss Junction	...	12 20	12 18	...	...	...	...	12 25	12 35	...	...
Bryn Hall Siding	...	...	...	...	...	...	...	X	...	...	
Garswood Hall Siding	...	12 25	...	...	...	...	...	X	...	...	
Bryn Junction ...arr	...		12 23	...	...	...	...	12 34	12 40	...	
Pemberton and Norley Branches: Bryn Junction ...dep.	...	...	...	...	...	...	...	...	...	...	
Park Lane Colliery arr	...	...		...	...	...	...		...	...	
Blundell's Pembrtn Col.	...	C		C	...	...	...	C	...	...	
Pemberton J., L. & Y.	...		Calls at Stone's Siding Garswood when required.		...	...	...		...	...	Does shunting at Prescot when required.
Norley Colliery arr.	...	...		...	...	...	...		...	...	
Norley Colliery dep.	...	...		...	...	12 30	...		...	...	
Pemberton J., L.&Y. ,,	...	...		...	...	...	...	Is a regular train on Mons.	...	...	
Blundell's Pembrtn Col.	...	...		...	...	12 58	...		...	...	
Park Lane Colliery ,,	...	...		...	...	...	...		...	...	
Bryn Junction ...arr.	...	...	...	...	...	...	...		...	...	...
Bryn Junction ...dep.	...	...	12 23	12 25	...	...	...	12 34	12 40	...	...
Bryn (for Ashton-in-Makfield)	...	...	...	...	...	...	...	...	...	1 22	...
Ashton Colliery Siding	...	...	...	...	...	...	...	...	...	...	...
Garswood	...	...	X	...	...	...	...	...	...	1 26	...
Carr Mill Junction	...	...	12 34	12 36	...		...	12 45	12 50	...	...
Carr Mill	...	...	...	...	12 40		...	...		1 30	...
Gerrard's Bridge Junc.	...	...	...	...	...		...	...		...	...
Pocket Nook Junc. arr	...	...	...	...	12 45	For Sandhills.	...	12 50	11.10 a.m., Hulton Siding to Garston.	...	...
Pocket Nook Junc. dep	...	...	...	...			...	1 55		...	...
St. HELENS arr	12 17	...	12 40	...	...		...	...		1 35	...
St. HELENS dep	12 18	...	12 50	...	...	...	1 15	2 0		1 36	2 0
Thatto Heath	...	...	...	...	...	...	...	...		1 40	...
Eccleston Park	...	...	...	...	...	...	...	...		1 43	...
Prescot	12 26	...	...	...	...	...	1 22	...		1 46	2 15
Huyton Junction	12 29	...	1 10	...	...	...	1 25			1 49	
Huyton	12 31	...	...		...	...	1 27		...	1 51	...
Roby	...	...	...	For Garston.	...	...	1 30	To Clock Face	...	1 54	...
Broad Green	...	...	...		...	...	...		...	1 59	...
Olive Mount Junction	...	...	1 20		...	...	...		...	...	...
LIVERPOOL EdgeH. arr	12 39	...	1 25		...	...	1 41		...	2 4	...
LIVERPOOL ,, dep	12 41	...		...	...	...	1 44		...	2 6	...
LIVERPOOL Lime S. arr	12 45	...	..	...	...	...	1 48		...	2 10	...

Week Days. DOWN. STATIONS.	73	74	75	76	77	78	79	80	81	82
	Minral	Minra		Exp. Goods.	Gd	PAS			Minral	Minral Empty
	265				103					
Preston to Wigan, see p. 4 to 36	S p m	p m		p.m.	P.M.	p m			P.M.	p m
WIGAN	...	W	...	W	...	2 20	...		...	...
Springs Branch	...	...	...	...	...	...	...	...	...	...
Ince Moss Junction	...	1 15	...	1 50	2 5	...	...	...	...	3 0
Bryn Hall Siding	...	...	...	...	2 10	...	...	...	...	...
Garswood Hall Siding	...	...	...	...	2 15	...	...	...	...	...
Bryn Junction ...arr	...	1 24	...	1 58	2 17	...	...	...	...	3 8
Pemberton and Norley Branches: Bryn Junction ...dep.	...	...	...	...	2 25	...	...	...	...	...
Park Lane Colliery arr	...	...	...	...	2 30	...	...	...	...	...
Blundell's Pembrtn Col.	C	C	...	C	2 40	...	...	...	C	...
Pemberton J., L. & Y.	...	...	...	...		...	...	...	...	...
Norley Colliery arr.	...	...	...	...	C	...	...	...	...	...
Norley Colliery dep.	...	...	...	...		...	...	...	2 0	...
Pemberton J., L.&Y. ,,	...	...	...	...	...	...	...	...	...	...
Blundell's Pembrtn Col.	...	...	...	...	...	...	...	...	2 20	...
Park Lane Colliery ,,	...	...	...	...	...	...	...	...	2 45	...
Bryn Junction ...arr.	...	...	...	...	...	...	...	...	...	...
Bryn Junction ...dep.	...	1 24	...	1 58	...	...	...	...	2 55	3 8
Bryn (for Ashton-in-Makfield)	...	...	...	...	...	2 28	...	...	...	...
Ashton Colliery Siding	...	...	...	...	...	...	...	...	...	...
Garswood	1 30	...	...	...	...	2 32	...	...	X	3 20
Carr Mill Junction	1 37	1 39	...	2 10	...	...	...	...	3 10	
Carr Mill	...	...	...	...	...	2 36	...	...	...	...
Gerrard's Bridge Junc.	...	...	...	...	...	...	...	...	...	...
Pocket Nook Junc. arr	1 42	...	...	...	...	...	...	...	...	...
Pocket Nook Junc. dep	2 7		...	...	...	...	...	...	...	...
St. HELENS arr	2 10		...	2 20	...	2 41	...	...	3 15	...
St. HELENS dep	2 25		...		...	2 43	...	...	3 45	...
Thatto Heath	...		...	...	...	2 48	...	...	...	...
Eccleston Park			...	...	...	2 51	...	...	...	...
Prescot			...	...	...	2 57	...	...	...	...
Huyton Junction		12.45 p.m. Abram Colliery to Garston	...		...	3 0	...	...		...
Huyton	For Clock Face.		...		...	3 2	...	...		...
Roby			...	11.40 a.m. from Blackburn.	...	3 5	...	...	For Clock Face.	...
Broad Green			...		...	3 9	...	...		...
Olive Mount Junction			...		...	...	...	...		...
LIVERPOOL EdgeH. arr			...		...	3 14	...	...		...
LIVERPOOL ,, dep			...		...	3 16	...	...		...
LIVERPOOL Lime S. arr	...	...	...	...	...	3 20	...	...	...	...

Week Days. DOWN. STATIONS.	83	84	85	86	87	88	89	90	91	92
	Minral	Minral	PAS	Minral	Exp. Gds.	Minral	Minral	Minral		Minral
	163	6		227				107		
Preston to Wigan, see p. 4 to 36	p.m.	MS p.m.	p.m.	p.m.	p m	p.m.	P.M.	p m		P.M.
WIGAN	W	3 10	3 45	...	W	...	W	...	...	W
Springs Branch	...	3 20	...	...	...	...	...	...	...	...
Ince Moss Junction	3 15	3 25	...	...	3 40	3 55	4 5	4 10	...	4 25
Bryn Hall Siding	...	...	...	...	...	...	...	...	...	...
Garswood Hall Siding	...	...	...	...	...	...	...	4 20	...	...
Bryn Junction ...arr	3 22	3 30	...	...	3 45	4 3	4 13	4 25	...	4 32
Pemberton and Norley Branches: Bryn Junction ...dep.	...	3 35	...	...	...	...	...	4 30	...	...
Park Lane Colliery arr	...	3 40	...	...		...	...	4 35	...	...
Blundell's Pembrtn Col.	...	3 45	...	...		C	C	4 55	...	C
Pemberton J., L. & Y.	...		...	...	12.55 p.m. from Blackpool (T.R.)			...	...	
Norley Colliery arr.	...	C	...	...		...	...	5 35	...	...
Norley Colliery dep.	...		...	3 15		...	...		...	...
Pemberton J., L.&Y. ,,	...	...	...	...		...	...	...	...	...
Blundell's Pembrtn Col.	...	...	...	3 35		...	...	...	...	...
Park Lane Colliery ,,	...	...	...	3 45		...	...	...	...	...
Bryn Junction ...arr.	...	...	...	...	...	...	...	...	...	...
Bryn Junction ...dep.	3 22	...	...	3 55	3 45	4 3	4 18	...	...	4 32
Bryn (for Ashton-in-Makfield)	...	...	3 53	...	...	...	...	...	...	...
Ashton Colliery Siding	...	...	...	...	...	...	...	...	...	...
Garswood	...	...	3 57	...	4 5	...	...	...	...	...
Carr Mill Junction	3 37	...	...	4 7	4 12	4 17	4 30	...	...	4 48
Carr Mill	...	...	4 1	...	...	...		...	...	
Gerrard's Bridge Junc.		...	...		...	...		...	...	
Pocket Nook Junc. arr		...	...		C			...	...	
Pocket Nook Junc. dep		...	...		...			...	...	
St. HELENS arr		...	4 6		...			...	...	3.28 p.m. Tyldesley to Garston.
St. HELENS dep		...	4 10	For Widnes.	4 17			...	...	
Thatto Heath		...	4 15		...	For Widnes.		...	...	
Eccleston Park		...	4 18		...		3.0 p.m. Hulton Siding to Garston.	...	...	
Prescot	11.35 a.m., Carnforth to Garston.	...	4 22	...	...			Leaves Blundell's Siding 5.0 p.m.	...	
Huyton Junction		...	4 25	...	4 35	...			...	
Huyton		...	4 27	...	...	...			...	...
Roby		...	4 30	...	...	...	...		...	...
Broad Green		...	4 34	...	...	...	...	...	...	...
Olive Mount Junction	...	...	...	...	...	...	...	...	...	...
LIVERPOOL EdgeH. arr	...	...	4 39	...	4 50	...	...	...	...	...
LIVERPOOL ,, dep	...	...	4 41	...		...	...	...	...	...
LIVERPOOL Lime S. arr	...	...	4 45	...	...	...	...	...	...	...

No. 81—Calls at Garswood on Saturdays and runs via Blackbrook when required. Is Engine and Van between Norley and Blundell's Siding.

No. 87—Arrives Garswood 3.55 p.m.

London & North Western c.1909

Wigan and Pemberton Branch to Liverpool. 163

Week Days. Down.

STATIONS.	93	94	95	96	97	98	99	100	101	102	103	104	105	106	107
	Gd	Minral	PAS	Minral	Minral	PAS	PAS	Minral Empty	Minral	Minral	Minral	Cattle	Minral	Minral	
	198	173			163					175			6		
			S	MO				S O		S O		S	MS	S O	
(Preston to Wigan, see pages 4 to 6)	p m	p.m.	p.m.	p m	p.m.	P.M.	p.m.	p m	P.M.	pm	P.M.	p m	P.M.	p.m.	
WIGAN ....dep	W	...	.	Arrives Garswood 4.35 p.m.	...	5 5	5 15	...	...	...	...	...	...	...	...
Springs Branch	...	...	..		...	...	...	W	...	...	W	W	...	...	...
Ince Moss Junction	4 0	4 30	...		5 0	...	...	5 20	5 25	5 30	5 40	5 50	...	6 0	...
Bryn Hall Siding	...	X	...		...	...	...	...	...	...	...	...	...	...	...
Garswood Hall Siding ...	...	...	...		...	...	...	...	...	...	...	...	...	...	...
Bryn Junction ....arr	4 10	4 41	...		...	...	...	5 30	5 33	5 38	5 49	5 56	...	6 10	...
(Pemberton and Norley Branches.) Bryn Junction ......dep	...	...	...		...	...	...	5 35	...	...	...	W	...	6 15	...
Park Lane Colliery arr	C	...	...		...	...	...	5 40	C	...	C	C	...	...	...
Blundell's Pembrtn Col.		...	...		...	...	...	5 50		...			...	6 25	...
Pemberton J. L&Y ,,		...	...	...	...	...	...		...	...	...		...	...	...
Norley Colliery arr	2.10 p.m. from Blackburn.	...	...	...	...	...	...	...	...	...	...	4.25p.m. from Oxheys.	...	...	...
Norley Colliery dep		...	...	...	...	...	...	...	...	...	...		...	...	...
Pemberton J. L&Y ,,		...	...	...	...	...	...	...	...	...	...		...	...	...
Blundell's Pembrtn Col		...	...	4 0	...	...	...	...	...	...	...		5 30	6 55	...
Park Lane Colliery ,,		...	...	4 15	...	...	...	...	...	...	...		5 45	7 55	...
Bryn Junction ......arr		...	...	4 20	...	...	...	...	...	...	...		5 50	...	...
Bryn Junction ......dep	4 10	4 41	...	4 25	5 6	...	...	...	5 33	6 0	5 49	5 56	5 55	8 0	...
Bryn (For Ashton-in-Makfield)	...	...	...	...	...	...	5 23	...	...	...	...	...	...	...	...
Ashton Colliery Siding...	...	...	...	...	...	...	...	...	...	...	...	...	...	...	...
Garswood.....................	X	...	...	5 18	...	...	5 27	3.30 p.m. from Preston.	...	...	...	...	6 35	...	...
Carr Mill Junction.........	4 28	4 53	...	5 25	5 13	...	...		5 50	6 15	6 10	6 10	6 41	8 18	...
Carr Mill	...	...	...	...	...	...	5 31		...	...	...	...	...	...	...
Gerard's Bridge Junction	...	...	...	...	...	...	...		...	...	4.30 p.m. Hulton Siding to Garston.	...	...	...	...
Pocket Nook Junc. arr	...	...	...	...	For Garston.	...	...		...	For Garston.		...	...	...	...
Pocket Nook Junc. dep	...	...	...	...		...	...		...			...	...	...	...
ST. HELENS ......arr	...	For Garston.	...	5 30		5 19	5 36		5 58			6 15	6 48	8 22	...
ST. HELENS ......dep	4 35		5 0	5 50		5 20	5 40		6 5			6 20	7 30	8 45	...
Thatto Heath	...		5 5	...		...	5 45	...	...			...	...	...	...
Eccleston Park	...		5 8	...	...	..	5 48	...	...			...	...	...	...
Prescot	X		5 12	...	...	5 29	5 52	...	...	...		...	...	...	...
Huyton Junction	4 55	...	15	6 9	...	5 32	5 56	...	6 23	...	...	6 35	7 49	...	...
Huyton	...	...	17	...	...	5 35	5 58	...	...	...	...	...	...	...	...
Roby	...	...	5 20	...	...	...	6 1	...	...	...	...	...	4	For Clock Face.	...
Broad Green	...	...	5 24	...	...	...	6 6	...	...	...	...	...	...		...
Olive Mount Junction ...	...	...	...	6 20	...	...	...	...	...	...	...	...	8 0		...
LIVERPOOL Edge H. arr	5 10	...	5 29	6 25	...	5 42	6 12	...	6 40	...	...	6 50	8 5		...
LIVERPOOL ,, ,, dp		...	5 31		...	5 44	6 14	...		...	...				...
LIVERPOOL Lime St. arr	...	...	5 35	...	...	5 48	6 20	...	...	...	...	...	...	...	...

STATIONS.	108	109	110	111	112	113	114	115	116	117	118	119	120	121	122	123
	PAS	Minr'l	Minral	PAS	Minral	Minral		L. & Y. Minral	PAS	Minral	PAS		Minral	Minral	PAS	Minral
		163	175						435				175			173
		S O	S		S O			S		S			MO	S		
(Preston to Wigan, see pages 4 to 6)	P.M.	p.m.	p m	p m	p m	p m		p m	p.m.	p.m.	p.m.		p.m.	p.m.	p m	p m
WIGAN ....dep	6 5	...	...	7 0	...	6 30	...	...	7 55	...	8 20	...	...	...	8 55	...
Springs Branch	...	...	W	...	...	7 20	...	...	...	...	...	...	...	..	...	W
Ince Moss Junction	...	6 15	6 30	...	7 10	7 22	...	...	...	8 5	...	...	8 35	8 40	...	8 50
Bryn Hall Siding	...	...	...	...	7 30	...	...	...	...	...	...	...	...	9 0	...	...
Garswood Hall Siding ...	...	...	...	...	7 40	...	...	...	...	...	...	...	X	9 20	...	...
Bryn Junction ....arr	...	6 21	6 38	...	7 45	7 27	...	...	...	8 15	...	...	8 42	9 25	...	8 58
(Pemberton and Norley Branches.) Bryn Junction ......dep	...	...	...	...	...	...	...	...	...	8 20	...	...	...	9 35	...	...
Park Lane Colliery arr	...	...	C	...	...	C	...	...	...	...	...	...	C	10 0	...	C
Blundell's Pembrtn Col.	...	...		...	...		...	...	...	8 30	...	...		10 10	...	
Pemberton J. L&Y ,,	...	...	...	...	...	...	...	...	7.0 p.m. from Blackpool.	...	...	...	...		...	...
Norley Colliery arr	...	...	...	...	...	...	...	8 30		...	...	...	...	...	...	...
Norley Colliery dep	...	...	...	...	...	...	...	8 45		...	...	...	...	...	...	...
Pemberton J. L&Y ,,	...	...	...	...	...	...	...	...		...	...	...	...	...	...	...
Blundell's Pembrtn Col	...	...	...	...	...	...	...	...		9 0	...	...	...	...	...	...
Park Lane Colliery ,,	...	...	...	...	...	...	...	...		9 55	...	...	...	...	...	...
Bryn Junction ......arr	...	...	...	...	...	...	...	...	...	...	...	...	...	...	...	...
Bryn Junction ......dep	...	6 21	6 58	...	7 45	7 27	...	...	...	10 0	...	...	8 42	...	...	8 58
Bryn (For Ashton-in-Makfield)	6 13	...	...	7 7	...	...	...	Works traffic for Park Lane Siding if required.	...	...	8 27	...	X	...	...	...
Ashton Colliery Siding...	...	...	...	...	...	...	...		...	...	...	...	...	...	...	...
Garswood.....................	6 17	...	...	7 11	...	...	...		...	...	8 31	...	...	...	...	...
Carr Mill Junction.........	...	6 35	7 10	...	8 5	7 35	...		...	10 17	...	...	8 55	...	...	9 20
Carr Mill	6 21	...	...	...	...	...	...		...	...	8 35	...	...	...	...	...
Gerard's Bridge Junction	...	...	...	...	For Widnes.	...	...		...	...	...	...	...	...	...	...
Pocket Nook Junc. arr	...	...	...	...		6.5 p.m., Broomfields to Garston	...		...	...	...	...	For Garston.	...	...	...
Pocket Nook Junc. dep	...	...	...	...			...		...	...	...	...		...	...	...
ST. HELENS ......arr	6 26	To Garston.	...	7 19			...		8 10	10 25	8 40	...		...	9 9	7.30 p.m., Howe Bdg. West to Garston.
ST. HELENS ......dep	6 28		...	7 21			...		8 11	10 45	8 41	...		...	9 10	
Thatto Heath	6 33		...	7 26			...		...	...	8 46	...		...	...	
Eccleston Park	6 36		...	7 29			...		...	...	8 49	...		...	...	
Prescot	6 40		...	7 33	...	...	...		8 18	...	8 52	...		...	...	
Huyton Junction	6 43	...	6.5 p.m., Lindsay to Garston.	7 36	...	...	...	7.35 p.m from Aintree.	8 21	...	8 55	...	...	...	9 19	
Huyton	6 45	...		7 38	...	...	...		...	For Clock Face.	8 57	...	...	...	...	
Roby	6 48	...		7 41	...	...	...		...		...	...	...	...	...	
Broad Green	6 52	...		7 45	...	...	...		...		...	...	...	...	...	...
Olive Mount Junction ...	...	...		...	...	...	...		...		...	...	...	...	...	...
LIVERPOOL Edge H. arr	6 58	...		7 50	...	...	...		8 29		9 4	...	...	...	9 24	...
LIVERPOOL ,, ,, dp	7 0	...		7 51	...	...	...		8 31		9 6	...	...	...	9 26	...
LIVERPOOL Lime St. arr	7 5	...		7 55	...	...	...		8 35	...	9 10	...	...	...	9 30	...

No. 93 (X)—Calls at Garswood when required to attach Empty Wagons, and at Prescot for ordinary Traffic.

No. 105—Arrives Garswood 6.5 p.m

164 Wigan and Pemberton Branch to Liverpool.

Week Days. Down.

Week Days.

STATIONS.	124	125	126	127	128	129	130	131	132	133	134	135	136	137	138	139	140	141
		Minral	PAS	Minral	Minral	Minral	Goods	Minral	Minral		PAS	Exp. Goods.	Minral		PAS	Exp. Goods.		Minral
					107	276	175					199	176			199		
						SO	M	S				F S				FO		S
Preston to Wigan, see pages 4 to 6	...	p.m.	P.M.	P.M.	P.M.	p.m.	p.m.	P.M.	p.m.		P.M.	p.m.	P.M.		p m	p.m.		p m
WIGAN	...	W	9 40	W	...	...	9 0	7 5	...	...	10 40	W	W	...	11 26	W	...	...
Springs Branch	...	...	...	...	...	9 35	...	...	...	...	...	...	...	...	...	...	...	...
Ince Moss Junction	...	9 10	Calls at Carr Mill on Saturdays only.	9 20	9 25	9 40	9 45	9 50	10 0	...	...	11 0	11 5	...	...	11 15	...	11 50
Bryn Hall Siding	...	...		...	...	...	See	...	...	...	...	...	...	...	...	...	...	...
Garswood Hall Siding ...	...	...		...	...	10 0	note	...	...	...	...	...	...	...	...	...	...	...
Bryn Junction ....arr	...	9 16		9 27	9 32	10 5	9 53	9 58	10 6	...	...	11 8	11 13	...	...	11 23	...	11 58
(Pemberton and Norley Branches.) Bryn Junction......dep	...	...		...	9 40	...	...	...	...	...	...	...	...	...	...	...	...	...
Park Lane Colliery arr	...	C		C	9 45	...	...	...	C	...	Calls at Garswood on Saturdays only.	...	C	...	...	...	...	...
Blundell's Pembrtn Col.	...				9 55	...	...	...		...		8.0 p.m. from Blackburn.		...	...	8.35 p.m. from Blackburn.	...	...
Pemberton J. L&Y ,,	...	8.40 p.m., Bickershaw to Garston.		8.50 p.m. from Rose Bridge	...	...	...	5.30 p.m. Crow Nest to Garston.	...	...			...	...	11 0p.m.from Preston.		...	...
Norley Colliery arr	...				...	...	...		...	...			...	...			...	...
Norley Colliery dep	...		...		...	...	...		...	...			...	...			...	...
Pemberton J. L&Y ,,	...		...		...	...	...		...	...			...	...			...	...
Blundell's Pembrtn Col	...		...		...	...	...		...	...			...	...			...	...
Park Lane Colliery ,,	...		...		...	...	...		...	...			...	...			...	...
Bryn Junction ......arr	...		...		...	...	...		...	...	...	...	...	...		...	...	...
Bryn Junction ......dep	...	9 16	...	9 27	...	10 5	9 53	9 58	10 6	...	...	11 8	11 13	...	...	11 23	...	11 58
Bryn (for Ashton-in-Makerfld)	...	...	9 47	...	...	...	...	...	...	...	10 47	...	...	...	...	...	...	...
Ashton Colliery Siding...	...	...	...	...		...	...	...	...	...	...	...	...	...	...	...	...	...
Garswood	...	...	9 51	...		10 20	...	...	...	...	10X51	...	...	...	...	...	...	...
Carr Mill Junction.........	...	9 30	...	9 50	Is "C" on Saturdays.	10 27	10 10	10 15	10 22	...	...	11 20	11 30	...	...	11 38	...	12 10
Carr Mill	...	...	9X55	...		...	...	...	...	...	...	...	...	...	...	...	...	...
Gerard's Bridge Siding...	...	...	...	...		...	...	...	...	...	...	...	...	...	...	...	...	11.15 p.m., Bamfurlong to Birkenhead.
Pocket Nook Junc. arr	...	...	...	...		...	...	...	...	...	...	...	...	...	...	...	...	
Pocket Nook Junc. dep	...	...	...	...		...	...	...	...	...	...	...	...	...	...	...	...	
St. HELENS .... arr	...	...	10 0	9 55		...	5.40 p.m. Fleetwood to Garston.	...	10 30	...	10 58	11 25	...	...	11 39	11 45	...	
St. HELENS .... dep	...	...	10 1	10 15		...		...	10 40	...	11 0	11 45	...	...	11 40	11 55	...	
Thatto Heath	...	...	10 5	...		...		...	...	...	11 5	...	10.30 p.m., Abram Colliery to Garston.	...	...	...	...	
Eccleston Park	..	...	10 8	...		...		...	...	...	11 8	...		...	...	...	...	
Prescot	...	...	10 11	...	...	...		...	...	...	11 12	...		...	...	...	...	
Huyton Junction	...	...	10 14	10 30	...	For Clock Face.		...	11 0	...	11 16	12 0		...	11 48	12 10	...	
Huyton	...	...	10 16	...	...			...	...	...	11 18	...		...	...	...	...	
Roby	...	...	10 20	...	...			...	...	...	...	...		...	...	...	...	
Broad Green	...	...	10 24	...	...			...	...	...	...	...		...	...	...	...	...
Olive Mount Junction ...	...	...	...	...	...		...	...	...	...	...	...		...	...	...	...	...
LIVERPOOL Edge H. arr	...	...	10 29	10 45	...		...	...	11 15	...	11 28	12 15		...	11 55	12 25	...	...
LIVERPOOL ,, dep	...	...	10 31		...	...	...	...		...	11 30			...	11 56		...	...
LIVERPOOL Lime St. arr	...	...	10 35	...	...	...	...	...	...	...	11 35	...	...	...	12 0	...	...	...

Sundays.

STATIONS.	1	2	3	4	5	6	7	8	9	10	11	12	13
	MAIL	Expres Gd		PAS	Cattle	Minrl	PAS		Expres Gd	PAS	PAS	Expres Gd	PAS
		*			*								
Preston to Wigan, see pages 4 to 6	A.M.	A.M.	...	A.M.	A.M.	a.m.	a.m.		a.m.	A.M.	P.M.	p m	P.M.
WIGAN	1 20	W	...	3 0	2 58	...	4 50	...	8 8	9 25	6 50	10 53	11 20
Springs Branch	...	...	...	...	3 15	...	...	...	...	...	...	10 56	...
Ince Moss Junction	...	3 X 43	...	...	...	3 50	...	...	...	...	...	10 59	...
Bryn Hall Siding	...	...	...	...	...	4 0	...	...	...	...	...	...	...
Garswood Hall Siding ...	...	...	...	...	...	4 25	...	...	...	...	...	...	...
Bryn Junction ....arr	...	3 48	...	...	3 25	4 28	...	...	8 20	...	...	11 3	...
(Pemberton and Norley Branches.) Bryn Junction......dep	...	...	...	...	10.0 p.m. Carlisle to Edge H. (via Stanley)	C	...	...	3.30 a.m. from Carlisle.	8.35 a.m.from Preston	6.10p.m.from Preston	5.45 p.m.from Carlisle.	...
Park Lane Colliery arr	...	9.35 p.m. from Kendal.	...	...			...	...					...
Blundell's Pembrtn Col.	...		...	...		...	...	...					...
Pemberton J. L&Y ,,	...		...	...		...	...	...					...
Norley Colliery arr	...		...	...		...	...	...					...
Norley Colliery dep	...		...	...		...	...	...	...	...	...	...	...
Pemberton J. L&Y ,,	...		...	...		...	...	...	...	...	...	...	...
Blundell's Pembrtn Col	...		...	...		...	...	...	...	...	...	...	...
Park Lane Colliery ,,	...		...	...		...	...	...	...	...	...	...	...
Bryn Junction ......arr	...	...	...	...		...	...	...	...	...	...	...	...
Bryn Junction ......dep	...	3 48	...	...	3 25	4 28	...	...	8 20	...	...	11 3	...
Bryn (for Ashton-in-Makerfld)	...	...	...	...	...	...	...	...	...	9.32	6 57	...	...
Ashton Colliery Siding...	...	...	...	...	...	...	...	...	...	...	...	...	...
Garswood	...	...	...	...	...	...	...	...	...	9 36	7 1	...	...
Carr Mill Junction.........	...	3 58	...	...	3 35	4 40	...	...	8 30	...	...	11 13	...
Carr Mill	...	...	...	...	...	...	...	...	...	...	...	...	...
Gerard's Bridge Siding...	...	...	...	...	...	...	...	...	...	...	...	...	...
Pocket Nook Junc. arr	...	...	...	...	...	...	...	...	...	...	...	...	...
Pocket Nook Junc. dep	...	...	...	...	...	...	...	...	...	...	...	...	...
St. HELENS .... arr	1 35	4 3	...	3 15	...	...	5 5	...	8 35	9 44	7 8	11 18	11 35
St. HELENS .... dep	1 36	4 10	...	3 16	3 40	4 50	5 10	...	8 50	9 48	7 10	11 50	11 37
Thatto Heath	...	...	...	...	...	...	...	...	...	9 53	7 15	...	...
Eccleston Park	...	...	...	...	...	...	...	...	...	9.56	7 18	...	...
Prescot	1 42	...	...	...	...	...	...	...	...	10 0	7 22	...	...
Huyton Junction	1 48	4 25	...	...	3 53	For Widnes.	...	...	9 3	...	...	12 4	11 47
Huyton	...	...	...	...	...		...	...	...	10 6	7 28	...	...
Roby	...	...	...	...	...		...	...	...	10 9	7 31	...	...
Broad Green	...	...	...	...	...		...	...	...	10 13	7 37	...	...
Olive Mount Junction ...	...	4 35	...	...	4 2		...	...	...	...	...	...	...
LIVERPOOL Edge H. arr	1 54	4 40	...	3 34	...		5 25	...	9 20	10 18	7 43	12 20	11 54
LIVERPOOL ,, dep	1 56		...	3 36	...		5 30	...		10 20	7 45		11 56
LIVERPOOL Lime St. arr	2 0	...	...	3 40	...	...	5 35	...	...	10 25	7 50	...	12 0

No. 127—Starts from Bamfurlong Sidings when required.
No. 130—Runs from Fleetwood to Ince Moss on Mondays.
No. 131—Arrives Ince Moss 7.15 p.m.

No. 1—Calls at Prescot for Postal purposes only.

London & North Western c.1909

WIGAN, CHORLEY AND BLACKBURN.

Week days.

	a.m. (Arrives Feniscowles at 5.53 a.m.)	a.m.	a.m.	a.m.	a.m.	a.m.	a.m.	a.m.	a.m.	a.m. (Saturdays only.)	From Llandudno.	a.m.	a.m.	p.m. (Saturdays only.)	p.m. (Saturdays excepted.)	p.m.	p.m.	p.m.
Liverpool (Lime Street) .. depart			5 55				8 15	9 50		11 0		11†0	11 0			1†50	2 20	
Wigan (L.N.W.) ,,			7 10				9 45	10 55		12 25			12 55				3 45	
Boar's Head			7 14				9 49	10 59					1 0				3 49	
Red Rock			7 17				9 52	11 2					1 3				3 55	
White Bear			7 23				9 58	11 8		12 37			1 9				4 1	
Liverpool (Exchange) ...... depart					6 50	7 58			9 22							1D7		4 0
Wigan (L&Y) ,,		5 57			8 5	9 6			10 50			12 25				2 52		4 40
Ince		6 0			8 8	9 9			10 53			12 28				2 55		4 43
Hindley		6 4			8 13	9 14			10 57			12 32				2 59		4 48
Dicconson Lane and Aspull		6 11			8 22	9 23			11 4			12 39				3 6		4 55
Hilton House		6 14			8 25	9 26			11 7			12 42				3 9		4 58
Blackrod		6 18			8 29	9 30			11 12			12 46				3 13		5 2
Adlington (L&Y)		6 22			8 33	9 34			11 16			12 50				3 17		5 6
Chorley ...... arrive		6 27	7 31		8 37	9 39	10 8	11 16	11 22	12 43		12 55	1 18			3 22	4 9	5 11
Manchester (Victoria) ... depart			5 20		7 50		8§50	9 45					12E3	1 0			3 15	
Bolton (Trinity Street) ... ,,		4 55	6 18		8 12		9 26	10 25					12E37				3 39	
Chorley ...... depart		6 30	7 34		8 38		10 9	11 18		12 44			1 20	1 50			4 10	
Heapey		6 36	7 40		8 44		10 15	11 24					1 26	1 58			4 17	
Brinscall	5 45	6 41	7 45	8 25	8 50		10 20	11 29		12 53			1 31	2 5			4 23	
Withnell	5 49	6 45	7 50	8 29	8 54		10 24	11 33					1 35	2 10			4 27	
Feniscowles	6 10	6 49	7 57	8 34	8 59		10 28	11 37					1 39	2 15	2 15		4 31	
Cherry Tree ¶	6 14		8 0	8 37	9 2		10 32	11 41					1 43	2 19	2 19		4 34	
Mill Hill ¶	6 17		8 3	8 40	9 5		10 36	11 44		1 2			1 46	2 22	2 22		4 38	
Blackburn ¶ ...... arrive	6 21		8 7	8 43	9 9		10 40	11 48		1 7			1 50	2 26	2 26		4 42	

Week days—continued.

	p.m.	p.m.	p.m.	p.m.	p.m.	p.m.	p.m.	p.m.	p.m. (Saturdays only.)
Liverpool (Lime Street) depart	4 20			6 15		7 15			
Wigan (L.N.W) ,,	5 50			7 30		9 35			
Boar's Head	5 55			7 34		9 39			
Red Rock	5 58			7 37		9 42			
White Bear	6 4			7 43		9 48			
Liverpool (Exchange) ... depart		4B43			7 15			9 50	
Wigan (L&Y) ,,		6 15			8 12			10 37	
Ince		6 18			8 15			10 40	
Hindley		6 22			8 19			10 44	
Dicconson Lane and Aspull		6 29			8 26			10 51	
Hilton House		6 32			8 29			10 54	
Blackrod		6 37			8 33			10 58	
Adlington (L&Y)		6 41			8 37			11 2	
Chorley ...... arrive	6 12	6 46		7 54	8 42	9 56		11 7	
Manchester (Victoria) .. depart	5 15		5Sx43	7 0		9 5			10 30
Bolton (Trinity Street) .. ,,	5 47		6Sx20	7 24		9 27			10 50
Chorley ...... depart	6 13		6 52	7 55		9 57	10 20		11 18
Heapey	6 19		6 58	7 59		10 3	10 26		11 24
Brinscall	6 25		7 3	8 5		10 8	10 31		11 29
Withnell	6 29		7 7	8 9		10 12	10 35		
Feniscowles	6 33		7 11	8 14		10 16	10 39		
Cherry Tree ¶	6 37		7 15	8 18		10 20	10 43		
Mill Hill ¶	6 40		7 18	8 21		10 23	10 46		11 39
Blackburn ¶ ...... arrive	6 44		7 22	8 26		10 27	10 50		11 43

Sundays.

	a.m.	p.m.	p.m.	p.m.	p.m.	p.m.
Liverpool (Lime Street) depart	8†0				6†45	
Wigan (L.N.W) ,,						
Boar's Head						
Red Rock						
White Bear						
Liverpool (Exchange) ... depart	7 55		2 15		5 30	8 50
Wigan (L&Y) ,,	9 42		3 30		8 5	9 35
Ince	9 46		3 34		8 9	9 39
Hindley	9 50		3 38		8 13	9 43
Dicconson Lane and Aspull	9 56		3 44		8 20	9 49
Hilton House	10 0		3 48		8 24	9 53
Blackrod	10 4		3 52		8 28	9 57
Adlington (L&Y)	10 9		3 57		8 32	10 2
Chorley ...... arrive	10 15		4 3		8 37	10 8
Manchester (Victoria) .. depart	9 15	2 10			7 30	
Bolton (Trinity Street) .. ,,	9 40	2 36			8 2	
Chorley ...... depart	10 17	3 15		4 50	8 38	
Heapey	10 24	3 21		4 56	8 44	
Brinscall	10 30	3 26		5 1	8 49	
Withnell	10 34	3 30		5 5	8 53	
Feniscowles	10 38	3 34		5 9	8 57	
Cherry Tree ¶	10 42	3 38		5 13	9 1	
Mill Hill ¶	10 45	3 41		5 16	9 4	
Blackburn ¶ ...... arrive	10 49	3 45		5 20	9 8	

Week days.

	a.m.	a.m.	a.m.	a.m.	a.m.	a.m.	a.m.	a.m. (Saturdays only.)	To Llandudno	a.m.	a.m.	a.m.	p.m.	p.m.	p.m.	p.m.	p.m.	p.m.
Blackburn ¶ ...... depart		5 20	6 30		7 20	7 28	8 5	8 50			9 58		12 15	12 50		1 20	1 48	
Mill Hill ¶		5 23	6 33		7 23	7 31	8 8	8 53			10 1		12 18	12 53		1 23	1 51	
Cherry Tree ¶		5 26	6 36		7 26	7 34	8 11				10 4		12 21	12 56		1 26	1 54	
Feniscowles		5 30	6 41	7 20	7 31	7 42	8 16				10 9		12 26	1 0		1 31	1 59	
Withnell		5 34	6 46	7 25	7 36	7 49	8 21				10 14		12 31	1 6			2 4	
Brinscall		5 38	6 52	7 30	7 40	7 56	8 26	9 7			10 20		12 35	1 10			2 9	
Heapey			6 57	7 36		8 2	8 31				10 25		12 41	1 14			2 14	
Chorley ...... arrive			7 3	7 42		8 8	8 37	9 17			10 31		12 47	1 20		Saturdays excepted.	2 20	
Bolton (Trinity Street) .. arrive			7 52			8 40	9 39				11 35		1 27	2 17			3 10	
Manchester (Exchange) ,,			8 27			8 50	9 58				12 0		1 32	2 49			3 35	
Chorley ...... depart	5 3		7 5	7 50		8 9	8 38	9 18		10 0	10 33	11 35	12 48		1 34		2 21	3 40
Adlington (L&Y)	5 9		7 12	7 56						10 6		11 41			1 40			3 46
Blackrod	5 14		7 17	8 0						10 10		11 46			1 44			3 50
Hilton House	5 18		7 20	8 3						10 13		11 50			1 47			3 53
Dicconson Lane and Aspull	5 21		7 23	8 6						10 16		11 54		Saturdays only.	1 50			3 56
Hindley	5 26		7 28	8 11						10 21		12 0			1 55			4 1
Ince	5 30		7 32	8 15						10 25		12 5			1 59			4 5
Wigan (L&Y) ...... arrive	5 33		7 35	8 18						10 28		12 11			2 2			4 9
Liverpool (Exchange) ... ,,	8 12		8 40	9 30						11 11		1 2			2Sx55			5 57
White Bear						8 20	8 46	9 24			10 39		12 54				2 27	
Red Rock						8 26	8 53				10 45		1 1				2 33	
Boar's Head						8 29	8 58				10 51		1 4				2 45	
Wigan (L.N.W) ...... arrive						8 35	9 3	9 39			11 0		1 10				2 50	
Liverpool (Lime Street) ,,	7†53						10 5	11 5			12 31		2 50		3†45		4 45	5†40

Week days—continued.

	p.m.	p.m.	p.m.	p.m.	p.m.	p.m.	p.m.	p.m. (Wednesdays only.)	p.m. (Saturdays only.)
Blackburn ¶ ...... depart	4 30	5 27	6 28		7 50		9 35	10 35	10 35
Mill Hill ¶	4 33	5 31	6 31		7 53		9 38	10 38	10 38
Cherry Tree ¶	4 36	5 34	6 34		7 56		9 41	10 41	10 41
Feniscowles	4 41	5 39	6 38		8 0		9 45	10 46	10 46
Withnell	4 46	5 43	6 44		8 5		9 50	10 51	10 51
Brinscall	4 51	5 47	6 49		8 10		9 55	10 55	10 55
Heapey	4 56	5 51	6 54		8 14		9 59		11 0
Chorley ...... arrive	5 2	5 56	7 0		8 20		10 5		11 5
Bolton (Trinity Street) .. arrive	5A53	6 34	7 50		8 45		11 7		11 56
Manchester (Victoria) ,,	6Sx27	6 57	8 52		9‡36		11 45		12 18
Chorley ...... depart	5 3	6 0	7 2	7 17	8 22	9 15			
Adlington (L&Y)		6 6		7 23		9 21			
Blackrod		6 10		7 27		9 25			
Hilton House		6 14		7 30		9 28			
Dicconson Lane and Aspull		6 18		7 33		9 31			
Hindley		6 24		7 38		9 36			
Ince		6 28		7 42		9 40			
Wigan (L&Y ...... arrive		6 31		7 45		9 43			
Liverpool (Exchange) ... ,,		7F53		9 2		11 30			
White Bear	5 9		7 6		8 28				
Red Rock	5 15		7 13		8 34				
Boar's Head	5 18		7 18		8 37				
Wigan (L.N.W) ...... arrive	5 24		7 27		8 43				
Liverpool (Lime Street) ,,	6 50	7†50	8 52		10 19				

Sundays.

	a.m.	a.m.	p.m.	p.m.	p.m.	p.m.
Blackburn ¶ ...... depart	7 25		1 50		5 35	8 10
Mill Hill ¶	7 28		1 53		5 38	8 13
Cherry Tree ¶	7 31		1 56		5 41	8 16
Feniscowles	7 36		2 1		5 46	8 21
Withnell	7 41		2 7		5 51	8 26
Brinscall	7 46		2 11		5 56	8 31
Heapey	7 52		2 16		6 1	8 37
Chorley ...... arrive	7 59		2 22		6 7	8 44
Bolton (Trinity Street) .. arrive	8 44		3 28		7 0	9 27
Manchester (Victoria) ,,	9 30		3 57		7 30	10 0
Chorley ...... depart		8 43		2 35	6 9	8 45
Adlington (L&Y)		8 49		2 42	6 15	8 53
Blackrod		8 53		2 47	6 19	8 58
Hilton House		8 58		2 52	6 24	9 1
Dicconson Lane and Aspull		9 1		2 55	6 27	9 4
Hindley		9 6		3 0	6 32	9 9
Ince		9 10		3 4	6 36	9 13
Wigan (L&Y ...... arrive		9 13		3 8	6 39	9 16
Liverpool (Exchange) ... ,,		10 3		6 29		10 23
White Bear						
Red Rock						
Boar's Head						
Wigan (L.N.W) ...... arrive						
Liverpool (Lime Street) ,,					8†7	

For other Trains between Cherry Tree and Blackburn, see pages 280 to 285.

Passengers cross between Wigan (L.N.W.) and Wigan (L.Y.) stations at their own expense.

‡—On Mons. and Sats. arrives Manchester (Vic.) 9.21 p.m.
§—Leaves Manchester (Vic.) 8.35 a.m. on Sats.
A—On Sats., arrives Bolton (Trinity St.) at 6.16 p.m.
B—On Sats., leaves Liverpool (Ex.) at 4.58 p.m.

D—On Sats. leaves Liverpool (Ex.) at 1.3 p.m.
E—Leaves Manchester at 12.20, and Bolton at 12.52 p.m. on Saturdays.
F—On Sats., arrives Liverpool (Ex.) at 7.58 p.m.
Sx—Saturdays excepted.

LMS c1923

BIBLIOGRAPHY

A Lancashire Triangle Part One. D.J.Sweeney. Triangle Publishing 1996 .

The Wigan Branch Railway. D.J.Sweeney. Triangle Publishing 2008.

Articles, Railway & Travel Monthly. S.M.Phillip. 1912.

Article, The Hunslet Austerity 0-6-0STs. Don Townsley. Locomotives Illustrated, Ian Allan 1988.

Articles, The Lancashire Union Railway, John Marshall. The Railway Magazine 1970.

LMS Engine Sheds Vol 1. C.Hawkins & G.Reeves. Wild Swan Publishing 1981.

Railways of Great Britain & Ireland. Francis Whishaw. 1842.

The Industrial Railways of the Wigan Coalfield Part One. C.H.A.Townley, F.D.Smith & J.A.Peden. Runpast Publishing 1991.

The Industrial Railways of the Wigan Coalfield Part Two. C.H.A.Townley, F.D.Smith & J.A.Peden. Runpast Publishing 1992.

Wigan Coal & Iron. D.Anderson & A.A.France. Smiths Books (Wigan) 1994.

W.T.T. information of colliery workings over Springs Branch supplied by the late Harry Townley.

Clinker's Register of Closed Passenger Stations. C.R.Clinker. Avon-Anglia Publications 1988.

Lancashire Union line plans c1865 & 1880, Wigan & Leigh Archives.

North Union line plan c1854, Courtesy of John Hall.

London & North Western line plan c1886, Courtesy of John Hall.

L.M.S. line plan, Bryn Junction c1929, Courtesy of Tony Graham.

ABBREVIATIONS

B.R.	British Railways
B.R.C.W.	Birmingham Railway Carriage & Wagon Co.
B.T.H.	British Thompson - Houston
C.L.C	Cheshire Lines Committee
C.WT.	Hundredweight
D.M.U.	Diesel Multiple Unit
E.W.S.	English Welsh & Scottish (Railways)
L.C.C.	Lancashire County Council
L.C.G.B.	Locomotive Club of Great Britain
L.M.S.	London, Midland & Scottish (Railway)
L.N.E.R.	London North Eastern Railway
L&N.W.	London & North Western (Railway)
LT&S.	London Tilbury & Southend (Railway)
L&Y.	Lancashire & Yorkshire (Railway)
M.G.R.	Merry-Go-Round
M.R.	Midland Railway
M.o.D	Ministry of Defence
M.o.S.	Ministry of Supply
M.S&L.	Manchester, Sheffield & Lincolnshire (Railway)
N.C.B.	National Coal Board
P.B.J.R.	Platt Bridge Junction Railway
P.W.	Permanent Way
R.C.T.S.	Railway Correspondence & Travel Society
R.E.C.	Railway Executive Committee
R.O.F.	Royal Ordnance Factory
R.S.J.	Rolled Steel Joist
S.B.	Signal Box
U.K.	United Kingdom
S.LS.	Stephenson Locomotive Society
U.S.A.C.	United Sulphuric Acid Company
W.C.M.L.	West Coast Main Line
W.D.	War Department
W.T.T.	Working Time Table
W.W.II.	World War II.

Imperial to Metric conversion

1in (inch) = 25.4mm.
1ft (foot) =304.8mm.
1yd (yard) =.944metres. (22yds = 1 chain).
1statute mile = 1.6093 kilometers.
1acre* (4,870 sq yds) = .4097 hectares.
20 cwt (hundredweight) = 1ton =1.016 tonnes.